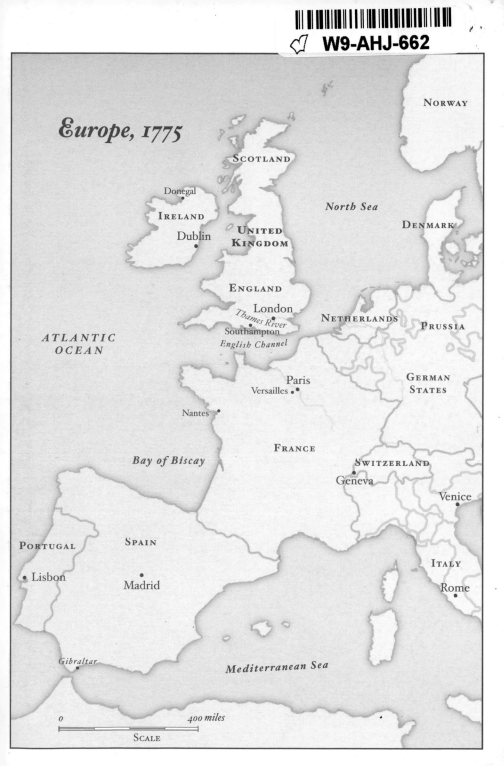

Europe, 1775

NORWAY

SCOTLAND

Donegal

IRELAND

Dublin

North Sea

DENMARK

UNITED
KINGDOM

ENGLAND

London

Thames River

Southampton

English Channel

NETHERLANDS

PRUSSIA

ATLANTIC
OCEAN

Paris

Versailles

GERMAN
STATES

Nantes

FRANCE

SWITZERLAND

Geneva

Bay of Biscay

Venice

PORTUGAL

SPAIN

ITALY

Lisbon

Madrid

Rome

Gibraltar

Mediterranean Sea

0   400 miles

SCALE

BEN FRANKLIN
INVENTING AMERICA

Benjamin Franklin

BEN FRANKLIN
INVENTING AMERICA

THOMAS FLEMING

STERLING PUBLISHING CO., INC.
New York

A FLYING POINT PRESS BOOK

Design: PlutoMedia
Front cover painting: Michael Deas
Frontispiece: The Granger Collection, New York

Library of Congress Cataloging-in-Publication Data

Fleming, Thomas J.
Benjamin Franklin : inventing America / Thomas Fleming. — Updated ed.
p. cm. — (Sterling point books)
Includes index.
ISBN-13: 978-1-4027-4523-2 (trade)
ISBN-10: 1-4027-4523-0 (trade)
ISBN-13: 978-1-4027-4143-2 (paper)
ISBN-10: 1-4027-4143-X (paper)
1. Franklin, Benjamin, 1706-1790—Juvenile literature. 2. Statesmen—United States—Biography—
Juvenile literature. 3. Inventors—United States—Biography—
Juvenile literature. 4. Scientists—United States—Biography—Juvenile literature.
5. Printers—United States—Biography—Juvenile literature. I. Title.

E302.6.F8F565 2007
973.3092—dc22
[B]
2006032142

2 4 6 8 10 9 7 5 3 1

Published by Sterling Publishing Co., Inc.
387 Park Avenue South, New York, NY 10016
Original edition published by Four Winds Press
Copyright © 1973 by Thomas J. Fleming
New material in this updated edition
Copyright © 2007 by Flying Point Press
Maps copyright © by Richard Thompson, Creative Freelancers, Inc.
Distributed in Canada by Sterling Publishing
c/o Canadian Manda Group, 165 Dufferin Street
Toronto, Ontario, Canada M6K 3H6
Distributed in the United Kingdom by GMC Distribution Services
Castle Place, 166 High Street, Lewes, East Sussex, England BN7 1XU
Distributed in Australia by Capricorn Link (Australia) Pty. Ltd.
P.O. Box 704, Windsor, NSW 2756, Australia

Sterling ISBN-13: 978-1-4027-4523-2
ISBN-10: 1-4027-4523-0

For information about custom editions, special sales, premium and
corporate purchases, please contact Sterling Special Sales Department at
800-805-5489 or specialsales@sterlingpub.com.

CONTENTS

CONTENTS

BEN FRANKLIN
INVENTING AMERICA

CHAPTER 1

THE APPRENTICE

ONE DAY IN 1771, WHILE VISITING FRIENDS IN the village of Twyford, not far from Southampton in southwestern England, Benjamin Franklin decided to write a letter to his son William. He sat down in the red brick summerhouse in the garden, with the door open and the August sunshine streaming in. "Dear Son," he began. The letter became famous because it grew over the next three weeks into a book. In this book, Franklin told his son many things William did not know about his father's boyhood in Boston.

"I do not remember when I could not read," Benjamin told his son. His father, Josiah, had decided that Benjamin's fondness for books meant he would make a good minister. Josiah sent Ben to the local grammar school where, in one year, he rose to the head of the class, and then skipped into the class above it.

But Ben's father had a big family—four children by his first wife and ten by his second wife. "I remember thirteen sitting at one time at his table," Benjamin wrote. He was the youngest son, but there were two younger daughters. Josiah Franklin decided he could not afford to send his son all the way through grammar school and college, and sent him to another school where the instruction was limited to writing and arithmetic. Benjamin very quickly learned to write, but he failed in arithmetic.

When Benjamin was ten, Josiah Franklin brought the boy home to work for him in his candle- and soap-making business. Ben cut wicks for the candles, filled the dipping mold, worked behind the counter in the shop where the candles and soap were sold, and ran errands for his father. Soon he had seen enough to know he "disliked the trade."

"What do you want to do?" his father asked. "Go to sea," replied Ben. This upset his father very much, for an older son, Josiah, had become a sailor and then drowned when his ship sank. His father tred to persuade young Benjamin to choose another trade, taking the boy for walks with him around Boston to let him watch bricklayers, carpenters and other tradesmen at work. Though Ben was fascinated by the skill with which these men handled their tools and learned how to use many of them himself, he did not find a trade that interested him.

Meanwhile, he enjoyed himself. Boston was surrounded by water and Ben had learned to swim almost as soon as he could walk. Like most children, he wanted to swim as fast as possible, and one day he decided to improve on his natural equipment. "I made two oval palettes, each about ten inches long and six broad, with a hole for the thumb, in order to retain it fast in the palm of my hand. They much resembled a painter's palettes. In swimming I pushed the edges of these forward, and I struck the water with their flat surfaces and I drew them back . . . I swam faster by means of these palettes, but they fatigued my wrists. I also fitted to the soles of my feet a kind of sandals; but I was not satisfied with them because I observed that the stroke is partly given by the inside of the feet and the ankles, and not entirely with the soles of the feet. . . ."

Then one day, while flying a paper kite near the bank of a big pond—nearly a mile wide—Ben got an even better idea. The water suddenly looked too good to resist, so Ben tied the string of the kite to a stake, tore off his clothes, and jumped into the pond. The kite continued to fly, and Ben decided to enjoy flying the kite and swimming at the same time. He climbed out of the water, seized the kite string and then jumped back in. Flipping over on his back, he held the string in his hands, and the kite continued to soar. Suddenly he noticed that the kite had become a sail, and he called to one of his friends on the bank of the pond and told him to carry his clothes over to the other side. "My kite . . . carried me quite over without the least fatigue and with the greatest pleasure imaginable," he wrote. "I was only obliged occasionally to halt a little in my course, and resist its progress, when it appeared that by following too quick I lowered the kite too much."

Among friends his own age, Ben was always the leader. In a boat or canoe, he gave the orders, "especially in any case of difficulty," though sometimes, he admitted, he led his friends into "scrapes." One of their pastimes was fishing for minnows on the edge of the pond, where the land was marshy. It often became "a mere quagmire" into which they sank, muddying their clothes. One day Ben decided they needed a wharf. Looking around, he saw "a large heap of stones which were intended for a new house near the marsh, and which would very well suit our purpose." In the evening, after the builders departed, Ben assembled a group of his friends, and, working "like so many ants," they lugged the stones down to the marsh and built their "little wharf." The next morning, the workmen were very annoyed to discover the stones missing, but they soon found out who had taken them. Benjamin's father gave his son a severe lecture, reminding him, against the boy's pleas about "the usefulness of the work," that "nothing was useful which was not honest." Benjamin loved and respected his father, and he never forgot that advice.

By the time Josiah Franklin had decided on a trade for Benjamin, James Franklin, Benjamin's older brother, was already in business as a printer in Boston. Printing seemed a very logical business for someone as interested in words as Benjamin, who continued to read every book he could find, even spending his own money on books. So at the age of twelve, Benjamin was "bound" as an apprentice to his older brother by an agreement which stipulated that he would have to remain an apprentice until he was twenty-one. Benjamin quickly learned how to set type and operate a printing press, but in his spare time he continued to read every book he could buy or borrow. "Often I sat up in my room reading the greatest part of the night," he said.

Benjamin soon decided that he wanted to become a writer. He was inclined to poetry, and wrote some "little pieces" which he showed his brother James, who urged him to compose some ballads. He wrote two, "The Lighthouse Tragedy," about the drowning of a ship's captain and his two daughters, and "A Sailor's Song" about the capture of Blackbeard the pirate. James printed these ballads and sent Benjamin around Boston to sell them. "The Lighthouse Tragedy" sold "wonderfully" because it was about a recent event. Benjamin was enormously flattered; he thought he was on his way to becoming a famous poet. Then Josiah Franklin took him aside for a father-to-son talk. He told Ben that his poetry was very poor stuff. Moreover, it was no profession for anyone born poor, for versemakers were generally beggars. Instead, he encouraged Benjamin to learn how to write good prose.

Around this time, Benjamin became friendly with another young Bostonian named John Collins, who was also a great reader. The boys were fond of arguing; sometimes they put their arguments into writing. Josiah Franklin pointed out that Ben's writing was far inferior to Collins', and Ben realizing he was right, thereafter grew more attentive to "the manner" in writing and worked daily to improve himself. He found a volume of *The Spectator*, the famous English newspaper written by Joseph Addison and Richard Steele, and thought "the writing excellent." After he read one of the essays, he made notes on each sentence and then would put them aside for a few days. Then, without referring to *The Spectator*, he tried to rewrite his notes and compared the result to the original essay. This helped him correct some of his faults, but he found his biggest problem was his limited vocabulary. Ben tried to solve this problem by turning *The Spectator* essays into rhyme. In order to "suit the measure" or find a different sound for a rhyme, he was constantly forced to use new words, thereby enlarging his vocabulary. Next he took all his notes and jumbled them together, and then tried to "reduce them into the best order" to teach himself "method in the arrangement of thoughts." Again, he compared his work to the original essay in *The Spectator*, and criticized the results.

While struggling to improve himself as a writer, Benjamin did not neglect his other talents. He was ashamed of his failure to learn arithmetic, and on his own he bought a textbook and taught himself all that he needed to know in that field. At the same time he acquired another skill. After reading "Memorable Things of Socrates," by the Greek historian Xenophon, Benjamin decided he liked Socrates' way of arguing by asking questions. Dropping his habit of "abrupt contradiction and positive argumentation" and instead pretending to be a "humble enquirer and doubter," Ben soon became "very artful and expert in drawing people even of superior knowledge into . . . difficulties out of which they could not extricate themselves." Often, he admitted, he obtained victories "that neither my self nor my cause deserved."

Meanwhile, James Franklin had begun to publish a newspaper, *The New England Courant.* Along with printing the news, James had the clever idea of asking his friends to write amusing little essays for the paper. These writings made it more popular, and Benjamin decided he would like to get into the act. Although he was only a boy, Ben already sensed that his brother was jealous of his skill as a writer. So Ben carefully disguised his handwriting, wrote an unsigned essay and slipped it under the door of the printing house one night. James Franklin showed the essay to his writing friends; and while young Benjamin worked away at his typesetting, he listened with "exquisite pleasure" while the older men praised the quality of the writing and tried to guess who was the author.

The name Franklin had signed to the bottom of the letter was "Silence Dogood." He pretended to be the widow of a country minister, and commented on the manners and morals of New England. Harvard College came in for some very sharp comments in Mrs. Dogood's fourth essay. Noting that most parents consulted only their purses instead of their children's capacities in deciding whether to send their children to this "temple of learning," she observed that, as a result, at graduation "every beetle-scull seem'd well satisfy'd with his own portion of learning, tho' perhaps he was e'en just as ignorant as ever." [After graduation, what happened?] "Some . . . took to merchandising, others to traveling, some to one thing, some to another, and some to nothing; and many of them . . . liv'd as poor as churchmice, being unable to dig, and asham'd to beg, and to live by their wits it was impossible." No wonder so many of them became ministers, Mrs. Dogood concluded. All they had learned at Harvard was how to "carry themselves handsomely, and enter a room genteely (which might as well be acquir'd at a dancing school)." She ended her essay by urging parents not to be so "blind to their children's dulness, and insensible of the solidity of their sculls."

Mrs. Dogood contributed fourteen essays to *The New England Courant,* and then her creator, Benjamin Franklin, triumphantly revealed his identity to his brother and his friends. James Franklin was not pleased; he became even more jealous of Benjamin. The two brothers were soon quarreling constantly, and taking their disputes to their father for settlement. Josiah Franklin tended to favor Benjamin, so James decided to settle future arguments with his fists. Benjamin took these beatings "extreamly amiss" and soon found himself "continually wishing" for a chance to shorten his apprenticeship.

CHAPTER 2

THE RUNAWAY

BENJAMIN'S OPPORTUNITY TO LEAVE HIS BROTHER arrived a few months later, when James Franklin criticized the Massachusetts Assembly and was imprisoned for a month. Freedom of the press as we now know it in America and other democratic nations did not exist in those days. While his brother was in jail, Benjamin ran the *Courant*. The Assembly finally released James Franklin, but they ordered him to stop printing his paper. To circumvent this oppressive ruling, James transferred the ownership of the paper to Ben. To make this maneuver legal he had to release Benjamin from his apprenticeship. Secretly, he had Benjamin sign a new "indenture," as the terms of an apprenticeship were called.

Within a matter of months, a new argument erupted between the brothers and James once more resorted to his fists. Angrily, Benjamin informed his brother that he considered himself a free man and was quitting his job. He knew that James would not dare to enforce the secret indenture that he had signed. In a resentful fury, James Franklin did the next worse thing and went to every printer in Boston, warning them not to give Benjamin any work. His father disapproved of Benjamin's decision, and since he was only seventeen his family could legally force him to stay in Boston. So he decided to run away.

Benjamin's friend Collins arranged for his passage to New York on a sloop and Benjamin sold some of his books to raise a little money. In three days he was in New York, "near three hundred miles from home . . . without the least recommendation to or knowledge of any person in the place." There was no work for printers in New York, and Benjamin struggled on to Philadelphia.

The trip turned into a miserable ordeal. Stormy weather harassed the boat that took him from New York to Perth Amboy, turning a journey of two or three hours into thirty hours without food or water. The runaway trudged across central New Jersey on foot, through soaking rain, and finally arrived in Philadelphia at 9 o'clock on Sunday morning, filthy and exhausted. He bought some bread and wandered around town eating it, then went to church with some Quakers and fell asleep in the middle of their service. A friendly Quaker took him to the Crooked Billet Tavern on Water Street, where Ben rented a room and slept most of the day and all of the night. The next morning he cleaned himself up and went looking for work.

All Benjamin could find was part-time work with a weird character named Keimer, whose printing equipment consisted of "an old shatter'd press" and one small worn-out font of English type. Keimer had a full-length beard, long hair and wore dirty tattered clothes, and, to complete the picture of an eccentric, he lived in a house with no furniture.

Keimer loved to argue about religion, but he found young Ben too much for him. "I us'd to work him so with my Socratic method," Ben said, "and trepann'd him so often by questions apparently so distant from any point we had in hand and yet by degrees led to the point . . . that at last he grew ridiculously cautious and would hardly answer me the most common question without asking first, *What do you intend to infer from that?*" Keimer was so impressed with Ben as a disputer that he asked him to join in establishing a new religion. Keimer would preach the doctrines, and Ben would refute all the opponents.

Meanwhile, they found very little printing to do. With funds running low, Ben suggested they become vegetarians. He had experimented with this kind of diet before he left Boston, and knew he could put up with it. But Keimer was "a great glutton" and he found the diet almost unendurable, in spite of a list of forty dishes which Ben had a neighborhood woman prepare for them at different times. Finally, Keimer could stand the vegetarian meals no longer, and ordered a roast pig. He invited

Ben and two women friends to dine with him, but the neighborhood cook brought the pig before the guests arrived. Keimer, Ben said, "could not resist the temptation" and ate the whole pig before they came.

Ben's adventures with Keimer were interrupted by the appearance of his brother-in-law Robert Holmes, captain of a sloop that traded between Boston and Delaware. Holmes had heard that Ben was in Philadelphia and wrote him a letter, urging him to return to Boston. Ben replied by mail, and Holmes showed his letter to Sir William Keith, the Governor of Pennsylvania, hoping that he would urge the runaway to go home. Instead, Keith declared himself most impressed by Ben's skill as a writer, and announced that he wanted to set him up as a printer in Philadelphia. Keith went to Keimer's shop and conversed with Ben "in a most affable, friendly and familiar manner imaginable." The Governor invited the young man to his home for dinner, and explained what he had in mind. Ben was naturally delighted, and he soon went back to Boston with a letter in his pocket from Governor Keith, urging his father to loan him the money he needed to set up a printing shop.

Josiah Franklin read the Governor's letter, but "said little of it" to Ben for some days. When Captain Holmes returned, Josiah asked him what he thought of Keith. Holmes did his best to give a favorable impression, but Josiah finally spoke his mind: The Governor must be a man of "small discretion" to think of setting an eighteen-year-old boy up in business. To

Ben's chagrin, Josiah wrote a polite letter to Keith, thanking him for the offer, but declining to risk the money. The cost of equipping a small print shop was a hundred pounds—the modern day equivalent being $14,000.

Ben's brother James refused to hire him again, so Josiah gave his son permission to return to Philadelphia. He urged Ben to "avoid lampooning in the Silence Dogood style," work hard and save his money. By the time he was twenty-one, he ought to have nearly enough money to set himself up in business and if he "came near the matter" Josiah would give him the rest.

Ben's friend John Collins decided to return to Philadelphia with him. Ben went overland to New York and met Collins there. To Ben's amazement he discovered his friend had acquired a great fondness for brandy and had been drunk every day since his arrival in New York. Collins had lost his money gambling, and Ben had to pay the bill at his boarding house and put up money for the rest of the journey to Philadelphia. There, Collins had trouble finding work, and continued to drink and live off Ben. Liquor made him belligerent, and the friends almost always quarreled when Collins drank.

One night while rowing in a boat on the Delaware, their friendship came to an end. There were several other young men in the boat, and each had taken a turn at the oars. But Collins had been drinking, and he suddenly announced, "I will be rowed home."

"We will not row you," Ben said.

13

"You must or stay all night on the water," Collins said.

The others were inclined to give up the argument. "Let us row him," they said. But Ben refused. Collins became more and more ugly tempered, finally swearing he would make Ben row or throw him overboard. Collins lurched to his feet and came toward Ben, swinging his fists. Ben grabbed Collins by the seat of the pants and threw him head first into the river.

Collins was a good swimmer, so he was in no danger of drowning. But before he could reach the boat, Ben ordered his fellow oarsmen to put it out of his reach. Every time Collins came close to the boat, they asked him if he would row. "No," he would cry and they would pull away from him again. "He was ready to die with vexation," Ben reported. But Collins obstinately refused to row. Finally he began to tire, and Ben dragged him into the boat "and brought him home dripping wet in the evening.

"We hardly exchanged a civil word afterwards," Ben said. A few weeks later Collins went to the West Indies as a tutor for the sons of a wealthy planter there. He promised to pay back Ben the money he owed him. "But I never heard of him after," Ben said.

Meanwhile, Governor Keith remained determined to set Ben up as a printer. "Give me an inventory of the things necessary to be had from England," he said, "and I will send for them. You shall repay me when you are able."

Ben did not have "the least doubt of his meaning what he said," and he gave the Governor an inventory of what he needed. But then Keith had another idea. Why didn't Ben go to England and choose the types and other equipment personally? He might also be able to make arrangements with booksellers and stationers to import and sell their books and paper. The offer was irresistible to an adventurous young man. An opportunity to see London, capital of the British Empire, to an American colonist the greatest city in the world! Ben eagerly accepted, and thereby made one of his first serious mistakes, or, as he called them in printers' language, "errata."

For some time he had been seeing a young girl his own age— Deborah Read, the daughter of a Philadelphia shopkeeper. They were in love and already talking about marriage. But the prospect of going on a long voyage made Ben decide to put off marriage until his return from England. So he left poor Deborah, obviously heartbroken, behind him and sailed for England. In the ship's mailbag, Governor Keith assured him, were numerous letters of recommendation from him to important men in England, which would enable Ben to buy all the equipment he needed, on the Governor's credit.

After a long, stormy voyage, the ship finally reached London on the 24th of December, 1724. The Captain opened the mailbag and Ben was puzzled to discover no letters with his name on them. But he picked out several that seemed to be in the Governor's handwriting. He trudged into the city from the Thames River docks and presented his first letter to a stationer. The man opened it and said, "Oh, Riddlesden; I have lately found him to be a complete rascal and I will have nothing to do with him nor receive any letters from him." He handed the letter back to Ben and turned to wait on a customer.

Ben swiftly discovered that none of the letters were from Governor Keith. Baffled, he sought out a friend he had made on the voyage, a Philadelphia merchant named Thomas Denham. Haltingly, Ben explained why he was in London. (He had kept the purpose of his trip a secret at the Governor's advice.) Denham laughed heartily at the idea that Governor Keith could give Ben a letter of credit to buy equipment. He had, said Denham, "no credit to give." Why had the Governor played such a trick on a poor ignorant boy? It was, Mr. Denham explained, a habit he had acquired. "He wished to please everybody, and having little to give, he gave expectations."

"What should I do?" Ben asked in bewilderment. He was 3,000 miles from home, without a cent in his pocket.

CHAPTER 3

THE SWIMMING INSTRUCTOR

THERE WAS ONLY ONE THING TO DO—BEN WENT to work as a printer. To his delight, he found he was easily the equal of English printers. In fact, he could work harder and longer than most of them. By now Ben was a husky eighteen-year-old, almost six feet tall with extremely muscular arms and shoulders. While most printers needed both hands to carry one large form of type up and down stairs, Ben carried a form in each hand. The master printer, noting his quickness at composing, gave Ben all the work which required speed. He thus made more money than his fellow journeymen.

Ben tried to save his money, but he had a problem similar to the one Collins had given him in Philadelphia. Another friend, James Ralph, who had made the voyage with him, wanted to become a poet or a playwright. But he found it very difficult to get any work at all, and so he lived off Ben's earnings.

Although Ralph had a wife in Philadelphia, he fell in love with a young woman who ran a millinery shop. They lived together as man and wife, and she lost her friends and her business. Ben was soon supporting both of them. In desperation, Ralph took a teaching job in the country. His English "wife" continued to visit Ben, who found himself falling in love with her. When Ben suggested that he take Ralph's place, the lady angrily rejected him, and informed Ralph, who rushed back to London, denounced Ben and grandly informed him that he considered all his debts canceled. By now these amounted to some 27 pounds, no small sum at the time. (In today's money it was about $2,700 of purchasing power.)

Thereafter, Ben struggled mightily to save every possible cent to pay for his voyage back to Philadelphia. Saving this money was a long, slow struggle, lasting almost two years. Without Ralph's company he was lonely and homesick.

Toward the end of this period, Ben almost gave up printing and opened a swimming school. He had become friendly with another young printer, who had received a good education and read Latin and spoke French. Ben taught him and a friend how to swim in only two visits to the Thames.

One day, on a trip down the river with this young man and a number of his other friends, the young printer began telling everyone what a remarkable swimmer Ben Franklin was. Although England was a seafaring nation, few people could swim, and everyone became very curious to see Ben perform. Agreeably, he stripped off most of his clothes, leaped into the

Thames and swam from Chelsea to Blackfriar's—a distance of about three and a half miles. He dove like a porpoise, floated on his back, and swam under water, all of which "surpriz'd and pleas'd those to whom they were novelties."

A wealthy Englishman heard about this performance, and asked Ben to call on him. His sons were preparing to leave on a tour of Europe, he explained, and he would like them to be taught swimming. The sum of money he offered Ben made the young man's head spin, and Ben suddenly realized that he could make a great deal of money teaching Englishmen how to swim. But reluctantly he gave up the idea, and told his wealthy customer that he could not teach his sons. Ben was going back to America.

Thomas Denham, the merchant who had told Ben the truth about Governor Keith, had kept in touch with his young friend over the past year and a half. Now he offered to take Ben back to Philadelphia with him, and give him a job as his clerk in a store he planned to open there. Ben had accepted the offer, before the idea of a swimming school had occurred to him. Perhaps he would have accepted Denham's offer anyway. "I was grown tired of London," he said, "remember'd with pleasure the happy months I had spent in Pennsylvania, and wish'd again to see it."

On the long voyage back to Philadelphia, Ben kept a journal. In it he described the various English towns they passed while going down the Channel, and once on the ocean, the weather, the fish they caught, and the characters of his fellow voyagers.

For the first time he revealed one of the talents that was to make him famous—the keen, observing eye of a scientist.

"This afternoon we took up several branches of gulfweed," he wrote on September 28th, 1726. Gulfweed was the vegetation which grew in the Gulf Stream, the great ocean river that runs from the Gulf of Mexico across the Atlantic.

One of these branches had something peculiar in it. In common with the rest, it had a leaf about three-quarters of an inch long, indented like a saw, and a small yellow berry, filled with nothing but wind; besides which it bore a fruit of the animal kind, very surprising to see. It was a small shellfish like a heart, the stalk by which it proceeded from the branch being partly of a grizzly kind. Upon this one branch of the weed, there were near forty of these vegetable animals; the smallest of them, near the end, contained a substance somewhat like an oyster, but the larger were visibly animated, opening their shells every moment, and thrusting out a set of unformed claws, not unlike those of a crab; but the inner part was still a kind of soft jelly. Observing the weed more narrowly, I spied a very small crab crawling along it, about as big as the head of a tenpenny nail, and of a yellowish color, like the weed itself. This gave me some reason to think that he was a native of the branch; that he had not long since been in the same condition with the rest of those little embryos that appeared in the shells, this being the method of their generation; and that, consequently, all the rest of this odd kind of fruit might be crabs in due time. To strengthen my conjecture, I have resolved to keep the weed in salt water, renewing it every day till we come onshore, by this experiment to see whether any more crabs will be produced or not in this manner.

The next day, as he was changing the water, Ben found another crab much smaller than the one he had previously noticed, and this convinced him that his hypothesis about the weed was correct. But the weed could not live in a small pot of water; the rest of the embryos died. The following day Ben hauled in more gulfweed with a boathook, and found "three living, perfect crabs, each less than the nail of my little finger." He also noticed that one of them had "a thin piece of the white shell which I before noticed as their covering while they remained in the condition of embryos, sticking close to his natural shell upon his back."

Along with keen observation, Ben did some thinking about his own life. He was almost 21, and he decided it was time to reflect upon his experience and draw some conclusions from it. Thus far, he decided, his life had been like a bad play—"a confused variety of different scenes." He was now entering upon a new scene, and he decided to make some resolutions.

"1. It is necessary for me to be extremely frugal for some

time, till I have paid what I owe. [Thomas Denham had loaned him the money for the voyage home.]

"2. To endeavour to speak truth in every instance; to give nobody expectations that are not likely to be answered, but aim at sincerity in every word and action—the most amiable excellence in a rational being.

"3. To apply myself industriously to whatever business I take in hand, and not divert my mind from my business by any foolish project of growing suddenly rich; for industry and patience are the surest means of plenty.

"4. I resolve to speak ill of no man whatever, not even in a matter of truth; but rather by some means excuse the faults I hear charged upon others, and upon proper occasion speak all the good I know of everybody."

Arriving safely in Philadelphia, Ben discovered the "erratum" he had made with Miss Read had grown worse. In the confusion of his first months in London, he had written her only one letter, implying that it would be a long time before he came home. She had therefore contracted a marriage with another man, who turned out to be a drunkard. He soon fled Philadelphia for the West Indies, leaving behind him a small mountain of debts.

Seeing how unhappy he had made this young woman, Ben began thinking about why it had happened. He decided that his bad conduct had something to do with his skeptical attitude toward religion. He noted that his arguments against religion had convinced his friends Collins and Ralph, and each of them had "afterwards wrong'd me greatly without the least compunction." Governor Keith was another freethinker. In his skeptical days Ben had liked to argue that there was no such thing as morality. Now he began to think that certain actions might not be bad because God had forbidden them or good because He commanded them, but they might be forbidden because they were bad for us, or commanded because they were beneficial to us as human beings. Thus he became convinced, he told his son William, "that truth, sincerity and integrity in dealings between man and man were of the utmost importance."

Back in Philadelphia, Ben Franklin began practicing these principles. But he soon saw that bringing order and honesty into his personal life was only a first step. A single person, though sincere and industrious, could not accomplish very much. So Franklin formed a club, the Junto. He got the idea from a book by Cotton Mather, a famous Boston minister. The Junto met each Friday evening, and the rules that Franklin drew up required every member in turn to produce a set of queries on some important subject—such as politics, science or morality. These queries were discussed by the group, under the direction of a president. Once every three months, each member had to produce an essay on a subject that interested him. This too was discussed and debated by the group. Drawing on his own experience as a debater, Franklin had formulated rules which

23

banned positive opinions and direct contradictions. Anyone who fell into either of these faults paid a small fine.

Along with the special queries that members were supposed to produce, there was a set of "standing queries," which members were asked to consider each week. Among them were the following:

"Hath any deserving stranger arrived in town since last meeting, that you heard of? And what have you heard or observed of his character or merits? And whether think you, it lies in the power of the Junto to oblige him, or to encourage him as he deserves.

"Do you know of any deserving young beginner lately set up, whom it lies in the power of the Junto any way to encourage?

"Have you lately observed any defect in the laws of your country? Or do you know of any beneficial law that is wanting?

"Have you lately observed any encroachment on the just liberties of the people?

These last two queries give us an interesting glimpse of what Ben Franklin was thinking around this time. Both of these ideas were to appear again and again in his life. Ben Franklin never stopped thinking about ways to improve the society in which he lived. And he never stopped worrying about the possibility that government, in the name of law and order, might take away the basic rights which every Englishman believed he had inherited at birth. Among these rights, or liberties, were trial by a jury of one's peers; the principle of habeas corpus, which forces a government to free a man from jail on the posting of reasonable bail; the right to petition the government for the redress of citizens' wrongs; and, above all, the right of free speech, which means that citizens can criticize the government in newspapers, in speeches and in conversations with their neighbors.

CHAPTER 4

THE NEWSPAPERMAN

MEANWHILE, BEN HAD TO COPE WITH SOME SUR-prising twists and turns in his career. Mr. Denham, the bene-factor who had brought him home from England, died six months after they returned to Philadelphia. Around the same time, Ben almost died too, from an attack of pleurisy. When he recovered, he decided to go back to the printing business again. He went to work as foreman for his old friend Keimer, but he soon saw that Keimer only planned to let him train his apprentices, and after they had learned printing, fire Ben, and so save the rather large salary he was paying him. Ben decided to go into business for himself.

He found a new friend, a Welshman named Hugh Meredith, who had a rather wealthy father. The older Meredith agreed to set them up in business as equal partners, if Ben would agree to train his son as a printer.

26

As soon as they opened their print shop, Ben began planning to publish a newspaper. There was only one paper in Philadelphia then, Andrew Bradford's *American Weekly Mercury*, a very inferior publication. But Keimer heard about Ben's plans, and rushed into print with another paper called *The Universal Instructor in All Arts and Sciences: and Pennsylvania Gazette*. Keimer could do nothing right—his paper was a disaster. It had little news in it; most of it was material reprinted from an encyclopedia. Franklin wrote a series of articles for the *Mercury*, ridiculing Keimer and his sheet, and soon the number of subscribers to the *Universal Instructor* . . . dwindled to the vanishing point. Within a year, Keimer announced he was leaving Pennsylvania, and sold the paper to Franklin and Meredith. Franklin promptly shortened Keimer's absurd title to *The Pennsylvania Gazette*, and went to work.

Already, Franklin had amazed easygoing Philadelphians with his energy. He regularly worked between twelve and fifteen hours a day. Meredith gave him little help. Printing bored him, and he preferred to sit around in nearby taverns drinking with friends. But because Meredith's father had put up the money to launch them, Franklin never criticized his lazy partner.

At first, Philadelphia's older merchants were sure that Franklin and Meredith would fail, because there were already two print shops in town. But one of the city's leading doctors, Patrick Baird, vigorously disagreed. "The industry of Franklin is superior to anything I ever saw of the kind," he said. "I see him still at work when I go home, and he is at work again before his neighbors are out of bed."

Finally, two friends went to Franklin separately, each unknown to the other, and offered him enough money to buy out his partner. Shrewdly, Franklin accepted half of each man's money, and easily persuaded Meredith to sell his share of the business. Meredith had realized he was not cut out to be a printer, and he and Ben parted in the friendliest fashion. Meredith took Franklin's money and bought a farm in North Carolina, where he lived happily for the rest of his life.

Franklin swiftly built the *Pennsylvania Gazette* into the best-known, most successful newspaper in America. One of the secrets of its popularity was the kind of wit which Franklin had already displayed in his Silence Dogood letters. The *Gazette* was always full of letters to the editor, some of which the editor wrote himself. There was Anthony Afterwit, who told sad stories about how his wife spent him into bankruptcy. Cecilia Single was a born shrew who lectured the editor in scorching terms because, she said, he was partial to men. Alice Addertongue said she was organizing a kind of stock exchange for the sale and transfer of calumnies and slanders.

Franklin carried on a long, lively war with his chief newspaper opposition, the *Mercury*. As usual, he scored points by making his readers laugh at his rival. He printed a letter from a man who declared himself the author of some verses published in the last edition of the *Mercury*. The fellow complained that for some unknown reason the editor of the *Mercury* had printed only the first two letters of his name, BL. "I request you to inform the publick that I did not desire my name should be concealed," declared the supposed author, "and that the remaining letters are O, C, K, H, E, A, D." Another letter pointed out that the *Mercury* had reported two prominent European soldiers had been killed by a single cannon ball—a remarkable achievement considering one of them was fighting in the Rhineland, and the other in Italy.

Equally important to the success of the *Pennsylvania Gazette* was Franklin's courage. In one of his first issues, he printed a story about the dispute which the assembly of Massachusetts was having with the royal governor, William Burnet. Franklin strongly supported the defiant stand of his native province, whose inhabitants insisted on their right to pay the Governor what they thought he needed and deserved. Boldly, the young editor applauded Massachusetts' refusal to knuckle under to the "menaces of a Governour fam'd for his cunning in politicks." Franklin said it was proof that Americans still retained "that ardent spirit of liberty, and that undaunted courage in the defense of it, which has in every age so gloriously distinguished BRITONS & ENGLISHMEN from all the rest of mankind." Later, Franklin proudly recalled how his bold stand had "struck the principal people" in Philadelphia and won him numerous new subscribers.

Inevitably, Franklin's independent attitude led him into conflict with the rulers of Pennsylvania. The province was a proprietary colony. Unlike a royal province, which was run by a governor appointed by the King, Pennsylvania was ruled by the sons of William Penn, the original proprietor, who had obtained the colony as a grant of land from the King, and then sold the lands within it to settlers, retaining millions of acres for his own property. As proprietors, Penn's two sons, Richard and Thomas, had the right to appoint the governor and his council, judges and other officials.

The proprietary party did not like criticism, and when Franklin began pointing out things that were wrong with the government, several friends advised him to follow a more cautious course. They warned that he and his paper would never be successful in Pennsylvania, without the power of the Penns behind him.

Franklin listened to this advice and invited these pessimists to dinner at his house that night. They sat down to a bare table, and the only food served to them was some strange looking mush in wooden bowls. Franklin poured some water into his bowl and began eating. His guests tried to follow his example, but the stuff tasted so terrible that they could barely swallow it. Finally, they asked him what in the world they were eating. "Sawdust meal and water," Franklin said. "Now go tell the rest of Philadelphia that a man who can eat that for supper doesn't need to be beholden to anyone."

Around this time, Franklin decided to marry. His choice was Deborah Read, the girl he had jilted when he went to London. He felt sorry for her and wanted to correct the "erratum" he had made in his relationship with her. He had also made another mistake since he returned to Philadelphia, which made it important for him to find an understanding wife. In spite of his resolution to lead a moral life, Franklin admitted in his *Autobiography* that he found it very difficult to control his sexual desires. Before he returned to Deborah, he had had a love affair with a very poor and rather ignorant woman. According to one story, she was an "oyster wench," selling oysters from a basket or a pushcart in the streets of the city. From this love affair, a son was born. Franklin named the boy William, and accepted complete responsibility for him. A child born out of wedlock is called illegitimate; people who speak more bluntly would call him a bastard. Franklin did not want his son to be raised with that label on him, and marriage to the boy's mother was out of the question. So, on September 1, 1730, Franklin married Deborah Read and brought his son into their household.

Deborah was grateful to Franklin for rescuing her from a lonely life and she did her best to accept William as her own son. She also worked hard for Franklin, who later recalled "how she assisted me cheerfully in my business, folding and stitching pamphlets, tending shop, purchasing old linen rags for the papermakers, etc., etc." He also proudly recalled that in those days he had been "clothed from head to foot in woolen and linen of my wife's manufacture." Deborah was also Franklin's financial bookkeeper and also ran the shop attached to his printing office, where he sold books and stationery.

Franklin was deeply grateful to Deborah, and showed it by writing a love song for her. One night, at the Junto, he and his friends had begun discussing how many love songs were written to mistresses, but no one had been able to think of a single song written in praise of a wife. The next day, Franklin gave this song to one of his friends, and asked him to memorize it and sing it at the next Junto meeting.

Of their Chloes and Phillises poets may prate
    I sing my plain country Joan
These twelve years my wife, still the joy of my life;
    Blest day that I made her my own.

Not a word of her face, or her shape, or her eyes
    Or of flames or of darts you shall hear;
Tho' I beauty admire 'tis virtue I prize
    That fades not in seventy year.

Some faults have we all, and so has my Joan
    But then they're exceedingly small;
And now I'm grown us'd to 'em, so like my own
    I scarcely can see 'em at all . . ."

CHAPTER 5

FIRST CITIZEN OF
PHILADELPHIA

TWO YEARS AFTER HIS MARRIAGE, WITH HIS
paper thriving, Franklin launched an even more successful
publication—*Poor Richard's Almanack*. Every newspaper publisher in the colonies tried to produce an almanac. It was an
ideal way to use up "dead time" when the presses were standing
idle, and if the book caught on it could also be profitable.

The success of an almanac depended upon the appeal of
the "philomath"—the resident astrologer who did the writing
and predicting. Franklin decided to become his own philomath. He realized that most people read an almanac for
amusement and that they did not really believe that anyone
could predict the weather and other events with any accuracy,
a full year ahead. So Franklin created a philomath named

Richard Saunders, who wrote a funny introduction to the first almanac. Poor Richard explained that he only had taken to writing because his wife was sick of watching him gaze at the stars. She had ordered him to make some money, or she was going to burn all his books and instruments.

Franklin's competition in this field was an almanac written by a philomath named Titan Leeds. Solemnly, Poor Richard explained that he would have written almanacs long ago, but he hated to cut into his friend Titan's profits. Now, it was all right for him to publish, because Titan was about to die.

Richard explained that according to his reading of the stars, Titan would expire on October 17th, 1733, while Titan's calculations inclined him to think he would survive until the 26th of the same month. Naturally, Titan Leeds was infuriated, and wrote a nasty reply, insisting he was very much alive, and calling Poor Richard a fraud. The next year, Poor Richard replied. Titan Leeds was certainly dead, he declared, because in the almanac that appeared under his name for the year 1734 "I am treated in a very gross and unhandsome manner . . . I am called a false predictor, an ignorant, a conceited scribbler, a fool and a lyar." His good friend Titan would never have treated him this way. Titan continued to sputter insults, but his almanac soon faded in popularity, while Poor Richard's soared.

The main reason for Franklin's success were the proverbs which he strung throughout *Poor Richard's Almanack*. He took them from many books, including the Bible, but he often rewrote them to sharpen their wit or their point.

He's a fool that makes his doctor his heir.
Fish and visitors smell in three days.
The worst wheel of a cart makes the most noise.
Experience keeps a dear school, yet fools will learn at no
other.
It is hard for an empty sack to stand upright.
Sal laughs at everything you say; why? because she has
fine teeth.

Franklin also made fun of philomaths who pretended they could really predict the future. "I find that this will be a plentiful year of all manner of good things for those who have enough," he wrote, "but the orange trees in Greenland will go near to fare the worse for the cold. . . ."

Meanwhile, Franklin was working hard to improve Philadelphia. With the help of the Junto and the *Gazette,* he founded the city's first volunteer fire department and reorganized "The Watch," the city's policemen, who patrolled the streets at night. To give everyone a better chance to educate themselves, he founded a subscription library, the first in America. He was also the guiding spirit behind the creation of the Pennsylvania Hospital and the Philadelphia Academy, which eventually became the University of Pennsylvania. He helped to organize the colony's first militia, the Philadelphia Associaters, to provide a defense against a threatened French and Spanish invasion. At the same time, he served as clerk of the Pennsylvania Assembly.

In all of these areas, Franklin practiced a very unusual strategy of leadership. When he first began soliciting subscriptions for the library, he met with "objections and reluctances." He swiftly saw that others envied him, because they thought that he was tackling the job solely to get the credit for it. From that moment, Franklin put himself "as much as I could out of sight," and described the project as "a scheme of a number of friends" who had requested him to gather the support of "lovers of reading." The library was soon thriving, and henceforth, Franklin stayed behind the scenes, never attempting to take the credit or the glory for anything he achieved.

Only one thing marred Franklin's happiness. Two years after his marriage, Deborah had given birth to a son, whom Franklin named Francis Folger. At the age of four, the little boy died of smallpox. After this sad loss, Deborah became more and more jealous of William. She resented the attention Franklin showered on his only son. Franklin was a generous father. He bought William expensive presents, such as a pony, which the boy let wander away. Even after her daughter, Sarah, was born in 1743, Deborah still resented William's presence in the house. As he grew older, William could not help but notice that his stepmother did not like him, for Deborah had a very sharp tongue. Franklin did his best to soothe their quarrels, but he was not always successful.

At the same time, Franklin was thinking about his own

future. By 1745, he was a successful, moderately wealthy man, with an income of well over 2,000 pounds, or about $50,000, a year. (An ordinary working man considered himself lucky to make fifteen pounds a year.) He owned several houses in Philadelphia, and received rents from them. But Franklin saw no point in continuing to pile up more and more money. He called this "the pursuit of wealth to no purpose" and told a funny story about it. One day he visited a very wealthy Philadelphia friend, who took him through his expensive new house. The rooms were huge, and each time Franklin asked him why he had given himself so much space, the man replied, "Because I can afford it." Finally, Franklin smiled and said, "Why don't you buy a hat six times too big for your head? You can afford that too."

That kind of empty life was not for him, Franklin concluded. Instead, at the age of 42, he decided to retire from business. Not long before this he had hired a new printer, a Scotsman named David Hall. He was a very competent man and Franklin liked him, and he offered Hall a chance to become his partner, and run the business, if Hall would agree to pay Franklin half the profits from the *Pennsylvania Gazette* and *Poor Richard's Almanack* and other work done by the print shop for the next twenty years. At the end of that time, Hall would become the full owner of the business. Naturally, Hall leaped at the chance.

People in Philadelphia wondered what Franklin was going

to do. Some of his friends thought he was crazy to give up a profitable business that could have made him one of the richest men in America. They were even more amazed to discover that the retired Franklin was working harder than ever, but now he was not trying to make money. He was trying to solve the mysteries of electricity.

CHAPTER 6

SCIENTIST AND INVENTOR

TWO YEARS BEFORE, WHILE VISITING RELATIVES in Boston, Franklin had attended a lecture by Dr. Archibald Spencer, a Scottish scientist who had performed some electrical experiments. Later that year, Spencer had come to Philadelphia and sold most of his apparatus to Franklin. Franklin then bought more equipment through Peter Collinson, a Quaker friend in London who was a member of the Royal Society, the powerhouse of the British scientific world. Soon he was writing to Collinson, "I never was before engaged in any study that so totally engrossed my attention and my time as this has lately done."

At that time, scientists knew very little about electricity. They produced it by rubbing glass tubes with silk, or wool with resin. In 1746, at the University of Leyden, in the Netherlands, they discovered how to store electricity in a special bottle lined with strips of tin, that was soon called the Leyden jar. Most scientists thought there were two kinds of electricity, vitreous (from silk) and resinous (from resin). Franklin, experimenting in his Philadelphia laboratory, soon concluded that electricity was a single "fluid." But he noticed that sometimes it attracted, and sometimes it repelled. Why?

To answer that question, Franklin conducted the following experiment. He gathered three volunteers in his laboratory and had two of them, whom we shall call A and B, stand on wax squares, which insulated them from the ground. Then A rubbed a glass tube, thereby transferring some of the electricity in his own body to the tube. He then held the tube out to B, and immediately, an electric spark jumped from the tube to B's hand. Now A had less electricity than he normally possessed, and B had more than his usual share. Franklin now ordered B to hold out his hand to C, who was standing on the ground. Immediately, a spark leaped from B to C. Then Franklin repeated the experiment. However, this time he ordered B to ignore C, and to hold out his hand to A. A much greater electric spark jumped from B back to A.

The explanation? B's body, once he received the charge from A, had more electricity in it than he normally possessed. He was charged "positively," Franklin said. A, with less electricity, was charged "negatively." To simplify the explanation even more, Franklin called the positive charge plus and the negative charge minus. This was a major breakthrough in the history of electricity. It enabled scientists to understand for the first time how electrical current traveled from one body to another.

Franklin also noticed that a sharply pointed object, such as a knitting needle, drew off electricity from a positively charged body much more rapidly, and from a greater distance, than a blunt object.

Then, on November 7th, 1749, Franklin moved even closer to his greatest discovery. In a journal he was keeping of his experiments, he wrote, "Electrical fluid agrees with lightning in these particulars. 1. Giving light. 2. Colour of the light. 3. Crooked direction. 4. Swift motion. 5. Being conducted by metals. 6. Crack or noise in exploding. 7. Subsisting in water or ice. 8. Rending bodies it passes through. 9. Destroying animals. 10. Melting metals. 11. Firing inflammable substances. 12. Sulphureous smell. The electric fluid is attracted by points. We do not know whether this property is in lightning. But since they agree in all particulars wherein we can already compare them, is it not probable they agree likewise in this? Let the experiment be made."

Nine months later, he sent to Peter Collinson a letter summarizing his electrical discoveries and suggesting the experiment which he hoped would "make truth useful to mankind." He suggested erecting "on top of some high tower or steeple . . . a kind of sentry box." It would contain a man and an insulated stand. From the middle of the stand, an iron rod would rise and then, bending at right angles, pass out the door and go up again, twenty or thirty feet to a very sharp point. If clouds contained electricity, as Franklin suspected they did, the pointed rod would draw off the "fluid."

Franklin's letter was published in England as a small book entitled, *Experiments and Observations on Electricity, Made at Philadelphia in America*. It was translated into French, and soon two French electricians conducted Franklin's experiment, successfully drawing electricity from clouds. British electricians repeated the performance a few weeks later.

In America, meanwhile, Franklin tried another, more famous approach. Since there was no high ground or church steeple in or near Philadelphia, Franklin made a kite out of a silk kerchief, attached a pointed wire to the tip, and, accompanied only by his son William, went out to the Philadelphia commons, or public grazing grounds, on the edge of the town. There William got the kite aloft in a gathering thunderstorm. For insulation, Franklin tied the kite string to a silk ribbon which he held in his hand. Just above the ribbon he attached a key to the string.

At first, the kite dove and looped in the gathering storm, and nothing seemed to happen. But then, a scattering rain began to fall, and wet the string. Immediately, the fibers of the string stood erect, proof that they were positively charged. Franklin touched his knuckle to the key and received a mild electric shock. He then held the tip of a Leyden jar to the key, and drew off a large supply of electrical "fluid." He had been right. Clouds were full of electricity, and lightning and electricity were undoubtedly the same thing.

A few months later, in *Poor Richard's Almanack,* Franklin published the practical application of his idea. "It has pleased God in his goodness to mankind at length to discover to them the means of securing their habitations and other buildings from mischief by thunder and lightning." He then described how people could erect lightning rods on the roofs of their houses, and run them down the side of the building to the ground. The same thing could be done for ships, by running a wire from a rod on the mast down one of the shrouds to the water. The rod would thus "ground" to carry off the lightning charge harmlessly, instead of letting it hit the house or ship. Franklin made no attempt to patent his invention. He gave it to the world free of charge, as he did with many other things he invented, including the Pennsylvania fireplace, often called the Franklin stove. This was the first fireplace that kept most of the warm air in the room, instead of letting it escape up the chimney. Franklin also invented the first electrical battery. And he redesigned the street lights of Philadelphia, substituting four flat panes of glass for a globe, which quickly became smoky and gave little light. All of these things he gave to the world, free of charge, remarking that he had profited in his life from the inventions of other men, and that was why he had no desire to make money from his own inventions.

Franklin's electrical discoveries, particularly his work with lightning and the lightning rod, made him world famous. The King of France sent his personal congratulations across the ocean. The British Royal Society elected him a member by unanimous vote and bestowed upon him its highest award, the Copley Medal. Yale and Harvard gave him honorary degrees. Immanuel Kant, the greatest philosopher of the time, compared him to Prometheus, the Greek god who had brought down fire from heaven and gave it to mankind. In 1750, most people still believed that there was something divine about lightning, associating it with the vengeance of an angry God. The man who tamed it readily acquired an awesome, almost superhuman image.

But Franklin declined to act like a superman. Instead, he delighted in entertaining his friends with electrical tricks. He would electrify a many-legged piece of wire, and make it walk like a spider. He darkened the room, and electrified the gold border of a book. He electrified the gold crown on a painting of England's king, George II. Anyone who touched it received a very strong shock. He put a glass of brandy on one side of the Schuylkill River and sent an electric current across the river to set it ablaze. He electrified the gold rims of glasses, and then let his friends drink wine from them, giving them a tingling shock. He killed turkeys with a shock from his electric battery, and roasted them on an electric jack. Once, to show electricity's power, he knocked down three strong men with a single charge.

During one of these exhibitions, Franklin almost killed himself. He was showing a group of visitors how he could kill a turkey. Conversing with them while he prepared his apparatus, he accidentally touched the positive and negative poles at the same time. There was a loud crack, and Franklin's body vibrated like that of a man having a convulsion. He blacked out completely for several seconds, but, amazingly, did not fall. The hand that received the electric charge was dead white, and there was a bruise on his breastbone as if he had been hit there by a rock. Otherwise, he was unharmed, and he made a joke out of the incident. "I was going to kill a turkey," he said, "but it seems that I almost killed a goose."

Stories about Franklin's experiments attracted curiosity-seekers by the dozens. They would lurk around his house, trying to catch a glimpse of the electrician in his laboratory. One day Franklin electrified the rail fence on which they leaned, and sent a hefty charge surging down it. The gawkers vanished in a cloud of dust, certain that the devil himself had gotten inside them.

Franklin spent four years studying electricity, and at the end of that time he had transformed it from a curiosity into a branch of science. If he had been able to continue his study of it, he might have achieved even more scientific triumphs.

But there were political problems in Pennsylvania which badly needed solving, and Franklin could not resist his friends when they asked for his help. He believed that solving political and moral problems was more important than making scientific discoveries. He was fond of saying that if Isaac Newton, one of England's greatest scientists, had been the captain of a ship, he would not have been justified if he deserted the helm in a crisis to make even the greatest of his scientific discoveries.

The welfare of a colony such as Pennsylvania, which had over 300,000 people in it, was an even heavier responsibility. Franklin felt that every citizen in a free society shared the responsibility for its safety and health. Franklin also felt deeply grateful to Pennsylvania for giving him a chance to rise from poverty and obscurity to modest wealth and fame, and he wanted to give others the same opportunity. So, when his fellow citizens elected him to the Assembly as a representative from Philadelphia, Ben Franklin more or less abandoned his laboratory and put his powerful mind and considerable energy to work on the politics of Pennsylvania.

The Penns were the big problem in Pennsylvania. They owned millions of acres of land in the colony, but they refused to pay any taxes on them. Each time a governor was sent from England, he had specific instructions to veto any bill passed by the Assembly taxing the proprietors' estates.

Particularly annoying was the Penns' refusal to share the expenses of dealing with the Indians. Each year Pennsylvania and the other colonies gave the tribes on their respective frontiers expensive presents to keep them loyal and at peace. The French, in possession of Canada, began competing for the Indians' support with even more expensive presents. This was an unfortunate development for the colonies because the French, united in a single colony with the immense wealth of the French king behind them, were easily able to outbid individual colonies, such as Pennsylvania. One of Franklin's first duties as an assemblyman was to serve as a commissioner to negotiate new treaties of peace with Pennsylvania's Indians. When he and his fellow commissioners found out that the Indians considered their offerings inadequate, they promptly advanced their own money to buy more goods "at the Philadelphia price" on the frontier.

Franklin returned from this conference deeply worried about the future of England's colonies in America. He thought their very existence was imperiled by France's aggressive plans to move down the Ohio and seal off the colonies between the Appalachian Mountains and the Atlantic Ocean. It was time for the English colonies to unite. He pointed out to his friends that the Iroquois, a confederation of six Indian tribes, was the strongest power in the Indian world. Why didn't the English follow their example?

"It would be a strange thing if six nations of ignorant savages should be capable of forming a scheme for such an union, and be able to execute it in such a manner as that it has subsisted ages and appears indissoluble; and yet that a like union should be impracticable for ten or a dozen English colonies, to whom it is more necessary and must be more advantageous. . . ."

More and more, Franklin began thinking of the thirteen English colonies as a nation that must be formed.

CHAPTER 7

THE POSTMASTER

EVEN BEFORE HE BEGAN STUDYING ELECTRICITY, Franklin had tried to unite Americans who had a common interest in science by founding the American Philosophical Society. Its purpose was to pool scientific knowledge and to speed up its application to American life. The response was disappointing, partly because of the wretched mail service in the colonies. It took as long as six weeks for a letter to travel from Boston to Philadelphia, and letters were frequently lost by careless post riders and postmasters. It was hard to unite people who had trouble communicating with each other, and Franklin soon began thinking of ways to improve the postal service.

First he took the job of postmaster in Philadelphia, partly to make sure that his newspaper, which had the largest circulation of any on the continent, was regularly and safely mailed to subscribers. Then in 1751, the Deputy Postmaster General for America died, and Franklin applied for his job. He got the appointment, and swiftly went to work to transform the American postal system. For four years he worked at it without making a cent of money. Only if the system showed a profit would he get paid, and for decades it had been operating at a loss.

Like the scientist that he was, Franklin preferred to learn from first-hand observation, and within a few months after his appointment, he set out on a ten-week journey "to the East," as he called it, in the language of the born Bostonian. He traveled across New Jersey, through New York, and up into Connecticut, Rhode Island, and Massachusetts.

The improvements Franklin achieved in the postal service were nothing less than spectacular. He reduced the traveling time of a Boston-Philadelphia letter from six weeks to three. Abolishing the old monopolistic system by which each postmaster sent the newspaper of his choice through the mail free, he opened the service to all papers, for a small charge. He insisted on postmasters keeping precise accounts of their revenues and ordered them to print in the newspapers the names of persons who had letters waiting for them—a practice he had long followed in Philadelphia. People who did not call for their letters on the day they arrived had them delivered the following day, and were charged an extra penny. Again, this was an innovation Franklin had tried first in Philadelphia, and it made the post office much more popular. Too often in many cities, letters were allowed to lie around for weeks, and were liable to be lost, or read by idlers. After three months, unclaimed letters were forwarded to the central post office in Philadelphia—thus creating the first dead-letter office.

On the post roads, Franklin had milestones erected, so that post riders could pace themselves better. By talking with riders and postmasters face to face, Franklin established an esprit de corps, which had much to do with getting a new vitality into the service. He consulted the post riders and postmasters on new roads, fords, and ferries. In three years, the service was completely overhauled, and its new speed and reliability won it a popularity it had never known before. In the fourth year of Franklin's administration, it paid a profit for the first time in its history, collecting more revenue in 12 months than it had in the previous 36.

Traveling was a rugged business in the 1750s, and only someone with Franklin's tough constitution could have endured the bad weather, the terrible roads (too often either quagmires of mud or suffocating dust storms), the innumerable rivers which the traveler had to ford or ferry. Taverns and inns were few and often overcrowded. To get a place by the fire, after hours on the road in rain or cold, was difficult.

Once Franklin used his wit to overcome this particular challenge. Stopping in a Rhode Island tavern on a raw, blustery, rainy day, he found two dozen locals and travelers crowded around the room's only fire.

"Boy," Franklin said in stentorian tones to the tavern-keeper's son, "get my horse a quart of oysters."

"A quart of oysters?" gasped the boy.

"You heard me, a quart of oysters," Franklin boomed.

The boy obeyed, and there was a general stampede out the door to see this incredible phenomenon, a horse who ate oysters. The horse snorted and snuffled in indignation, and refused to have anything to do with the oysters. Baffled, the curiosity-seekers trooped back into the tavern, to find Deputy Postmaster General Franklin sitting serenely in the chair closest to the fire.

While Franklin traveled around America, his mind was not idle. In fact, moving from colony to colony inspired him to set down on paper one of his most important scientific insights, published a few years later under the title, "Observations Concerning the Increase of Mankind, Peopling of Countries &c." With a brilliant combination of mathematics and social observation, Franklin noted that there were now well over 1,000,000 Englishmen in North America. Yet little more than 80,000 had emigrated from England. This fact alone showed a radical difference between the New World and the Old World, where population was relatively stable. America, with its almost unlimited land and productive capacity, placed no barrier to marriage and the raising of families, as the economically cramped Old World did. For this reason, Franklin predicted that the population of America would double every 20 or 25 years—a prophecy which was fulfilled with scientific exactitude until 1860, when massive immigration created even more rapid growth. For Franklin, contemplating this increase in the early 1750s, it meant one significant thing— America will "in another century be more than the people of England, and the greatest number of Englishmen will be on this side of the water."

Franklin did not see this as a threat to the mother country. He boldly spoke and wrote as an Anglo-American and loyal member of the Empire. "What an accession of power to the British Empire by sea as well as land! What increase of trade and navigation! What numbers of ships and seamen!" Underlying this emotion, however, was a more uniquely American sentiment. In 1750, Parliament had restricted the manufacture of iron in Pennsylvania, because British ironmasters had complained that American-made iron was competing with their products. This made no sense to Franklin, because the population of the colonies was increasing so fast that there was sure to be an ever-growing market for manufacturers, whether British or American. "A wise and good mother," Franklin said, placed no distressing restraints on her children. "To distress is to weaken, and weakening the children weakens the whole family."

Franklin was not afraid to speak boldly when he confronted British stupidity. Shortly after he finished his essay on population, he sarcastically suggested a way for Americans to stop another bad British practice. Whenever their jails became overcrowded, the British deported their criminals to America.

Often these evildoers continued their life of crime in the New World, committing numerous robberies and murders. The best way to solve the problem, Franklin suggested in the *Pennsylvania Gazette,* was to return the compliment. From now on, let the Americans regularly export all their rattlesnakes to England.

Because as Deputy Postmaster General he was one of the few Americans who thought in terms of the entire continent, Franklin was appointed by Pennsylvania to be a delegate to the Albany Congress, convened in 1754 to work out a common intercolonial defense against the threatening French and Indians. Typically, he did more than think defensively. He proposed a plan of union which would have created a Governor General and a Grand Council consisting of members chosen by the assemblies of each colony. Although the delegates to the conference approved the plan, it received short shrift both from the colonial assemblies and from England. The colonial assemblies thought that it conceded too much of their local power to the General Council and especially to the Governor General, who would be appointed by the King. London thought it came too close to creating a political body strong enough to challenge the power of Parliament.

Disappointed, Franklin nevertheless continued to try to drum up interest in the idea wherever he went. He found an ardent listener in William Shirley, the royal governor of Massachusetts. The two men had many conversations together and also exchanged several letters on the subject.

Shirley's approach, natural enough for a man who saw the colonies through the eyes of the Crown, was to have the Grand Council work out plans for common defense and pay for them from taxes laid on the Americans by an act of Parliament. Worse, Shirley's Grand Council consisted largely of Royal Governors and their councilors, all of whom were appointed by the King, or at least required his approval.

Franklin immediately warned Shirley that Americans would never tolerate this approach. "Excluding the people of the colonies from all share in the choice of the Grand Council would probably give extreme dissatisfaction, as well as the taxing them by act of Parliament where they have no representation." In three searching letters, which were really political essays, Franklin explained to the Governor why Americans would not pay taxes voted by Parliament, and why they resented England's interference in their internal affairs. More than two decades later, James Madison, reading these letters, declared that Franklin had summed up the entire argument of the American Revolution "within the compass of a nutshell" 20 years before it occurred to anyone else.

CHAPTER 8

FATHER

PENNSYLVANIA, AND HIS FAMILY, REMAINED AT least as important to Franklin during these years as his postmastering and continental politicking. When Franklin took his seat in the Pennsylvania Assembly, he resigned his job as Assembly clerk, which he had held for over a dozen years. The Assembly promptly appointed William Franklin as his replacement. It was one more evidence of the central place William held in Franklin's affections. If a single word had to be chosen to describe Benjamin Franklin, paternal would come close to saying it all. This burly, broad-shouldered man seemed to fulfill himself most when he was in fathering role, sharing his strength, his wisdom, his generosity, and his humor with other people. Inevitably, this brought a special intensity to his relationship with his only son.

Another reason for this intensity was William's uneasy

position in Philadelphia society. As Franklin's political power increased, he became more and more critical of the petty grasping policy of the Penns. This made him an antagonist of the members of the proprietary party, who held the judgeships and other positions of power and honor which the Penns could bestow. Unable to wound Franklin personally, they struck at him through his son. There were constant snide whispers about William's illegitimate birth. When he fell in love with pretty, poetically talented Elizabeth Graeme, and asked for her hand in marriage, her wealthy parents haughtily rebuffed him. Inevitably, it saddened Franklin to see his son forced to cope with such unpleasant experiences.

Another reason why Franklin worried over William was the young man's relationship with Deborah, who continued to unleash her shrew's temper on her stepson.

A young clerk named Daniel Fisher, who lived in Franklin's house for a time, has left us a vivid picture of Deborah Franklin's feelings toward William. In his diary, Fisher wrote of seeing young Franklin pass through the house "without the least compliment between Mrs. Franklin and him or any sort of notice taken of each other." One day, as Deborah was chatting with Fisher, and William Franklin passed them in silence as usual, Deborah Franklin exclaimed, "Mr. Fisher, there goes the greatest villain upon earth." While Fisher stared in bewilderment, Deborah proceeded to denounce William Franklin "in the foulest terms I ever heard from a gentlewoman." Young Fisher eventually quit his job and moved out of the Franklin household. He simply could not stand Deborah Franklin's "turbulent temper."

Deborah and her husband had slowly moved apart, in the years since their marriage. She remained the shopkeeper's daughter, practically illiterate. She would sign her letters to him, "Your affecthone wife." He always began his letters to her: "My dear child." More and more jealous of the time he gave to public affairs, she told Daniel Fisher, "All the world claimed a privilege of troubling her Pappy," her family name for Franklin.

Eventually, Franklin gave up trying to control Deborah's wild tongue. With his father's permission, as soon as William obtained his first salary as clerk of the Assembly the young man moved into separate quarters to escape his quarrelsome stepmother.

In his teens, William had toyed with escaping Philadelphia and Deborah for good. He had tried to run away as a sailor aboard a privateer. Returned home through Franklin's intervention, he had badgered his father into getting him an army commission and had marched off to fight the French in Canada. The war ended before he heard a shot fired in anger, but he came home with a military style in his bearing, and an aura of adventure which gave him more self-confidence in his relationships with young Philadelphians his own age.

Almost immediately, William embarked on another, far more significant adventure. With fur trader George Croghan, he traveled west to an Indian conference on the Ohio. Like many other Americans of his generation, young Franklin was struck by the fabulous richness of the land beyond the Alleghenies, and the almost boundless abundance of it. He poured out his story about "the country back of us" to his father, who listened with keen interest, and was so impressed he sent copies of William's journal to friends in England.

William was convinced that a fortune was waiting for the men who first possessed these lands, then so haphazardly "owned" by small bands of Indians, who regarded them only as hunting preserves. In fact, when he returned home, he talked of nothing but ways of organizing trading companies and colonizing expeditions which would establish England's grip on the territory. For a while, Ohio seemed to be the only thing that interested him, aside from the pursuit of Philadelphia's belles at the Assembly Balls.

Finally, Franklin took William aside, and bluntly informed him that Ohio, fascinating and important as it might some day become, was at the moment about as substantial as a castle in the clouds. What Franklin feared was the possibility that William was assuming he could invest his time in fantasies and Assembly Balls because he was eventually coming into a handsome inheritance. Gently, Franklin told his son that he planned to spend the modest estate he had accumulated on himself. William had better start thinking about choosing a profession.

Shortly after the great kite experiment, William began studying law in the office of Franklin's good friend and political lieutenant, stocky, learned Joseph Galloway. At the same time, Franklin wrote to England and asked friends there to register William in the Inns of Court, where the elite of the British legal profession studied the common law. Hopefully, he said, he would make the trip to England with William when the time came for him to go.

CHAPTER 9

FRONTIERSMAN

BEFORE THEY WENT TO ENGLAND, HOWEVER, Franklin and his son shared a wild adventure on the Pennsylvania frontier. The French had built a fort on the site of the present-day city of Pittsburgh. To drive them out, the British sent Major General James Braddock and an army of 2,500 red-coated regulars. Pennsylvania and the other colonies were supposed to contribute money to purchase supplies for this army, but instead, the Pennsylvanians got into their usual wrangle with the Governor about taxing the Penns' estates. This made Braddock very angry with Pennsylvania, and the Assembly sent Franklin and his son William to Frederick, Maryland, where Braddock was organizing his troops and gathering his supplies, to explain the situation.

The Franklins arrived to discover General Braddock almost

insane with fury. The supplies sold to the army by American contractors were rotten, and there were only 25 wagons collected to transport tents and supplies for 2,250 men. Braddock was damning everyone involved, from the ministers in England who thought up the expedition to the haggling farmers who would not risk a wagon in the service of their country. The two Franklins watched while earnest young George Washington of Virginia, who was serving as General Braddock's aide, argued in vain with the General, trying to defend America's reputation.

Hoping to calm the general down, Franklin assured him that there were plenty of wagons available in Pennsylvania. The desperate general seized him by the arm. "Then you, sir, who are a man of interest there can probably procure them for us, and I beg you will undertake it." The General took a hundred pounds in hard cash from his money box and told Franklin to get to work.

The two Franklins immediately conferred with Sir John Sinclair, Braddock's quartermaster general. He had just returned from Pennsylvania, and he was angrily criticizing everything about the colony. Franklin noticed that Sinclair had a special uniform, which resembled that of a Hussar, the fearsome light cavalry of the Austrian and German armies, famous for their love of plunder.

Quickly Franklin dashed off a handbill, and had several thousand copies printed for distribution throughout Lancaster, York and Cumberland counties. He offered 15 shillings a day (perhaps $100 in modern money values)—a good price for a wagon, four horses and a driver. But the heart of Franklin's message was his warning that if the farmers of Pennsylvania did not accept "such good pay and reasonable terms" their loyalty would be "strongly suspected." This would put the King's "brave troops" in an exceedingly bad mood, and their march through the counties would almost certainly be "attended with many and great inconveniences."

If General Braddock did not get the necessary number of wagons in fourteen days, "I suppose Sir John Sinclair, the Hussar, with a body of soldiers, will immediately enter the province . . . which I shall be sorry to hear, because I am very sincerely and truthfully your friend and well-wisher."

Since most of the farmers in these counties were German immigrants, the word "Hussar" had an almost magical effect on them. Well within the deadline, over 150 four-horsed wagons, plus 259 pack horses, streamed into Braddock's camp.

The two Franklins became General Braddock's favorite dinner guests. He discussed his battle strategy with them, and Benjamin Franklin did not like what he heard. He warned the General that his army, struggling through the thick forests and over the swift streams of western Pennsylvania, would be easy to ambush. General Braddock laughed at this remark. "The savages may indeed be a formidable enemy to your raw American militia," said the British commander in chief, "but upon the King's regular and disciplin'd troops, sir, it is impossible that they should make any impression."

Benjamin and William Franklin rode home to Philadelphia, their minds still troubled by doubts. A few days later, two doctors, old friends of Franklin, came to him asking him to donate money to buy several hundred pounds of fireworks to celebrate the capture of Fort Duquesne, Braddock's objective in western Pennsylvania. Franklin let his glasses slip down a little on his nose and said, "I think it will be time enough to prepare the rejoicing when we know we have a reason to rejoice."

The doctors looked amazed. Like General Braddock, they assumed that British regulars were invincible. "Why the devil," said one of them, "you surely don't suppose that the fort will not be taken."

"I don't know that it will not be taken," Franklin said, "but I know that war is a very uncertain business."

The doctors abandoned their fund-raising. A few days later, a messenger rushed into Philadelphia carrying the stunning news that Braddock had been ambushed only a few miles from Fort Duquesne and two-thirds of his army killed or wounded. The survivors, under the command of Colonel Thomas Dunbar, were in headlong retreat.

The British did not stop running until they got to Trenton, New Jersey, on the eastern side of the Delaware. Obviously, it was up to Pennsylvania to defend its frontiers as best it could. All Braddock had accomplished was to build a handsome road down which the French and Indians could now pour, unrestrained, to slaughter hapless farmers and their families in their lonely cabins.

But not even desperate necessity could reconcile the Penns and Pennsylvania's Assembly. Again and again, the family's appointed representative, Governor Robert Hunter Morris, vetoed every tax bill which included the Proprietors' estates. Throughout the summer and the fall, debate raged, while the Indians on the frontier picked off isolated farms and single travelers in small, probing raids. When not even a sign of resistance appeared, the savages grew bolder. Large raiding parties poured into Berks and Northampton counties, and people died under the hatchet and scalping knife less than eighty miles from Philadelphia.

Most of the victims were Germans. Frantically they begged Governor Morris for help and when they got no answer, more than a thousand of them marched on Philadelphia, carrying a wagon full of scalped corpses which they parked before the Governor's mansion. Fortunately, the Penns had only a few days earlier offered to donate 5,000 pounds to the defense of the colony, if the Assembly would agree to a money bill that did not tax their estates. Under Franklin's leadership, the Assembly voted 60,000 pounds to raise and equip troops. But volunteers came forward very slowly. The bill exempted Quakers from serving—it was against their religion to serve in the army—and most other Pennsylvanians were reluctant to risk their lives to defend these apostles of nonviolence.

Franklin attacked the problem in the *Pennsylvania Gazette,* in the form of a dialogue among citizens X, Y, and Z.

"For my part," said Z, "I am no coward; but hang me if I'll fight to save the Quakers."

X replied, "That is to say you won't pump ship because it'll save the rats as well as yourself."

Then late in November came the worst news yet from the still defenseless frontier. The German village of Gnaden-hutten had been surprised by a Shawnee war party and every living soul slaughtered except a handful who escaped to the woods. The victims had all been pacifists, like the Quakers. Pure terror swept Pennsylvania. Farmers and their families abandoned their homesteads and crowded into the villages. Governor Morris was forced to beg Franklin to raise and organize a force of 300 rangers and lead them to the frontier.

Franklin accepted. He knew little about military affairs, but he knew how to lead men. With William Franklin taking care of the military details, Franklin marched his Rangers to the frontier, organized militia in a number of panic-stricken towns, and then advanced to Gnadenhutten, slogging through bitter cold and sleety rain. He spent his 50th birthday in a German farmer's barn, soaking wet from an all-day march in the rain. Indians sniped at them from a distance, but the braves had no stomach for taking on Franklin's well-armed force.

The Indians watched from the hills while Franklin and his son directed the little army in the building of a sturdy fort.

Franklin noticed that on the days that the men worked hard they were "good-natured and cheerful," while on days when rain forced them to be idle, they were mutinous and quarrelsome, "finding fault with their pork, the bread, etc., and in continual ill-humour."

The small army had a chaplain, a Presbyterian named Charles Beatty, who came to Franklin complaining that the men "did not generally attend his prayers and exhortations." As a stern soldier of the Lord, he was probably hoping that Franklin would issue an order, forcing the men to worship under threat of punishment. Instead, Franklin suggested that the chaplain double as steward of the rum. (The men were guaranteed a gill of rum a day, half in the morning and half in the evening.) He advised Chaplain Beatty to deal out the rum after prayers, and the chaplain took his advice. "Never were prayers more generally and more punctually attended," said Franklin.

The frontier secured, the Franklins returned to Philadelphia. There they found only more bitterness between the Assembly and the Proprietary Party. The 5,000 pounds which the Penns had supposedly donated to the war effort consisted of back rents in Pennsylvania which the Assembly would have to collect. Franklin led the Assembly in a mass march through the streets to deliver a scorching "remonstrance" to the Governor. When that official insisted on following his instructions, the Assembly ripped off another resolution, "That a commissioner or commissioners be appointed to go home to England, in behalf of the people of this province, to solicit a removal of the grievances we labor under by reason of Proprietary instructions." Benjamin Franklin was chosen to tackle this job. He asked William to go with him, to serve as his chief assistant—and also to complete his law studies at the Inns of Court, in London.

CHAPTER 10

SPOKESMAN FOR PHILADELPHIA

THE FRANKLINS RENTED ROOMS IN A HOUSE ON Craven Street, just off The Strand, one of the most fashionable streets in London, and only a few blocks away from the government offices in Whitehall Palace and the Houses of Parliament. The house was owned by a charming widow, Margaret Stevenson, who had a pretty young daughter, Polly. Franklin soon converted the Stevensons into a second family; Polly became a daughter to him. She was a brilliant girl, and Franklin encouraged her to study science, and to ask him questions about it. During the next several years he wrote her numerous letters about scientific topics, such as why black cloth absorbs more heat than white cloth. But as usual, he did not believe anyone should study science to the point where they did not lead a normal life. He urged Polly to marry and raise a family, soon making it clear, in fact, that he had strong hopes that William would propose to her, and that she would become his daughter-in-law.

But William was too busy enjoying London's high life. He did not particularly like an independent, studious girl like Polly. He preferred a more clinging, dependent woman and he soon found one in Elizabeth Downes, the daughter of a West Indian planter. She was pretty, and had a sweet, gentle disposition. But she declined to marry William as long as he had no visible means of support. William had to depend on Benjamin Franklin for all his considerable expenses. At one point, perhaps a little shocked by adding up how much he had spent recently, William told his father, "I am extremely oblig'd to you for your care in supplying me with money," and assured his father he would never forget his "paternal affection."

William continued his studies in the law at the Inns of Courts. Like his father before him, he found it hard to control his sexual drives, and soon he was forced to inform Franklin that he was a grandfather. A son, whom William named William Temple, had been born to a woman whom historians have never identified. Franklin insisted that his son accept complete responsibility for the boy, and advanced him the money needed to place the child with a good family in the country, who would raise him until it was time for him to go to school.

Meanwhile, with William's help, Franklin easily routed the

Penns, and forced them to agree to let their lands be taxed by the Pennsylvania Assembly. To this triumph, Franklin added a personal one. Through numerous friends around the British throne, he won for William an appointment as the Royal Governor of New Jersey.

William's appointment was part of a master plan that Franklin was evolving, to run the Penns out of Pennsylvania and replace them with a royal governor directly under the rule of the Crown. What better argument for royal government, than to be able to point to the honest, stable, peaceful regime of that staunch son of Philadelphia, William Franklin, Governor of New Jersey?

Finally, there was another, even larger dream. Franklin had never forgotten William's vivid description of the Ohio Valley. With the French defeated, this now was English territory. Already he had discussed with powerful friends in England the possibility of founding a colony there as William Penn had founded Pennsylvania. What better way to train his son in the uses of power, than to inherit the immense responsibility which this political experiment would leave him?

Perhaps the best example of Franklin's amazing ability to win friends in England was the letter which William Strahan, the richest and most powerful printer in London, publisher of an influential newspaper and of books such as Samuel Johnson's famed dictionary, wrote to Franklin's partner David Hall. In Franklin's six years in England, his friendship had become the most important relationship in Strahan's life, outside of his family.

Strahan began by telling "Dear Davie" (Hall had worked as an apprentice for him before joining Franklin in Philadelphia) that Hall would never have seen Franklin's face on his side of the water "had my power been in any measure equal to my inclination." It was amazing, Strahan went on, the way Franklin with all his remarkable talents and abilities which had won the admiration and affection of "the greatest geniuses of this country" was equally beloved by simple businessmen such as himself. Franklin knew how "to level himself for the time to the understandings of his company, and to enter without affectation into their amusements and chitchat." This was how he made people from all walks and levels of life "his affectionate friends."

As for himself, Strahan said, "I never found a person in my whole life more thoroughly to my mind . . . It would much exceed the bounds of a letter to tell you in how many views, and on how many accounts, I esteem and love him . . . Suffice it to say that I part with him with infinite regret and sorrow. I know not where to find his equal, nor can the chasm his departure leaves in my social enjoyments and happiness ever be filled up. There is something in his leaving us even more cruel than a separation by death; it is like an *untimely death,* where we part with a friend to meet no more, with a *whole heart,* as we say in Scotland." Strahan went on for pages, lamenting "a separation so much the more bitter and agonizing, as it is likely to be endless."

Franklin's affection for Strahan was deep enough. He told him, in his farewell letter, that he felt so depressed on leaving England, he had to admit that Strahan's "persuasions and arguments" had had their effect. "The attraction of reason is at present for the other side of the water, but that of inclination will be for this side. You know which usually prevails. I shall probably make but this one vibration and settle here forever. Nothing will prevent it, if I can, as I hope I can, prevail with Mrs. F. to accompany me."

Back in America, Franklin supervised the installation of William as Royal Governor of New Jersey, and did his utmost to persuade Deborah to return to England with him. He had fallen so totally in love with the mother country, he was serious about spending the rest of his life there. In a letter to an English friend he exclaimed, "Why should that petty island, which compared to America is but like a stepping stone in a brook, scarce enough of it above water to keep one's shoes dry; why, I say, should that little island, enjoy in almost every neighborhood, more sensible, virtuous and elegant minds, than we can collect in ranging a hundred leagues of our vast forests?" From Philadelphia he assured Strahan, "In two years at farthest I hope to settle all my affairs in such a manner, as that I may then conveniently remove to England, provided we can persuade the good woman to cross the seas."

But the good woman absolutely refused to consider an

ocean crossing. Deborah had an hysterical fear of ships and water, similar to the phobia that prevents many people from flying today. So, regretfully, Franklin began building a handsome new house in Philadelphia, and Governor William Franklin was soon telling the disconsolate Strahan that his father was obviously planning to spend his old age in America.

By now Franklin was 59, definitely old in a century when most men died in their 40s and 50s, with only a handful reaching the biblical three score and ten. Yet Franklin did not look or act old. He still had the burly, bulky vigor of his middle age, in spite of a paunch which sometimes prompted him to call himself "Dr. Fatsides."

When an Indian war erupted on the Pennsylvania frontier, the need to tax the Penns' estates again became a ticklish problem in the colony's Assembly. Franklin, who had been elected in absentia during his years in England, prepared the taxation bill in strict accordance with the agreement he had reached with the Penns. Then, to his disgust he discovered that the Penns had instructed their governor not to permit any taxation on their lands that exceeded the lowest taxes paid by individual owners on the poorest, cheapest land in the colony.

Infuriated but calm, Franklin marshaled his forces, and rammed through a bill petitioning the King to take the government of Pennsylvania out of the venal hands of the Penns, once and for all. Over the desperate opposition of the proprietary party, the Assembly appointed Franklin their delegate to take the petition to London and win its approval from the King and his Privy Councilors. Franklin assured the agitated Deborah that he would be back within twelve months. Then, escorted by no less than 300 men on horseback, he rode down to Chester on the Delaware, where the ship, *King of Prussia,* was waiting for him. Cannon, borrowed from the Philadelphia armory, boomed as he went aboard and the crowd sang an improvised version of "God Save the King."

O LORD our GOD arise,
Scatter our Enemies,
   And make them fall.
Confound their Politicks,
Frustrate such Hypocrites,
Franklin, on Thee we fix,
   GOD Save us all
Thy Knowledge rich in Store,
On Pennsylvania pour,
   Thou (*sic*) great Blessing
Long to defend our Laws,
Still give us greater Cause,
To sing with Heart and Voice,
   GEORGE and FRANKLIN
GOD Save Great GEORGE our King;
Prosper agent FRANKLIN:
   Grant him Success:
Hark how the Vallies ring;
GOD Save our Gracious King,

From whom all Blessings spring,
    Our Wrongs redress.

Franklin's devoted political lieutenant, Joseph Galloway, and two other close friends, Thomas Wharton and Abel James, both prominent Philadelphia merchants, went on board ship with him and sailed down the Delaware to New Castle. Franklin was deeply touched by this outpouring of affection and loyalty. On the night of November 8th, alone in his cabin aboard the *King of Prussia,* he had only one worry which still nagged at his mind: his daughter, Sarah, whom he called Sally. At 21, she was almost certain to be exposed to the same kind of humiliating snubs and petty insults from her father's political enemies that had made William Franklin unhappy. Benjamin had wanted to take Sally with him to England, to put her beyond the reach of this revenge, at least for the year he expected to be gone. But Deborah Franklin had absolutely refused to part with her.

Before the ship sailed, Franklin wrote Sally a letter, assuring her of his love and giving her some wise advice. He urged her to ignore the nasty things his enemies were saying about him. Even the pastor of the church that Sally attended was anti-Franklin, and made cruel remarks about him from the pulpit. Nevertheless, Franklin urged Sally to continue to attend church. Otherwise, his enemies would use her absence to accuse her of being a bad woman, like her evil father. Finally, he urged her to acquire "those useful accomplishments, arith-

75

metick and bookkeeping." With the Philadelphia establishment so thoroughly aroused against the Franklins, there was
not much chance that Sally would marry a wealthy scion. So
Franklin was attempting to prepare her for becoming a
tradesman's wife, and wanted her to be able to give her husband the kind of valuable help Deborah had given him.

Franklin had no need to worry about William, of course.
He was happily married to the Englishwoman he had met in
London, and making a great success of his governorship in
New Jersey. Franklin was tremendously proud of him.

When the elder Franklin sailed, he had every reason to
believe that his mission would be successful. With the many
friends he had acquired in England, he was confident he could
drive the Penns out of Pennsylvania, and get the government's
approval of a new colony in the Ohio Valley. Together, he and
his son would build a model society there. Benjamin Franklin
had no way of knowing that instead he was sailing into a mael-
strom that would destroy his relationship with William—the
deepest and most important personal relationship in his life.

CHAPTER 11

PERSUADER OF PARLIAMENT

WHEN FRANKLIN REACHED ENGLAND EARLY IN December, 1764, he found himself involved in a completely unexpected political uproar. The British government was deeply in debt, for it had cost over 200 million pounds to defeat France in the Seven Years War. British politicians shuddered at the thought of trying to impose more taxes in England, Scotland or Ireland. Everyone there was already complaining that the taxes were too high.

It was also costing the British a lot of money to maintain an army in America to control the Indians, and they decided to make the Americans pay for this expense, by taxing them. When Franklin arrived, he found Parliament preparing to pass a Stamp Act for America. All legal documents, marriage licenses, wills, contracts, as well as newspapers and many other items, would henceforth be required to carry a Royal stamp, which the government would sell. A similar law was already in existence in England.

Franklin and three other Americans went to see George Grenville, England's First Minister (the leader of the British cabinet, now called the Prime Minister), to advise him against passing the law. They warned him that Americans would resent it. They did not believe that Parliament had a right to tax them, because they had no representatives in Parliament. But Grenville did not listen to them. He presented the bill to Parliament, and it was passed with practically no debate. Franklin advised his American friends to be patient. He and other Americans in England would begin work to get the law repealed, but it might take a long time.

The reaction in America was much more impatient. In almost every colony, assemblies condemned the bill. In Virginia, Patrick Henry, a young backwoods orator, arose in the House of Burgesses to thunder, "Caesar had his Brutus, Charles I his Cromwell, let George III profit from their example." In Boston and New York, mobs rioted, destroying the houses of government officials, and forcing commissioners appointed by the Crown to sell the stamps, to resign. In Philadelphia, Franklin's proprietary party enemies spread a vicious rumor that he was in favor of the Stamp Act, and had even helped the British government draft the law. A mob gathered in the streets, and threatened to attack his house.

Franklin, in London, heard the story from Deborah, in vivid, if badly spelled letters. For nine days, she said, she was kept in "one contineued hurrey" by people urging her to flee with her daughter Sally to Governor William Franklin's home in Burlington, New Jersey. But other friends and relatives staunchly supported them. One of Deborah's cousins arrived to tell her that "more than twenty pepel" had told him it was his duty to stay with her. She told him she was "pleased to receive civility from aney bodey."

Toward nightfall, Deborah told her cousin to "fech a gun or two" and also to summon her brother to assist in the defense of the house. "We maid one room into a magazin. I ordored sum sorte of defens up stairs such as I cold manaig my self," Deborah told her husband. When neighbors again advised her to flee, she refused. "I sed . . . I was verey shuer you had dun nothing to hurte aney bodey nor had I not given aney ofense to aney person att all nor wold I be maid unesey by aney bodey nor wold I stir or show the leste uneseynis." Reinforcements from other relatives and Franklin's friends and neighbors, all well armed, discouraged the mob, and Franklin's house was not attacked.

In London, Franklin redoubled his efforts to get the Stamp Act repealed. He had letters from friends in America published in the newspapers, warning the English that they were in danger of losing the colonies. Franklin himself spent long hours at his desk, answering the arrogant and opinionated assaults on Americans that began appearing in the English press. He also worked tirelessly to influence members of Parliament. Almost every hour of the day, Franklin told one friend, was spent in "forming, explaining, consulting, disputing" with Britain's lawmakers. He worked closely with a committee of 28 London merchants who pressured Parliament to repeal the Stamp Act. Americans had signed non-importation agreements, pledging themselves to buy no English goods until the tax was repealed. The merchants sent circular letters to 20 other British towns and cities urging them to petition Parliament to abandon the Stamp Act before it wrecked the British economy.

At first, Franklin seemed to make little progress. Many members of Parliament saw the Stamp Act as a test of Parliament's right to tax Americans. "A peppercorn, in acknowledgement of the right, was of more value than millions without," one said.

Edmund Burke, a brilliant Irish-born member of Parliament who wanted to repeal the Stamp Act, decided Parliament needed to be better informed. "Ignorance of American affairs," he declared, had misled them. So he summoned a series of experts before Parliament to testify about America. One of these was Benjamin Franklin.

Franklin made sure that his testimony would have a real impact. With the help of several friends in Parliament, he drew up and carefully rehearsed a list of questions and answers that he hoped would refute the Stamp Act once and for all.

On February 13, 1766, Franklin appeared before the House of Commons. His testimony demolished the supporters of the

Stamp Act. Refuting the notion that America was rich, and relatively untaxed, Franklin told how many taxes Americans were already paying to their colonial assemblies. Even more effective was the way he showed that the Stamp Act was not only unjust, but totally impractical. In the thinly populated back settlements along the frontier, and in Canada (now an English possession), there was no mail service, and people could not get stamps—which meant they could not marry, make their wills, or buy or sell property without taking long journeys and "spending perhaps three or four pounds, that the Crown might get sixpence."

At one point, Franklin won a bitter exchange with George Grenville himself, the man who had proposed the Stamp Act. Out of office now, Grenville was angry at anyone who dared to criticize his brainchild. "Do you think it right that America should be protected by this country and pay no part of the expense?" he demanded.

"That is not the case," Franklin replied. "The colonies raised, clothed, and paid during the last war, near 25,000 men, and spent many millions."

"Were you not reimbursed by Parliament?"

"We were only reimbursed what in your opinion we had advanced beyond our proportion, or beyond what might reasonably be expected from us; and it was a very small part of what we spent. Pennsylvania, in particular, disbursed about 500,000 pounds and the reimbursements in the whole did not exceed 60,000 pounds."

Grenville sat down, looking very uncomfortable.

In answer to the prepared questions from his friends, Franklin presented some significant statistics about the population of America, and how much the colonists imported from Britain. There were 300,000 men in America between 16 and 60—more than enough to make a formidable army. Pennsylvania alone imported 500,000 pounds of British goods each year. The implication was obvious. Not only would a war with these people be dangerous; it would be highly uneconomic.

On and on the questions and answers rolled, drawing from Franklin answers that made the Stamp Act look more and more like the greatest piece of idiocy in Parliament's history. The supporters of the Stamp Act become so enraged, they began asking stupid questions.

Would the colonies acquiesce in the authority of Parliament if the Stamp Act was repealed? One man huffed.

"I don't doubt at all that if the legislature repealed the Act the colonies will acquiesce in the authority," said Franklin with a twinkle in his eye.

But Franklin closed his performance with a solemn warning.

"If the Act is not repealed, what do you think will be the consequences?" asked one of his friends.

"A total loss of the respect and affection the people of America bear this country, and of all the commerce that depends on that respect and affection."

A week later, the House of Commons voted to repeal the

Stamp Act. In America, the news touched off a wave of celebrations. Franklin's testimony before Parliament was reprinted in almost every colony, and his popularity soared. The proprietary party in Pennsylvania had to eat the slander they had been spreading, that Franklin had aided and abetted the Stamp Act.

But in London, the man who made the victory possible was not so optimistic about the future. He noted wryly that Parliament had also passed a Declaratory Act, in which it insisted that it had the right to enact laws binding the British colonies "in all cases whatsoever." Only a few weeks later, Parliament renewed the law that gave England the power to export convicts to the colonies. Franklin quietly circulated among his friends another bill, which would have given the colonies the right to export their convicts to Scotland. Most of the members of Parliament who saw it laughed, and considered it a joke. Obviously, they did not get Franklin's basic message, which was serious. The Americans were not going to let the British push them around indefinitely.

CHAPTER 12

AGENT

AFTER THE STAMP ACT UPROAR, THERE WAS NO hope of driving the Penns out of Pennsylvania and substituting a Royal Governor. But Franklin stayed on in London, as Pennsylvania's agent. The people felt that no one could do a better job of representing them before the various boards and committees that ran the empire.

Also, he was working on a plan to create a paper currency for all the colonies in America. Not only would it help to unify them, but it would also increase the circulation of money, and thus stimulate business. In Franklin's plan, the British government would derive a small profit from selling the money to the colonies, which would be a painless and invisible form of taxation. But as usual, he found it hard to get anyone in the British government to take his advice. America was only one part of the great British Empire. There were also the colonies in India, Africa, and the West Indies which claimed much of the government's attention. And the English political scene was very turbulent, with new cabinets and new First Ministers coming in and out almost every year.

At the same time, Franklin worked to create one of his oldest dreams, a new colony in the Ohio River Valley. William Franklin was now even more deeply involved in this dream. In America, Governor Franklin had joined some friends his own age in a company that negotiated a treaty with the Indians, giving them access to some of this land. In London, Franklin tried to win the British government's approval. Eventually, he persuaded William and his friends to dissolve their American company and merge it with a larger British company, which Franklin and his friends formed in London. Franklin drew into this company some of the biggest names in the British establishment. Lord Gower, the president of the King's Privy Council, was a partner. Slowly, patiently, for five years Franklin worked on this project.

Almost every year, he would tell his wife or his son William that he was discouraged and eager to return home. But something always happened to keep him in England for another year. If it was not the hope of some progress on the Ohio colony, it was new turmoil between England and America.

In 1768, Charles Townshend, one of the more lightheaded members of Parliament, proposed a series of new taxes. Instead of the internal tax of the Stamp Act, the Townshend Acts placed heavy duties on paper, lead, glass and other commodities that the colonies imported from England. Americans resented these taxes, and immediately began agitating for their repeal. Again, Franklin was busy writing articles in British newspapers, defending America against bitter accusations from angry Britons.

More and more, he became a spokesman for all Americans, and not just for Pennsylvania. Georgia asked him to be their agent in London, and then New Jersey, no doubt prompted by Governor William Franklin, made the same request. Then came a real surprise. Massachusetts, the most rebellious of all the colonies, asked Franklin to represent them.

Actually, it was the Massachusetts Assembly that made this request. The Assembly had been feuding furiously with the Royal Governor, Thomas Hutchinson, over the Townshend Acts and other matters. When the London agent for Massachusetts died, the choice of a new agent became part of the wrangle. It soon became obvious that the Governor and the Assembly could not agree on a new man, so the Assembly chose Franklin as its representative, and told the Governor to get his own agent.

Franklin knew that serving as agent for Massachusetts was a very dangerous job. Since they were the most independent of all the colonies, anyone who represented them was bound to be disliked by the men in power in London. Accepting the job was doubly painful for him, because he knew it might ruin his chances of getting approval for the Ohio colony. But he accepted the appointment, because he believed that the people of Massachusetts and their fellow Americans in other colonies were right, and the British were wrong, in the debate over Parliament's power.

Franklin found out just how much trouble Massachusetts was likely to cause for him when he went to see Wills Hill, Lord Hillsborough, the Minister in charge of the American colonies. Franklin had already tangled with him over the Ohio colony, which Lord Hillsborough did not approve. He had huge estates in Northern Ireland, and he was afraid that a new colony in America might lure workers away from that country. But Franklin had pushed the project steadily, in spite of Lord Hillsborough's disapproval, and had made considerable progress when he went to call on his lordship, on January 16th, 1771, to present his credentials as the agent for the Massachusetts Assembly. Here is a blow-by-blow account of the stormy interview, written by Benjamin Franklin only a few hours after it took place.

I was shown into the levee room, where . . . several other gentlemen were there attending, with whom I sat down a few minutes, when Secretary Pownall came out to us, and said his Lordship desired I would come in.

I was pleased with this ready admission and preference, having sometimes waited three or four hours for my turn; and, being pleased, I could more easily put on the open, cheerful countenance, that my friends advised me to wear. His Lordship came towards me and said, "I was dressing in order to go to court; but, hearing that you were at the door, who are a man of business, I determined to see you immediately." I thanked his Lordship, and said that my business at present was not much; it was only to pay my respects to his Lordship, and to acquaint him with my appointment by the House of Representatives of Massachusetts Bay to be their agent here, in which station if I could be of any service—(I was going to say—"to the public, I should be very happy"; but his Lordship, whose countenance changed at my naming that province, cut me short by saying, with something between a smile and a sneer,)

L.H. I must set you right there, Mr. Franklin, you are not agent.

B F. Why, my Lord?

L.H. You are not appointed.

B.F. I do not understand your Lordship; I have the appointment in my pocket.

L.H. You are mistaken; I have later and better advices. I have a letter from Governor Hutchinson; he would not give his assent to the bill.

B.F. There was no bill, my Lord; it was a vote of the House.

L.H. There was a bill presented to the governor for the purpose of appointing you and another, one Dr. Lee, I think he is called, to which the governor refused his assent.

B.F. I cannot understand this, my Lord; I think there must be some mistake in it. Is your Lordship quite sure that you have such a letter?

L.H. I will convince you of it directly. *(Rings the bell.)* Mr. Pownall will come in and satisfy you.

B.F. It is not necessary, that I should now detain your Lordship from dressing. You are going to court. I will wait on your Lordship another time.

L.H. No, stay; he will come immediately. *(To the servant.)* Tell Mr. Pownall I want him.

(Mr. Pownall comes in.)

L.H. Have not you at hand Governor Hutchinson's letter, mentioning his refusing his assent to the bill for appointing Dr. Franklin agent?

Sec. P. My Lord?

L.H. Is there not such a letter?

Sec. P. No, my Lord; there is a letter relating to some bill for the payment of a salary to Mr. De Berdt, and I think to some other agent, to which the governor had refused his assent.

L.H. And is there nothing in the letter to the purpose I mention?

Sec. P. No, my Lord.

B.F. I thought it could not well be, my Lord; as my letters are by the last ships, and they mention no such thing. Here is the authentic copy of the vote of the House appointing me, in which there is no mention of any act

89

intended. Will your Lordship please to look at it? *(With seeming unwillingness he takes it, but does not look into it.)*

L.H. Any information of this kind is not properly brought to me as Secretary of State. The Board of Trade is the proper place.

B.F. I will leave the paper then with Mr. Pownall to be—

L.H. *(Hastily.)* To what end would you leave it with him?

B.F. To be entered on the minutes of that Board, as usual.

L.H. *(Angrily.)* It shall not be entered there. No such paper shall be entered there, while I have any thing to do with the business of that Board. The House of Representatives has no right to appoint an agent. We shall take no notice of any agents, but such as are appointed by acts of Assembly, to which the governor gives his assent. We have confusion enough already. Here is one agent appointed by the Council, another by the House of Representatives. Which of these is agent for the province? An agent appointed by act of Assembly we can understand. No other will be attended to for the future, I can assure you.

B.F. I cannot conceive, my Lord, why the consent of the governor should be thought necessary to the appointment of an agent for the people. It seems to me that—

L.H. *(With a mixed look of anger and contempt.)* I shall not enter into a dispute with YOU, Sir, upon this subject.

B.F. I beg your Lordship's pardon; I do not presume to dispute with your Lordship; I would only say, that it seems to me, that every body of men, who cannot appear in person, where business relating to them may be transacted, should have a right to appear by an agent. The concurrence of the governor does not seem to me necessary. It is the business of the people, that is to be done; he is not one of them; he is himself an agent.

L.H. *(Hastily.)* Whose agent is he?

B.F. The King's, my Lord.

L.H. No such matter. He is one of the corporation by the province charter. No agent can be appointed but by an act, nor any act pass without his assent. Besides, this proceeding is directly contrary to express instructions.

B.F. I did not know there had been such instructions. I am not concerned in any offence against them, and—

L.H. Yes, your offering such a paper to be entered is an offence against them. *(Folding it up again without having read a word of it.)* No such appointment shall be entered. When I came into the administration of American affairs, I found them in great disorder. By *my firmness* they are now something mended; and, while I have the honor to hold the seals, I shall continue the same conduct, the same *firmness.* I think my duty to the master I serve, and to the government of this nation, requires it of me. If that conduct is not approved, *they* may take my office from me when they please. I shall make them a bow, and thank them; I shall resign with pleasure. That gentleman knows it, *(pointing to Mr. Pownall,)* but, while I continue in it, I shall resolutely persevere in the same FIRMNESS. *(Spoken with great warmth, and turning pale in his discourse, as if he was angry at something or somebody besides the agent, and of more consequence to himself.)*

B.F. *(Reaching out his hand for the paper, which his Lordship returned to him.)* I beg your Lordship's pardon for taking up so much of your time. It is, I believe, of no great importance whether the appointment is acknowledged or not, for I have not the least conception that an agent can *at present* be of any use to any of the colonies. I shall therefore give your Lordship no further trouble. *(Withdrew.)*

Franklin soon evened the score with Lord Hillsborough, however. He forced him to hold a hearing on the Ohio colony. The Board of Trade, which Hillsborough also headed, issued a report disapproving the project. Franklin requested the Privy Council to review this decision, and they repudiated Hillsborough's report. Completely humiliated, Hillsborough resigned. But he remained a powerful enemy, and his friends in the government stalled the final decision on the colony.

On April 6th, 1773, Franklin wrote an amusing letter to his friend and partner, Joseph Galloway, about this slow progress. "The affair of the [Ohio] grant goes on but slowly. I do not yet clearly see land. I begin to be a little of the sailor's mind when they were handing a cable out of a store into a ship, and one of 'em said: ' 'Tis a long heavy cable. I wish we could see the end of it.'

" 'D——n me,' says another, 'if I believe it has any end; some-body has cut it off.' "

CHAPTER 13

THE JOKER

WHILE HE WAS FIGHTING ON ALL THESE FRONTS, Franklin also managed to enjoy himself, and to remain keenly interested in his family and friends, keeping in close touch with his wife and daughter, in America. Only after a good deal of hesitation did he agree to Sally's marriage to Richard Bache, an emigrant from Yorkshire, in England. Bache returned to England to introduce himself to his father-in-law, and Franklin loaned him money to help him get started as a merchant in Philadelphia. Later came news that delighted him: Sally had made him a grandfather, and named the boy Benjamin Franklin Bache.

Franklin immediately warned his wife not to spoil the new arrival. He told her a story of two little boys in the street. "One was crying bitterly; the other came to him to ask what was the matter? I have been, says he, for a penny worth of vinegar, and

I have broke the glass and spilt the vinegar, and my mother will whip me. No, she won't whip you, says the other. Have then you got ne'er a grandmother?"

At Craven Street, where he stayed with the Stevensons, Franklin was equally pleased when Polly married a gifted young doctor, William Hewson. When she had a child, she promptly made Franklin the godfather. She wrote Franklin regularly, telling him of the child's progress. Franklin, in turn, gave her amusing advice on how to raise him. "Pray let him have everything he likes; I think it of great consequence while the features of the countenance are forming; it gives them a pleasant air, and, that being once become natural and fix'd by habit, the face is ever after the handsomer for it, and on that much of a person's good fortune and success in life may depend. Had I been cross'd as much in my infant likings and inclinations as you know I have been of late years, I should have been, I was going to say, not near so handsome; but as the vanity of that expression would offend other folks' vanity, I change it, out of regard to them, and say a great deal more homely."

Franklin was always teasing Polly and her friends to give him a kiss or a hug. His favorite among these friends was Dolly Blount, a very pretty young woman. Next door to Franklin lived James Hutton, one of the leaders of the Moravian Church in England, who also enjoyed pursuing Miss Blount for a kiss. One day, another of Polly's friends informed Franklin and Hutton that Dolly had made a vow to marry whichever one of them became a widower first. "It is impossible to express the various agitations of mind appearing in both their faces on this occasion," Franklin wrote, laughing at himself as much as at Hutton. "Vanity at the preference given them over the rest of mankind; affection to their present wives, fear of losing them, hope, if they must lose them, to obtain the proposed comforts; jealousy of each other in case both wives should die together, &c, &c,—all working at the same time jumbled their features into inexplicable confusion. They parted at length with professions & outward appearances indeed of ever-during friendship, but it was shrewdly suspected that each of them sincerely wished health & long life to the other's wife; & that however long either of these friends might like to live himself, the other would be very well pleas'd to survive him."

When he was not enjoying himself at Craven Street, Franklin often visited the homes of wealthy and powerful Englishmen. Among these, his two favorites were William Petty, Lord Shelburne, and Francis Dashwood, Lord le Despencer, the head of the British post office. Shelburne was sympathetic to America's side in the argument with Parliament, and he had favored the Ohio colony, until a shift in the political power structure had driven him out of office. He was now a member of the opposition, as the British called the party out of power in Parliament.

One weekend at Bowood, Shelburne's estate (which still stands, not far from London), Franklin played a joke on the assemblage of famous guests, including members of Parliament and the noted actor David Garrick. Walking in the "park," the broad landscaped gardens of the estate, Franklin remarked that he had acquired unusual powers, thanks to some scientific experiments he had been making. For instance, he now could transform rough water into calm water, at a wave of his cane. Of course, no one believed him. They pointed to a nearby brook, where a breeze was stirring up many small waves, and told him to prove it. Franklin walked over to the side of the brook and passed his cane over it a few times. The spectators gasped with disbelief—the surface of the water suddenly became calm, and as glassy as a mirror.

A workman, who was standing nearby, was sure that Franklin had just demonstrated supernatural powers. "What should I believe?" he cried.

"Only what you see," Franklin said.

The rest of the spectators rushed to the bank, and begged Franklin to tell them how he had done it. Only then did he reveal that the botton of his cane was hollow, and in the hollow he carried a small vial of clear oil. Franklin had been experimenting with the use of oil to calm storms at sea, in the hope of aiding vessels in distress. He found that it did not work very well on the ocean, but it did an excellent job on smaller bodies of water.

Another weekend at Lord le Despencer's, Franklin enjoyed the pleasure of seeing one of his best political jokes throw everyone into a turmoil. In one of the London papers under the heading of foreign news, he published, "An Edict from the King of Prussia." The Edict, supposedly signed by Frederick the Great of Prussia, declared that henceforth Prussia was going to exercise more control over its colony, England. The right to call England a colony was based, the King said, on the fact that it had been settled hundreds of years ago by German tribesmen. The King proceeded to forbid the manufacture of iron and numerous other products in exactly the same way that the English Parliament forbade their manufacture in America. All goods shipped by England had to pass through the German port of Koningsberg, just as all American ships had to touch first at London, and pay a duty on their cargoes before going on to other countries. Finally, the Edict declared, "We do hereby also ordain and command, that all the *thieves,* highway and street robbers, housebreakers, forgers, murderers . . . and villains of every denomination, who have forfeited their lives to the law in Prussia; but whom we, in our great clemency, do not think fit here to hang, shall be emptied out of our gaols into the said island of Great Britain, for the better peopling of that country."

Franklin was sitting in the breakfast room at Lord le Despencer's estate, when a visiting writer, Paul Whitehead, rushed into the room with the newspaper containing the Edict in his hand. "Here," he said, "here's news for ye! Here's the King of Prussia, claiming a right to this kingdom."

All stared with astonishment, and Franklin managed to look as surprised as the rest of the company.

Whitehead proceeded to read two or three paragraphs. "Damn his impudence," roared another guest, "I dare say, we shall hear by next post that he is upon his march with 100,000 men to back this." But then Whitehead, noticing the frequent references to Britain and the American colonies in the Prussian king's justification of his Edict, suddenly squinted at Franklin and said, "I'll be hanged if this is not some of your American jokes upon us."

Franklin cheerfully admitted his guilt, and Whitehead proceeded to read the rest of the Edict to roars of laughter. Everyone agreed that it was "a fair hit." Lord le Despencer liked the piece so much he had it cut out of the paper and preserved in his library.

In the summer or the fall of each year, Franklin took a trip, for he found that it improved his health to escape from London's sooty atmosphere for five or six weeks. But even on these trips, he found it more and more difficult to avoid politics. This was especially true in the fall of 1771, when he made a tour of Ireland and Scotland. He was appalled by the poverty he saw, especially in Ireland which was completely dominated by the English. To a friend in Rhode Island, he wrote vividly of what he had seen and why it convinced him that America must maintain its rights in the face of Parliament's grasping power.

"I have lately made a tour thro Ireland and Scotland. In those countries, a small part of the society are landlords, great noblemen, and gentlemen, extreamly opulent, living in the highest affluence and magnificence: the bulk of the people tenants, extreamly poor, living in the most sordid wretchedness, in dirty hovels of mud and straw, and cloathed only in rags.

"I often thought of the happiness of New England, where every man is a freeholder, has a vote in public affairs, lives in a tidy, warm house, has plenty of good food and fewel, with whole cloathes from head to foot, the manufacture perhaps of his own family. Long may they continue in this situation!"

Because he was determined to keep America free, Franklin decided to do something very risky. During one of his visits with English friends, a powerful member of the British government began arguing with him about the feud between Massachusetts and the Crown. To Franklin's amazement, the man assured him that the harsh policies which the British government had adopted—stationing troops there, forcing the Assembly to meet at inconvenient places, making judges independent of the people by having the Crown pay their salaries— had all been suggested by Americans, men living in Massachusetts. Franklin demanded proof, and his British friend produced for him letters which Governor Thomas Hutchinson and his Lieutenant Governor Andrew Oliver had written to a British official, recommending these and even harsher measures. "There must be some abridgment of what is called English liberty" in the colonies, Hutchinson had written.

Franklin, satisfied that the letters were authentic, decided to send them to his friends in Massachusetts. He felt it was his duty as agent to do so, in spite of the fact that the letters had obviously been stolen from the house of the man to whom they had been written, shortly after his death. Franklin said he hoped to make Americans realize that the quarrel between England and America was not all England's fault.

Franklin's strategy might have worked, if there had been time for Americans to think about what the Hutchinson-Oliver letters meant. But other things happened, almost at the same time, which combined with the letters to help start the Revolution.

CHAPTER 14

THE REVOLUTIONARY

DISTURBED BY AMERICAN RESISTANCE TO THE Townshend Acts, Parliament had repealed all of them except the tax on tea. This was retained to "uphold the right"—the right of Parliament to tax the colonies. The tax was very small, only threepence to a pound, but Americans refused to pay it as a matter of principle. Sales of British tea, imported from India by the East India Company, plummeted. Americans preferred to drink illegal tea, smuggled from the French and Dutch West Indies.

The East India Company lost millions of pounds, as tea piled up in its warehouses in England. Its stock tumbled on the London Exchange, and many people who had bought it went bankrupt.

Watching the spectacle, Franklin blamed the whole thing on British pride and greed. More and more, as he watched the

British government's behavior toward America, he became convinced that the English were scheming to reduce Americans to the kind of brutal poverty they had inflicted on Ireland. They wanted to create a vast network of government jobs which they could parcel out to their friends as they regularly did jobs in the Irish government.

Franklin stated this opinion boldly in the British newspapers, and in letters to friends in America. By this time the government was interrupting his mail regularly. The British soon began to regard Franklin as the man behind the entire American resistance. To some extent this was true. His letters were reprinted regularly in newspapers up and down the continent. As Deputy Postmaster General, he could send letters free by writing "Free B. Franklin" on them. But now, to make sure Americans got his message, he began writing "B. free Franklin."

Meanwhile, the Thomas Hutchinson letters which Franklin had sent to Massachusetts created political explosion in that colony. Franklin had asked his friends to show them only to a handful of influential leaders. But some of these men circulated them far beyond this small group, and soon they were printed in the newspapers. The Massachusetts Assembly passed a resolution demanding Hutchinson's removal as governor and sent it to Benjamin Franklin for presentation to the King. Franklin submitted it, and the Privy Council scheduled a hearing on the matter.

While Franklin was out of town, two men, one an American,

the other the brother of the man to whom the letters were written, fought a duel over them. The brother, whose name was Thomas Whately, accused the American, John Temple, of stealing them. The duel ended with Whately slightly wounded and demanding another match. Franklin, anxious to avoid bloodshed, published a letter in London's leading newspaper, admitting he had procured the letters and sent them to America. This admission aroused all his enemies in the British government.

Then came even more inflammatory news from America. The British government, trying to help the East India Company, had given them permission to sell their tea at a price so low that Americans would find it hard to resist. The tax remained on the tea, however. This angered many Americans who were determined to deny Parliament's right to tax the colonies. So, when the tea ships arrived carrying their cargoes of specially priced tea, riots took place in numerous ports. Unfortunately for Franklin, the first news of these acts of defiance to reach England came from Boston. There, a group of rioters, disguised as Indians, had boarded the tea ships, broken open the chests of tea, and thrown the contents into the harbor.

The leaders of the British government, already angry with Franklin, were now totally furious. At the Privy Council hearing on the petition to remove Hutchinson, they arranged for his public humiliation. The government Solicitor General, a lean, sharp-tongued Scot named Alexander Wedderburn, was "hired" as Hutchinson's defense attorney. While the full Privy Council of 35 lords, as well as their numerous followers, lady friends, and courtiers, snickered and guffawed, Wedderburn called Franklin a thief, a liar, an intriguing revolutionary—just about every dirty name in the English language.

Franklin stood a few feet away, absolutely silent, his face expressionless, throughout this hail of abuse. One American who happened to be present, a hot-blooded South Carolinian, marveled at Franklin's self-control. "Had it been me that was so grossly insulted, I should instantly have repelled the attack, in defiance of every consequence," he said. Later, Franklin told his friends that he had never before appreciated the value of a good conscience. If he had not been absolutely convinced that what he had done with the Hutchinson letters was right, he could never have endured the ordeal.

The next day, Franklin was informed by letter that he was dismissed as Deputy Postmaster General for North America. His first thoughts were of the fatal consequences to the Ohio Colony, and to his son's career. He immediately resigned from the Ohio Colony board so that no one could use him as an excuse to deny the final approval of the grant of land.

In a letter to William Franklin written just after his humiliation before the Privy Council, Franklin advised: "As there is no prospect of your being ever promoted to a better government, and that you hold has never defrayed its expenses, I wish you were well settled in your farm. 'Tis an honester and a more honourable, because a more independent employment."

Two weeks later, however, he wrote to his son in a calmer frame of mind. "Some tell me that it is determined to displace you likewise, but I do not know it as certain . . . Perhaps they may expect that your resentment of their treatment of me may induce you to resign, and save them the shame of depriving you when they ought to promote. But this I would not advise you to do. Let them take your place if they want it, though in truth I think it is scarce worth your keeping . . . But one may make something of an injury, nothing of a resignation."

Already Franklin was convinced that a revolution was inevitable and that America would become an independent nation. He wanted his son William to play a large part in the government of this new nation. William could indeed "make something" of an injury from the British government.

But it soon became apparent that the British were planning to injure a lot of other Americans before they got around to William Franklin. To punish Boston for the Tea Party, the Ministry proposed and Parliament swiftly passed a series of bills which the Americans called the Intolerable Acts. One closed the port of Boston to all shipping, until the tea was paid for. Another provided that any Royal official accused of murder or a similar crime would be tried outside Massachusetts, or in England. A third bill virtually annulled the colony's charter, giving the Governor almost dictatorial powers, and making him answerable for his salary, and the exercise of his power, only to England.

Finally came a blow that was to some extent aimed directly at Franklin. The Quebec Act set up a government for the French in Canada, and extended the borders of Canada southward to the Ohio River, swallowing Franklin's proposed colony. The Americans immediately saw that the British were attempting to pin them between the mountains and the sea. Alexander Wedderburn admitted as much, when members of the opposition accused the government of this intention, in debates in Parliament over the bills to punish Boston. For Franklin these Intolerable Acts were additional proof that the British were planning to reduce America to the state of total oppression with which they reigned in Ireland.

In America, the Intolerable Acts had a dramatic and almost immediate effect on public opinion. Everyone realized that if the British could change one colony's charter, they could change every colony's charter. From Connecticut to Georgia, Americans rallied to Massachusetts' side in the argument. Food and money poured into Boston to sustain the thousands of people who were jobless, because of the closing of the port. At the same time, the leaders of the colonies decided to convene a Continental Congress in Philadelphia to discuss the crisis and to work out ways to maintain a united front against the British.

In London, the British government was stunned by this surge of American support for Massachusetts. Franklin kept his American friends informed. "The coolness, temper & firmness of the American proceedings; the unanimity of all the colonies . . . have a good deal surprized and disappointed our enemies," he wrote.

Franklin was more worried by ominous signs of trouble in his relationship with his son. Governor Franklin, as a Royal official, did not look on the Continental Congress favorably. Instead, he suggested a congress of Royal Governors to mediate the quarrel. He also urged his father to come home to tell Americans that they should make peace with England.

Franklin could barely conceal his annoyance. "You say my presence is wish'd for at the Congress," he wrote, "but no person besides in America has given me the least intimation of such a desire; and it is thought by the great friends of the colonies here, that I ought to stay till the result of the Congress arrives, when my presence here may be of use." Curtly, he told William, "I hear nothing of the proposal you have made for a congress of Governors, &c." Franklin also did not like a remark that William had made, that the citizens of Massachusetts ought to think of "doing justice before they ask it" and pay for the ruined tea. Franklin vehemently disagreed. "They have extorted many thousand pounds from America unconstitutionally, under colour of acts of Parliament, and with an armed force. Of this money they ought to make restitution. They might first have taken out payment for the tea, &c., and returned the rest. But you, who are a thorough courtier, see everything with government eyes. . . ."

Again and again, Franklin exhorted his countrymen to

maintain their resistance. "By its continuance, you will undoubtedly carry all your points: by giving way you will lose every thing. Strong chains will be forged for you, and you will be made to pay for both the iron and the workmanship . . . If you should ever tamely submit to the yoke prepared for you, you cannot conceive how much you will be despised here, even by those who are endeavouring to impose it on you."

Not everyone in the British government wanted war with America. When they saw that Americans were almost unanimously determined to resist Parliament's claim, several members of the government, including the First Minister Lord North, approached Franklin secretly, through private messengers. Two Quaker friends, David Barclay and Dr. John Fothergill, asked him if he would draw up a plan to settle the quarrel, stating the principal American demands in ways that might persuade the British to yield to them.

Another messenger from Lord North used a chess game to disguise his errand. Lord Howe, an admiral in the British navy and a member of Parliament, arranged for Franklin to be invited to play chess with his sister. After Franklin had played several games with her, Miss Howe said, "What is to be done with this dispute between Great Britain and the colonies? I hope we are not to have a civil war."

"They should kiss and be friends," said Franklin. "What can they do better? Quarreling can be of service to neither, but is ruin to both."

"I have often said," replied Miss Howe, "that I wished

government would employ you to settle the dispute for 'em. I am sure nobody could do it so well. Do you not think that the thing is practicable?"

"Undoubtedly, madam," said Franklin, "if the parties are disposed to reconciliation; for the two countries have really no clashing interests to differ about. 'Tis rather a matter of punctilio which two or three reasonable people might settle in half an hour."

He thanked Miss Howe for her good opinion of him as a peacemaker. "But the ministers will never think of employing me in that good work, they choose rather to abuse me."

"Ay," said Miss Howe, "they have behaved shamefully to you. And indeed some of them are now ashamed of it themselves."

The next time Franklin and Miss Howe met, she introduced her brother to him. Lord Howe soon made it clear that he was hoping to persuade Franklin to join him as a fellow commissioner, appointed by the Crown, to go to America and negotiate a truce. He hinted that if Franklin agreed, he could be sure of receiving every reward that the Crown of England had in its power to confer. Lord Howe was telling Franklin that he could win a knighthood or a baronetcy, and become a very rich man.

Franklin declined to sell out the rights of his country; he insisted on standing behind all America's claims. As he saw it now, Parliament had no right to tax Americans, or rule over them in any way. The only link between England and America was allegiance to the King. This, Americans might be willing to concede, if England gave them the right to rule themselves in every other way. Almost a hundred years later, England realized that Franklin was right, and granted this kind of independence to Canada, Australia and her other overseas dominions. But at this point in history, England refused to give up Parliament's claims.

In the midst of these negotiations Franklin received very bad news from home. His wife Deborah had died. He felt guilty about not having gone home sooner, and immediately prepared to leave. The negotiations to prevent the war dwindled away, as Parliament rejected several proposals by leading members of the opposition to make peace with America. Finally, Franklin's two Quaker friends came to him and told him that he was wasting his time negotiating, and might as well depart. Whatever "pretenses" were offered by the government, "they are all hollow . . . To get a larger field on which to fatten a herd of worthless parasites is all that is regarded."

War was very close, and Franklin knew it. The thought filled him with dread. Already he sensed, on the other side of the world, that his son William disagreed with him on the great political question of America's independence. On his last day in London, Franklin spent some time with an English friend, going over bundles of newspapers recently arrived from America. Franklin pointed out articles that might do America some good, if they were reprinted in English papers. "He was frequently not able to proceed for the tears literally running down his cheeks," the friend said later.

CHAPTER 15

DIVIDED FAMILY

ABOARD THE PENNSYLVANIA PACKET, BOUND FOR Philadelphia, Franklin took with him a young man named William Temple Franklin, William's illegitimate son. Throughout his years in England, Franklin had remained close to the boy, bringing him to Craven Street regularly for visits, and paying for his education at a good boarding school. Now he was 16, a handsome, intelligent young man with a gift for drawing and languages. Franklin did not expect to return to England, so he was taking Temple home with him.

The sea was calm, the voyage slow. Franklin spent much of his time writing the longest letter of his life. It began with those familiar words, "Dear Son," and it continued for 97 pages telling in detail the story of Franklin's secret negotiations with the British government. There was no better proof of Franklin's anxious desire to prove to William that America was right, and Britain was wrong.

When he was not writing, Franklin found time to investigate further the Gulf Stream, that great ocean river he had noticed on his first voyage back from England. Now he studied it much more carefully, dropping thermometers over the side of the ship, and pulling up samples of the water, which was bright with phosphoresence. He soon decided that a ship sailing from America to Europe could considerably increase its speed by using the Gulf Stream, since the current ran swiftly in that direction. Going from Europe to America, a ship could save days, even weeks, of sailing by avoiding the Stream. But Franklin decided to keep this discovery a secret, for the time being, because, if war broke out, it would be useful primarily to the English, who would be sending dozens of warships to America.

Upon Franklin's arrival in Philadelphia on May 5th, 1775, excited Americans swarmed aboard the ship to inform him that war had begun. Sixteen days before, the British had sent a military expedition to Concord, Massachusetts, to seize cannon, gunpowder and other supplies stored there. Fighting had broken out on the Lexington green at dawn on April 19th, and before the day was over 49 Americans were dead, 41 wounded, and 5 missing. The British retreated from Concord, pursued by hundreds of American Minutemen. Their casualties were 73 killed, 174 wounded and 26 missing. Immediately, Franklin asked the biggest question in his mind: Had William resigned? The answer was no. William felt "obliged" to the British government because they had not removed him from office, in spite of their anger at his father. Governor Franklin felt that both the Americans and the British were partly right and partly wrong. We do not know whether Franklin saw William as soon as he landed in Philadelphia, or if he had a letter from him. We do have a letter that Franklin wrote to him on May 7th, 1775, in which he told his son bluntly where he stood. "I don't understand it as any favour to me or to you, the being continued in an office by which, with all your prudence, you cannot avoid running behindhand, if you live suitably to your station. While you are in it I know you will execute it with fidelity to your master, but I think independence more honourable than any service, and that in the state of American affairs . . . you will find yourself in no uncomfortable situation, and perhaps wish you had soon disengaged yourself."

Franklin was urging William to resign and to join the growing revolution. But neither William, nor Joseph Galloway, Franklin's chief political lieutenant in Pennsylvania, agreed with him. Galloway had proposed a plan of union between England and America and the Continental Congress had voted it down. Declaring himself insulted, he had quit the Congress and gone home.

On May 10, a second Continental Congress met in Philadelphia. Franklin was appointed an extra member of the Pennsylvania delegation. He told everyone that he was for independence, and was stunned to discover that very few people agreed with him. Among these few was a young, lanky delegate from Virginia, Thomas Jefferson. Almost everyone else agreed with John Dickinson, the leader of the Pennsylvania delegation, who was determined to work out a way to reconcile England and America. Franklin had tried this in London, and knew it was a waste of time. But he could only keep silence in Congress, and accept the majority opinion for the time being.

Then came the shocking news of Bunker Hill. The Americans had seized high ground north of Boston, and the British army had attacked them. A tremendous battle erupted, leaving over a thousand British, amd more than 400 Americans, dead and wounded. The village of Charlestown, just below Bunker Hill, was set on fire by cannon balls from British warships, and over 300 houses were destroyed. The news set Franklin's Massachusetts blood boiling. He went home and wrote a scorching letter to his friend, William Strahan.

Philada July 5, 1775

Mr. Strahan,

You are a Member of Parliament, and one of that Majority which has doomed my Country to Destruction.—You have begun to burn our Towns, and murder our People.—Look upon your Hands!—You and I were long Friends:—You are now my Enemy,—and I am

Yours,
B. FRANKLIN

After he wrote the letter, Franklin decided not to mail it. But he realized its value as propaganda, and had it reprinted widely in newspapers.

In spite of his all-out support for the American cause, some people suspected that Franklin was a British spy. A large part of the reason was his son's refusal to join the revolution. The long years Franklin had spent in England, and his friendship with so many powerful men in Parliament, were other reasons why he was suspect. William Bradford, nephew of Franklin's old newspaper competitor, eagerly spread this slander. Richard Henry Lee of Virginia, one of the leading members of the Continental Congress, announced he was launching an investigation to find out if Franklin really was a traitor.

Even more dismaying to Franklin was the decision in Congress to accept John Dickinson's advice and submit another "humble petition" to the king. Called the "Olive Branch Petition," it was written by Dickinson with some help from Thomas Jefferson, and sent to London, in spite of the bloody news from Bunker Hill.

Franklin, totally convinced now that independence was the only solution, wrote a Declaration of Independence and Articles of Confederation, creating an American nation. But when he showed it to the delegates, they were, in Jefferson's words, "revolted at it." Congress was still convinced, in this summer of 1775, that war could somehow be avoided. Politically isolated, Franklin was reduced to uncharacteristic silence in the Continental Congress.

Meanwhile, he worried about his son William and his grandson William Temple. The boy was spending the summer with his father and stepmother in Perth Amboy, New Jersey, and was enjoying himself immensely. Governor Franklin apparently found no difficulty inducing his wife Elizabeth to welcome Temple as a son. The motherless boy had responded with deep affection, and was soon enjoying the lively, well-to-do society that clustered around the Governor in his handsome house.

Most of these people were like William, loyal to the King. Franklin was worried about the effect these people might have on Temple's young mind. He sent the young man many letters, urging him to continue his studies and sending him news from Philadelphia. He told him about Sally's children, who now numbered three. Will, the second one, "has got a little gun, marches with it and whistles at the same time by way of fife," Franklin wrote. He was really telling Temple that even toddlers were aware that war was brewing.

In other letters, Franklin discussed Temple's future with William. They finally decided to enroll the young man in the college at Philadelphia in the fall. William asked his father whether he should bring Temple back to Philadelphia, or would Franklin prefer to come to Perth Amboy to collect him?

With congressmen such as John Adams already talking about arresting Loyalists, the sight of William in Philadelphia would only make Franklin's political influence in Congress even smaller than it already was. He told William that he preferred to come to Perth Amboy.

On this visit, Franklin made one last try to persuade William to join the American side. But William did not think the Americans could win the war. He also did not believe that, if they achieved independence, they could govern themselves. Basically, William did not like America and Americans as much as he liked England and her people. Because of his illegitimate birth, he had never been really accepted in America, while in London (where this fact was unknown), he had been accepted and rewarded with a high government post. He did not share his father's faith in the future of America because he had not found his opportunity, his career in America.

Also there was still for William the golden gleam of the Ohio colony, and he could not help resenting the part his father had played in wrecking this dream. A few weeks after Franklin returned to Philadelphia with Temple, William wrote him a very significant letter. He pointed out that the English partners in the Ohio Company said they had received "the *strongest assurances* that as soon as the present great dispute is settled *our grant shall be perfected.*" William did his own underlining, hinting strongly to his father that Benjamin ought to work for a compromise and stop agitating for independence.

This dispute with his son made Franklin wish that war could be avoided, somehow. He journeyed to Cambridge, Massachusetts, with two other members of Congress, to confer with George Washington, who had taken command of the American army that was besieging the British in Boston.

118

From there, he wrote to his son-in-law Richard Bache, admitting that he wished "most earnestly for peace, this war being a truly unnatural and mischievous one."

Then William Franklin made a move that almost altered the course of the Revolution. Summoning the New Jersey Assembly, he made a speech to them about "the present unhappy situation of publick affairs." He urged the Assembly to accept the invitation of the British government and petition the King to settle the dispute. Lord North, the British First Minister, had announced in Parliament that they were ready to settle any and all disputes, if each colony petitioned the King separately. Actually the British were hoping to divide and conquer the Americans by breaking the united front they were maintaining in the Continental Congress.

William went on to tell the New Jersey Assemblymen that he was well aware that "sentiments of independency are . . . openly avowed." He called independence a "horrid measure" and asked the Assembly to pass a resolution forbidding the New Jersey delegates in the Continental Congress to vote for it. The Assembly agreed to both of Governor Franklin's requests.

In Philadelphia, the Continental Congress reacted with shock and alarm. If New Jersey's petition reached the King, and he responded with generous grants of money and other favors, more colonies might be tempted to repeat the performance, and American unity would become a "rope of sand." Congress resolved unanimously "that in the present situation

119

of affairs, it will be very dangerous to the liberties and welfare of America, if any colony should separately petition the King or either house of Parliament." They then appointed a committee of three men, and ordered them to rush to Burlington, where the New Jersey Assembly was meeting, to inform the members of this resolution.

After listening to the three congressmen, the Assembly decided to delay their petition until they saw how the King replied to the so-called "Olive Branch Petition."

While his son was trying to wreck the Revolution, Franklin was working harder than ever to make it succeed. Each morning, he arose at 6 a.m. and went to a meeting of the Committee of Safety for the state of Pennsylvania. He bought powder and conferred on the manufacture of guns and cannon. He gave advice on how to block the Delaware River with underwater barriers made of logs and iron, so British warships could not sail up it and bombard Philadelphia.

At 9 o'clock, Franklin trudged to Congress, which was meeting in the Pennsylvania State House. There he served on no less than ten different committees, in addition to his duties as America's first Postmaster General. He had to worry about conciliating the Indians of the "Middle Department" along Pennsylvania's and Virginia's borders, advise Congress on ways to protect the trade of the colonies, and confer with generals and engineers on supplying and equipping the American army.

By far the most important committee on which Franklin

served began its work during the same month of December, 1775, that saw William Franklin's attempt to thwart the Revolution. The elder Franklin and four other congressmen were appointed to a secret committee with "the sole purpose of corresponding with our friends in Great Britain, Ireland and other parts of the world."

A few days later, the French-born librarian of the Philadelphia Library introduced Franklin to an "Antwerp merchant" who had come to America "out of curiosity." The man was actually a French spy, sent by the French government to see how the American Revolution was progressing. Franklin and his fellow committee members met with this man several times during the month of December. They maintained the strictest secrecy about these meetings. Each time they met, they chose a different building, and each member of the committee traveled alone, by a different route. The French secret agent assured them that "France wished them well," but he hesitated to say that France was ready to support the Americans. "It was slippery business in the face of the English," he said. He agreed to help the Americans hire French military engineers, and buy muskets and ammunition in France.

On January 2nd, 1776, Congress passed a resolution calling on local authorities in the various colonies to restrain the "wicked practices" of those "unworthy Americans" who persisted in supporting the [Royal government.] Within three days, the commander of the American army in New Jersey arrested Governor William Franklin. He intercepted letters that William had sent to the British government, identifying all the leaders of the Revolution in New Jersey, and discussing the rebellion in detail. The Congress, embarrassed by the fact that he was Benjamin Franklin's son, decided to let William remain in his house; and New Jersey continued to pay his salary as Royal Governor.

William tried to win Temple's sympathy by writing a letter describing the rough way that the army had surrounded his house with bayonet-wielding soldiers at 2 o'clock in the morning. Elizabeth Franklin had been so frightened, the Governor was certain that "another alarm of the like nature will put an end to her life." William reminded Temple how affectionately Mrs. Franklin had accepted him as her stepson. "Let what will happen, I hope you will never be wanting in a grateful sense of her kindness to you," he said.

Temple was deeply disturbed by his father's letter, and wrote an immediate answer, full of apologies and sympathy. But Benjamin Franklin did not communicate with his stubborn son. He had done everything in his power to convince him to change sides before it was too late. Now William would have to take the consequences for his decision.

CHAPTER 16

HANGING TOGETHER— OR SEPARATELY

IN THE EARLY MONTHS OF 1776, MORE AND MORE Americans began to realize that Franklin was right— independence was America's only hope. The King had declared the colonies in revolt and outside his protection, forbade all nations to trade with them and authorized the seizure of American ships on the high seas.

Meanwhile, a close Franklin friend, Thomas Paine, published on January 10th, 1776, a two-shilling pamphlet of 47 pages called "Common Sense." It was a devastating attack on the two ideas that still prevented most Americans from voting for independence—loyalty to the King, and the British Constitution. The pamphlet was a sensational success—in less than three months, 120,000 copies were sold. Many people thought

Franklin had written it, and, indeed, Paine may have gotten many of his ideas for it from talking with Franklin, who had written letters of introduction for him when he emigrated to America from England in 1774. Paine gave Franklin the first copy of the pamphlet that came off the press.

On March 3rd, Franklin's committee sent a secret agent of their own to France. He was Silas Deane, a Connecticut merchant. Franklin gave him introductions to many of his friends in France, and wrote a long letter, carefully instructing Deane on how to deal with the French foreign Minister, Count de Vergennes.

A few weeks later, Congress called on Franklin to take an exhausting trip to Canada. An American army was attempting to bring that colony into the revolutionary confederation, but the British army there had counterattacked and seemed on the point of driving the Americans out of the colony. Franklin traveled up Lake George and Lake Champlain in open boats, through water thick with ice. The weather was bitterly cold, and he bought a fur hat to keep his balding head warm. Between the terrible weather and the long journey, Franklin thought at one point he was dying, and wrote letters of farewell to several friends.

In Canada, he found that the American army was disintegrating because they had no money. He turned around and struggled back down the lakes to New York. On his return journey, his legs swelled, and boils broke out all over his body. He might well have died, except for the help he received from

Father John Carroll, an American priest who had voluntarily joined the American mission, in the hope of persuading the Catholic French Canadians to side with the Americans. But the Catholic Bishop of Quebec preferred to stick with the British, and Father Carroll, seeing that he was wasting his time in Canada and realizing the seriousness of Franklin's condition, had offered to make the journey home with him. From New York, Franklin wrote friends in Albany, "I think I could hardly have got along so far, but for Mister Carroll's friendly assistance and tender care of me."

In New York, Franklin felt well enough to have tea with an old friend named Mrs. Barrow. Her husband had joined the Loyalists aboard the British ships in the harbor. Franklin had paid her a visit on his way to Canada, and she had told him she feared that the American soldiers in New York might abuse her, because of her husband's politics. Franklin had gone directly to George Washington, and made sure that she would not be molested. At tea, he asked "how our people had behaved" to her. She told him that everyone had treated her with the utmost decorum and respect.

"I'm glad of that," said Franklin. "Why if they had used you ill I would have turned Tory."

"In that case," she said, with a twinkle in her eye, "I wish they had."

Back in Philadelphia, Franklin found that his son William was still against the Revolution. On May 15th, 1776, Congress had passed a resolution abolishing all "oaths and affirmations" to the Crown of Great Britain, and called on Americans to suppress all aspects of Royal authority that remained in the colonies. Ignoring this clear warning, Governor William Franklin issued a call for the New Jersey Assembly to meet in Perth Amboy on June 20th.

Unfortunately for William, the Third Provincial Congress of New Jersey—the local revolutionary government—was already in session, and decided that William's call was "in direct contempt and violation of the resolve of the Continental Congress." The members declared that William was "an enemy of the liberties of this country" and ordered him arrested, and his salary as Royal Governor "from henceforth to cease." At the same time, they urged the arresting officers to conduct themselves "with all the delicacy and tenderness which the nature of the business could possibly admit." If Governor Franklin agreed to sign a parole guaranteeing his good conduct, he would be permitted to live unmolested on his farm at Rancocas Creek below Burlington.

But Governor Franklin was totally uncooperative. He defied the soldiers who arrested him, and told the committee of the Provincial Congress who examined him that they could "do as you please and make the best of it." The committeemen informed the Continental Congress that William was "a virulent enemy to this country." On Monday, June 24th, the Continental Congress resolved that "William Franklin be sent under guard to Governor Trumbull of [Connecticut]."

William Franklin, still fighting for Temple's allegiance, wrote a bitter letter to his son, describing his ordeal. He called the New Jersey committeemen "low mightinesses" and described how they ordered him to make the trip to Connecticut, in spite of his claim that he was too sick to travel. "Hypocrites always suspect hypocrisy in others," the Governor said. Then, shifting gears, he urged Temple "to be dutiful and attentive to your grandfather" and "love Mrs. Franklin for she loves you, and will do all she can for you if I should never return more."

Throughout the last two weeks in June, Benjamin Franklin used his weakened condition, a result of his trip to Canada, as a good excuse to avoid attending Congress. He took little or no part in the fight to pass a declaration of independence. Congress appointed him a member of the committee to prepare this document. As the most famous man in Congress, and a writer with a world-wide reputation, Franklin would seem to have been the logical man to write the Declaration. But the embarrassment of his Tory son cast a shadow over his appeal as a Revolutionary spokesman. So the committee members gave the job to 33-year-old Thomas Jefferson, who was from Virginia, the largest of the 13 colonies, and a delegate without political liabilities.

Franklin made only a few minor changes in the wording of Jefferson's great document. Perhaps the most important was where Jefferson had written "We hold these truths to be sacred and undeniable"—Franklin crossed out "sacred and undeniable" and substituted "self-evident."

Franklin roused himself and came to Congress to vote in

favor of independence on July 2nd. He sat next to Jefferson, on the following day, as Congress went over the Declaration and deleted several sections of it. Jefferson was very disappointed and annoyed by this surgery. When it was over, and the final shortened version had won a vote of approval, Franklin tried to cheer Jefferson up. "I have made it a rule," he said, "whenever in my power to avoid becoming the draftsman of papers to be reviewed by a public body." To explain why, Franklin told Jefferson a story from his journeyman printer days. One of his friends, an apprentice hatter, decided to open a shop for himself. "His first concern was to have a handsome signboard with a proper inscription. He composed it in these words: *John Thompson, hatter, makes and sells hats for ready money*, with a figure of a hat subjoined. But he thought he would submit it to his friends for their amendments."

The first man he showed it to thought the word "hatter" was superfluous because it was followed by the words "makes hats." Thompson agreed and struck it out. The next friend observed that the word "makes" might as well be omitted, because the customers would not care who made the hats, as long as they were good ones. Thompson agreed and struck it out. A third friend suggested eliminating "for ready money" because none of the local merchants sold on credit. Again Thompson bowed to the will of the majority, and now he had a sign which said: "John Thompson sells hats."

"Sells hats," said his next friend, "why nobody will expect you to give them away. What then is the use of that word?"

Again poor Thompson conceded. Moments later, the word "hats" went into oblivion when another friend pointed out that there was one painted on the board. And so he was left with a sign that said "John Thompson" beneath the painted hat.

It was like Franklin to tell a joke at the moment when he was voting for the Declaration that would make him a traitor, liable to be hanged, drawn and quartered under English law. Contrary to the myth, no one actually signed the Declaration on July 4th. Not until August 2nd was a final copy engrossed on parchment and signed by the members of the Congress. Then, Franklin reportedly told another joke. John Hancock, after placing his large scrawl at the head of the list of signers, as befitted the President of Congress, said, "We must be unanimous, there must be no pulling different ways; we must all hang together."

"Yes," Franklin replied, "we must indeed all hang together, or most assuredly we shall all hang separately."

When Franklin had written his own Declaration of Independence, in the summer of 1775, he had attached to it Articles of Confederation. Now he threw all his energy into persuading Congress to form a union as quickly as possible. But he could not get them to agree. The smaller states demanded an equal vote with the large states. Of course, they did not have as many men or as much money to contribute to the war effort. Franklin warned them that having "an equal vote without bearing equal burdens" meant that the confederation would "never last long." The smaller colonies replied that they were afraid the larger colonies would reduce them to "vassals." The weather was hot, and the arguments were ever hotter. Franklin tried to cool everyone off with a joke.

He told them a story he had heard in England about the opposition of Scottish peers to the union between England and Scotland. One nobleman predicted "that as the whale had swallowed Jonah, so Scotland would be swallowed by England." But there were soon so many Scotsmen in high places in the English government that it looked like "Jonah had swallowed the whale." An admiring Jefferson later recalled, "This little story produced a general laugh and restored good humour." But neither humor nor reason could persuade the large state and small state men to agree.

Meanwhile, the British were massing a huge army on Staten Island, and preparing to attack George Washington and his largely amateur soldiers, who were entrenched on Long Island and in New York. On August 27th, the British attacked the Americans on Long Island, and beat them badly. Only a near miraculous combination of good luck, British overconfidence and foggy weather enabled Washington to escape by night with most of his army to Manhattan Island.

Lord Howe, the British admiral who had tried to negotiate with Franklin in London, appeared in New York harbor as commander in chief of the British navy. He said he had a commission from the King, to negotiate peace. Franklin and two other congressmen met with Lord Howe on Staten Island, but the conference ended in failure, because Lord Howe only had power to issue pardons, if and when Americans made their "submission" to the King. Franklin told him that Americans did not feel they had done anything that needed pardoning. He also told him that independence was now an unchangeable fact, and Britain had better face it, and negotiate with Americans as a separate country.

The British reply was a new attack on Washington's army. They stormed ashore at Kips Bay in Manhattan, and routed the raw American recruits who were supposed to be protecting this landing place. The American army fled, leaving George Washington alone on the battlefield. More and more, it began to look as if William Franklin was right in his opinion that the Americans could not hope to defeat Britain's professional army and navy.

From France, around this time, came more bad news. Franklin's friends wrote him, assuring him that the French government and the French people were sympathetic to the American cause, but despairing that none of the King's ministers "will espouse it with warmth." France was "over head and ears in debt." Congress, terribly alarmed by American defeats, decided that an alliance with France was an absolute necessity. They had heard nothing from Silas Deane, the secret agent Franklin's committee had sent to France in March. So they decided to send a more impressive ambassador— Benjamin Franklin.

This decision meant that Franklin would have to endure a

winter voyage across the Atlantic. At his age, this might in itself be a death sentence. An additional danger were the British cruisers which swarmed the ocean, for if one captured him on such a mission, a traitor's death at the end of a hangman's rope in London would be a certainty. But Franklin was totally committed to the Revolution. Turning to young Dr. Benjamin Rush of Philadelphia, who sat next to him in Congress, Franklin said, "I am old and good for nothing; but, as the storekeepers say of their remnants of cloth, 'I am but a fag end, and you may have me for what you please,' just so my country may command my services in any way they choose."

Franklin's first thoughts as he planned the voyage were of William Temple Franklin, now staying with his stepmother in New Jersey. Already, the boy had written his grandfather an angry letter when Franklin had refused to let him take a trip to visit his father in Wallingford, Connecticut, where Governor Franklin was being held a prisoner. If he left Temple behind in America, the boy would almost certainly become a Loyalist. So Franklin decided to take Temple with him. Quickly, he rushed a note to him in New Jersey, urging him to return to Philadelphia immediately. "I hope . . . that your mother will make no objection to it, something offering here that will be much to your advantage if you are not out of the way."

Franklin also decided to take with him his six-year-old grandson Benjamin Franklin Bache. The war was disrupting schools in America, and Franklin wanted the boy to get the best possible education. So, with his two young friends for company, Franklin rode to Marcus Hook on the Delaware, where boats took them aboard the American sloop *Reprisal.*

Franklin's faith in America's future remained amazingly strong. The day before he sailed, he wrote to a friend in Boston, "I hope our people will keep up their courage. I have no doubt of their finally succeeding by the blessing of God, nor have I any doubt that so good a cause will fail of that blessing."

CHAPTER 17

EXTRAORDINARY DIPLOMAT

THE VOYAGE IN THE *REPRISAL* WAS A TERRIBLE ordeal. The seas were turbulent, with mountainous waves, and the weather bitterly cold. There was nothing to eat but salt beef and ship's biscuits. Franklin wore the fur hat he had acquired in Canada, but it did little good. The boils that had tormented him in Canada broke out again, and he felt himself growing more and more feeble. His only consolation was the speed that the ship was making.

One day toward the end of the fourth week, the captain of the *Reprisal,* Lambert Wickes, burst into Franklin's cabin and asked for permission to attack a British ship. Wickes had received orders from Congress to avoid all encounters with the enemy until he had deposited Franklin safely in France. But now they were close to the French shore, and the ship, a plodding merchantman, was a tempting plum. Franklin took one look, and nodded his permission. The crew of the *Reprisal* raced to quarters, and the British ship surrendered without a shot. A prize crew was swiftly put aboard her. A few hours later, Wickes repeated the performance with another British ship. Franklin was delighted to see Americans strike a blow at England in her home waters.

Six days later, the *Reprisal* anchored off Brittany, near the small fishing village of Auray. Franklin was so exhausted he could barely stand, but he immediately fired off a letter to Silas Deane in Paris. "I am weak, but hope the good air which I breathe on land will soon re-establish me," he said. It took 24 hours to find a carriage and two tired horses in a neighboring town, but finally Franklin and his two grandsons started down the road to the port of Nantes.

After resting in Nantes, Franklin joined Deane in Paris. He enrolled young Benjamin Franklin Bache in a local private school, where he was soon speaking French like a native. In fact, the boy learned the language so well, he almost forgot how to speak English. Franklin and William Temple Franklin moved into the Hotel de Hambourg with Silas Deane and the two men went to work.

Franklin was pleased to learn that the French government had set up a dummy company, and had loaned the Americans two million livres—about $400,000—to buy guns and supplies. Some ships had already sailed. But when the French heard the bad news about Washington's defeats on Long Island and around New York, they refused to permit other ships to sail, in spite of the fact that they were already loaded and ready to depart.

This made Deane and his assistant, a Marylander named William Carmichael, very angry with France. But Franklin understood why the French were cautious—England had beaten them very badly in the last war, and they had no desire to suffer another defeat. Before they publicly supported the United States, they wanted to make sure the Americans could fight.

In Paris, Franklin continued to wear his fur hat, which caused a great deal of comment among the fashion conscious French. They liked it. They saw it as proof that Americans were simple and honest, and did not bother with trivial matters, such as wearing the right wig, or the latest fashion in hats. Franklin also made a point of wearing very plain brown or black suits, and white shirts. One Frenchman vowed that everything about him typified "simplicity and innocence."

Franklin was neither simple nor innocent, but he recognized the importance of winning the French people to his side. So he continued to wear his fur hat. With the help of Jacques Chaumont, a French businessman who was working with Silas Deane to supply the American army, Franklin had a painting of himself wearing the fur hat printed on plates, pitchers and other pieces of crockery, which were produced by the thousands in ovens at Chaumont's estate. They sold at a tremendous rate, and Franklin was soon able to remark that his face was better known in France than the face of the man in the moon.

At the same time, Franklin coped shrewdly with British attempts to wreck his mission. When an American woman living in France warned him that he was surrounded by British spies, he replied that he had "no doubt" this was true. In fact, he said that if he were sure that his valet was a spy, "as probably he is, I think I should not discharge him for that, if in other respects I lik'd him." Franklin saw that it would be to his advantage if the British learned about French secret aid, for this might make them so angry that they would declare war on France. It did not particularly matter to him just how France became America's ally. In fact, one of Franklin's closest aides in Paris, Connecticut-born Edward Bancroft, was a double agent who took 600 pounds a year from the British Secret Service and reported everything Franklin was doing to George III.

The British did become very angry at the sight of Franklin in Paris. The British ambassador, Lord Stormont, protested violently to the French government. The British newspapers were filled with stories claiming that Franklin had fled to France to save his skin, because the Revolution was collapsing. In a letter to his young friend Polly Stevenson Hewson, who was still in England, Franklin wrote, "I must contrive to get you to America. I want all my friends out of that wicked country. I have just seen in the papers seven paragraphs about me, of which six were lies."

In March, 1777, Franklin moved out of the Hotel de Hambourg and retreated to the village of Passy, about a half hour's drive from Paris on the road to Versailles, the palace of Louis XVI and the center of the French government. He accepted the invitation of the Chaumonts to live rent free in one of the houses on their estate, the Hôtel de Valentinois.

Franklin was soon asking the French Foreign Minister, Count Vergennes, to come to America's aid with a formal alliance. But Vergennes was still not sure that the Americans could win the war. The news from the battlefields in America continued to be bad. Washington had won small victories at Trenton and Princeton, but the latest word indicated that the British were mustering all their strength to deliver a knockout blow. One British army, commanded by General John Burgoyne, was to invade the colonies from Canada, while the main army, based in New York, would attack Philadelphia. So Count Vergennes stalled, offering Franklin more secret aid, but declining to become a public ally.

Calmly, Franklin asked Vergennes if there was any objection against Captain Lambert Wickes doing a little cruising against British vessels, and bringing his prizes into French ports. Vergennes reluctantly replied that there was no objection if Wickes' ship was "a vessel in distress." As for the prizes, that would depend on how loudly the British yelled. Under Franklin's orders, Captain Wickes promptly stood out of Nantes and in a matter of days picked off four British merchantmen. Next, he captured the Royal mail packet to Lisbon, the H.M.S. *Swallow*. Then he opened his seacocks until there was enough water in his hold to prove his "distress" and sailed his prizes back into Nantes.

The British Ambassador Lord Stormont protested wildly. Vergennes cooled him off by ordering Wickes and his prizes out of French waters within 24 hours. Of course, by this time all the prizes had been sold, taken offshore and hastily repainted, and their cargoes transferred to other ships. Meanwhile, Franklin sent Wickes orders to make another raid in British waters before he returned to America.

At the same time, Franklin launched another tough sailor, Gustavus Conyngham, a hotheaded daredevil from County Donegal, to war on British shipping. On May 3rd, Conyngham captured the British mail packet *The Prince of Orange* loaded with confidential documents the government was sending to its ambassadors in Europe. The documents were full of lies about the coming collapse of the Revolution, and Franklin cheerfully published them, with his refutations.

This time Lord Stormont almost went berserk. He demanded the arrest of Conyngham and his crew as pirates. Vergennes, still trying to avoid a break with England, arrested them, but declined to surrender them to the British. With the aid of the captured documents, and his native wit, Franklin was able to make a fool of Lord Stormont. One day a French friend rushed to Franklin to repeat the latest story about America's collapse, which he had heard from the British ambassador. Six battalions in Washington's army had laid down their arms. Was it true? "Oh, no," replied Franklin gravely, "it is not the truth, it is only a Stormont." Within a day the story had swept Paris, and *stormonter* became a new French word for lying. Lord Stormont was so upset, one day he wrote no less than nine letters to London about Franklin's activities.

Around this time, Franklin found himself dining at the same inn as Edward Gibbon, the famous author of *The Decline and Fall of the Roman Empire*. Gibbon, a fat, nearsighted little man, was a member of Parliament who voted blindly in support of the government's policies. Franklin invited Gibbon to join him at his table, but the historian primly replied that a servant of the King could not have any conversation with a rebel. Franklin sent back his regrets—and then could not resist adding that if Mr. Gibbon ever decided to write a book on the decline and fall of the British Empire, he would be happy to supply him with "ample materials."

Then came more bad news from America. Burgoyne had captured Fort Ticonderoga, the key defense point on America's northern frontier; and Washington had been defeated by the British at the battle of Brandywine, near Philadelphia. In addition, many of the supply ships which Deane had sent had been captured by blockading British warships. Obviously, America was in desperate need of French support.

Franklin also received some very bad news of a more personal kind from America during this gloomy fall of 1777.

William Franklin had been caught signing and smuggling out of Connecticut official pardons which the British were using in New Jersey and had been thrown into the town jail in Litchfield, Connecticut. Meanwhile, the British army abandoned New Jersey and took William's wife Elizabeth with them. In New York, without funds or friends, Elizabeth soon fell ill, and died. Temple Franklin was very sad when he heard this news, for she was the only mother he had ever known. He could not help remembering the words his father had written to him, urging him to take care of her. Temple was torn between his desire to be loyal to his grandfather and to America, and his love for his father and stepmother. It had a bad effect on Temple, emotionally. He became very cynical, and tried to tell himself that love did not matter. He swore he would never marry, because marriage only produced unhappiness.

Franklin had little time to console William. The barrage of bad news from America continued, and this time it was bad news both for America and for Franklin. The British had captured Philadelphia. All Franklin's property and, as far as he knew, his beloved daughter and her children were in the hands of the enemy. He had to struggle to keep up a brave front when Frenchmen asked him what was happening to the American Cause. "Well, Doctor," one Parisian said to him, "Howe has taken Philadelphia."

"I beg your pardon, sir," said Franklin, "Philadelphia has taken Howe."

Less than a week after this dismal news, a rumor came

drifting into Paris from Nantes. An American ship had arrived with a messenger carrying official dispatches for Franklin and his associates. The Americans and their French friends gathered at Franklin's house at Passy to await the arrival of the courier.

The moment a carriage was heard rattling over the cobblestones of the courtyard, Franklin and the others rushed out of the house. Jonathan Loring Austin of Boston got out. "Sir," Franklin asked, "is Philadelphia taken?"

"Yes, sir," replied Austin.

Franklin nodded mournfully. He had been hoping that the story was another British lie. Then, as he turned away, young Austin spoke again. "But, sir, I have greater news than that. General Burgoyne and his whole army are prisoners of war!"

It was true. New England militiamen, armed in many cases with guns from a ship sent by Silas Deane which had broken through the British blockade, had trapped Burgoyne's army near Saratoga, and he had surrendered.

Franklin immediately rushed into the house and began writing dispatches and letters. Some went to friends in England, to give the opposition in Parliament ammunition against the Ministry. Other letters went to friends in Paris. The most important one went to Count Vergennes, the French Foreign Minister, urging an alliance between France and America. To make sure everyone in Paris heard the news, Franklin had printed in French a handbill telling the story, newspaper style.

"Mail arrived from Philadelphia at Dr. Franklin's home in Passy after 34 days.

"On October 14th, Burgoyne had to lay down his arms, 9200 men killed or taken prisoner. . . ."

Vergennes said he was now ready to sign a treaty of alliance. But first he needed the approval of Spain. The Spanish King was an ally, as well as a Bourbon relative, of France's King, Louis XVI. When Spain refused to sign the treaty, the alliance was threatened with more—possibly fatal—delay. Franklin proceeded to have dinner with the head of the British Secret Service in Paris, whereupon the French became vastly alarmed. They were afraid that he was thinking about signing a truce with England. They did not know, of course, what Franklin said to the spy at dinner. England, the spy told Franklin, was ready to fight ten years to prevent America from winning independence. America, Franklin shot back, was ready to fight sixty years to win it.

The French now practically implored Franklin to sign a treaty of alliance. He was reluctant to do so, because he knew that it would mean a longer and more bitter war. He waited until the last possible moment, hoping to hear from England that the opposition had brought down the government and a pro-American Ministry had taken power. To Thomas Walpole, an old friend from the proposed Ohio Company, he wrote, "Everything seems to be rejected by your mad politicians that would lead to healing the breach." To another English friend, on February 5th, 1778, he wrote, "Understanding that a certain person promised to make proposals for healing a certain breach, I postponed and delay'd a material operation till I shou'd hear what those proposals were. I am now told that he will not make them . . . Therefore, adieu, my dear friend."

The following day, Franklin went to the Ministry of Foreign Affairs and signed the treaty of alliance with France. Friends noticed he wore the same Manchester velvet suit that he had worn the day he had been abused by Wedderburn before the Privy Council. They asked him why. Franklin smiled and said, "To give it a little revenge."

CHAPTER 18

PEACE NEGOTIATOR

THE BRITISH REFUSED TO GIVE UP THE FIGHT, in spite of the French alliance, and the war dragged on. The other Americans who were supposed to be helping Franklin in Paris quarreled with each other, and with him, probably because they envied him his great fame. The chief trouble-maker was a Virginian, Arthur Lee, who suspected everyone of being a traitor, even Franklin. Nothing ever pleased him.

One day, Deane and Lee were dining with Franklin, whose French neighbors had sent in a large cake with the inscription, *Le digne Franklin* (The worthy Franklin).

"As usual, Doctor," Silas Deane said, "we have to appropriate your present to our joint use."

Seeing a sour look on Arthur Lee's face, Franklin said, "Not at all. This must be intended for all the commissioners; only

BEN FRANKLIN

these French people cannot write English. They mean, no doubt, Lee, Deane, Franklin."

"That might answer," growled the humorless Lee, "but we know that whenever they remember us at all, they always put you first."

Eventually, Congress recalled Deane and Lee and gave Franklin the sole responsibility for representing the United States in Paris. This meant a lot more headaches. Franklin had to buy all the guns and other supplies for the American army. He had to be a part-time admiral, and supervise the activity of American warships in European waters. He had to worry about over a thousand American seamen who had been captured and were starving to death in British jails. He had to interview hundreds of officers from France, Germany and other countries who wanted to volunteer to fight in the American army. All these were extra duties, piled on top of his most important job—maintaining harmony between France and America, and persuading the French government to continue to loan money to the bankrupt Americans.

There were times when the European volunteers almost drove Franklin crazy. "Great officers in all ranks, in all departments; ladies great and small . . . worry me from morning to night," he complained. "The noise of every coach now that enters my court terrifies me. I am afraid to accept an invitation to dine abroad, being almost sure of meeting with some officer or officer's friend, who, as soon as I am put in good humour by a glass or two of champaign, begins his attack upon me. . . ."

As usual, Franklin saw the humorous side of the situation. One day he cooked up a "model of a letter of recommendation of a person you are unacquainted with." The letter, which he actually gave to some people going to America, explained that Franklin did not know the person, but he recommended him "to those civilities which every stranger of whom one knows no harm has a right to."

Around this time Franklin heard a story from England that cheered him up. Before the war, George III had permitted Franklin to install lightning rods on St. James Palace in London, where the royal family lived. A British electrician, Benjamin Wilson, told the King that Franklin's pointed lightning conductors were inferior to blunt ones. The King asked Franklin's old friend, Sir John Pringle, the physician to the royal family, for his opinion. Pringle replied that natural laws were not changeable by royal pleasure. George flew into a rage, barred Pringle from the palace, removed him as president of the Royal Society and replaced all the pointed conductors on St. James with blunt ones.

The wrangle inspired the following verse from a London wit.

While you Great George, for safety hunt
And sharp conductors change for blunt
    The nation's out of joint.
Franklin a wiser course pursues
And all your thunder fearless views
    By keeping to the *point*.

Franklin worried constantly over the American seamen in British jails. Through friends in England, he set up a fund which was supposed to pay them small amounts of money each week so they could buy decent food. The man in charge of this fund was a Maryland merchant, Thomas Digges, who had been selected by Arthur Lee. Unfortunately, Digges was a British agent. He took the 400 pounds—over $2,000—which Franklin sent to England, and instead of passing it on to the prisoners each week, he kept it in his own pocket.

Franklin condemned Digges in a scorching letter. "He that robs the rich even of a single guinea is a villain; but what is he who can break his sacred trust, by robbing a poor man and a prisoner of 18 pence given in charity for his relief and repeat that crime as often as there are weeks in a winter, and multiply it by robbing as many poor men every week as made up the number of near six hundred? We have no name in our language for such atrocious wickedness. If such a fellow is not damned, it is not worthwhile to keep a devil."

A British friend wrote a worried letter to Franklin, because he had heard a rumor that the secret agents of George III were planning to assassinate him. Franklin declined to be frightened by the story. "I thank you for your kind caution," he wrote, "but having nearly finished a long life, I set but little value on what remains of it . . . Perhaps the best use such an old fellow can be put to, is to make a martyr of him." No more was heard of an assassination plot.

At Passy, Franklin became warm friends with all his neighbors. The ladies especially loved him, and called him "mon cher Papa." His two favorites were Madame Brillon, a pretty, very gifted musician of 35, and Madame Helvetius, a widow of over 50, still rather beautiful, the daughter of an aristocrat. Franklin loved to tease Madame Brillon about being in love with her. But she regarded him as her "spiritual father." He finally agreed to adopt her as his "daughter," and in his letters he always called her that. When she had trouble with her husband, Madame Brillon fled to Franklin for advice. She depended on him, exactly as many daughters depend on their fathers.

With Madame Helvetius, Franklin had a different relationship. He actually fell in love with her and proposed marriage. But she said that she wished to remain faithful to the memory of her husband, and refused his offer. Franklin proceeded to write her a little story, in the hope of changing her mind. He said he had dreamt that he had died and gone to heaven, where he met Mr. Helvetius. Gravely, Helvetius informed Franklin that he had taken a new wife in Paradise. At that moment, the wife appeared, and Franklin was amazed to discover it was his wife on earth, Deborah. "Come," he said to Madame Helvetius, "let us revenge ourselves." But Madame still said no.

These loving friends helped to ease Franklin's pain when he heard more depressing news about his son William in America. The Continental Congress finally agreed to exchange William for a captured British general. In New York, William became head of the Board of Associated Loyalists, an organization that recruited men to fight on the British side. They began launching guerrilla raids against Americans loyal to Congress, in New Jersey, on Long Island, and in Connecticut. This hurt Franklin deeply. It was bad enough to have his son refuse to stand by him in the fight for American independence, but now he was fighting against his fellow Americans, in the meanest, cruelest way, killing people from ambush and burning homes and barns. To Franklin it meant that he could never again feel a father's love for William.

Franklin hoped that William Temple Franklin would take William's place. But Temple was emotionally wounded by the decision he had to make between his father and his grandfather. Part of the time he worked for Franklin, but most of the time he preferred to be a playboy, wearing the latest fashions and ogling the girls in Paris. At home in America, Arthur Lee tried to strike at Franklin through Temple, by accusing the young man of being a Loyalist, and possibly a spy. "Is it enough that I have lost my son; would they add my grandson?" Franklin cried in a letter to his son-in-law, Richard Bache. If Congress ordered him to fire Temple as his secretary, Franklin declared, he would quit.

As for his other grandson, Ben Bache, once he had learned French, Franklin sent him to school in Geneva, Switzerland. "He is a good, honest lad and will make, I think, a valuable man," Franklin said. He was right—Ben became a very successful newspaper editor.

Franklin wrote Ben many letters while the boy was in

Geneva. He always urged him to study hard. "I think of you every day," he wrote in one letter, "and there is nothing I desire more than to see you furnished with good learning [so that you can become] an honourable man in your own country."

The war dragged on and on. Then, in the fall of 1781, Franklin got an unexpected letter from Count Vergennes. He thought it might be a complaint, because the Americans were trying to borrow more money from France. Instead the letter contained the best possible news. The Americans had trapped another British army at Yorktown, Virginia, and the best British general in America, Charles Lord Cornwallis, had surrendered to George Washington. Franklin told Vergennes that King Louis XVI was *le plus grand faiseur d'heureux* (the greatest creator of happiness) in the world.

In the spring of 1782, the upheaval in the British Parliament which Franklin had been hoping to see for so many years finally took place. The opposition voted Lord North and his ministers out of power. The new Foreign Minister was William Petty, Lord Shelburne, Franklin's old friend. He immediately sent a personal representative to Franklin, telling him that England wanted peace. Franklin urged Shelburne to do more than negotiate a peace treaty. "Reconcile England and America," he advised him. How? Along with granting the thirteen colonies independence, Franklin said, Shelburne ought to give them as a gift Canada and Nova Scotia. This land could be used to pay for the millions of dollars of damage that England's armies and fleets had done to America's towns and cities. Shelburne's representative at the peace conference, Richard Oswald, agreed completely with this idea. If Franklin had been able to push the negotiations through, alone, America might have won complete control of the North American continent.

But Franklin was not the only peace negotiator on the American side. Two other men had been appointed by Congress, John Jay and John Adams, both lawyers who tended to see everything in legal terms. Jay refused to negotiate with the British until they formally recognized the independence of the United States. Adams sided with Jay, so Franklin was overruled. For over two months the Americans wrangled with the British over this point. During this time, the British won two victories in the war. Their fleet fought a battle in the West Indies with the French fleet, and beat them badly. Spain, which had entered the war late on France's side, tried to capture Gilbraltar with a massive assault. But the Spanish army was beaten off, and a British fleet broke through with supplies. These victories made the British much tougher bargainers at the peace table.

In the end, the Americans were glad to settle for all the territory between the seacoast and the Mississippi River, with boundaries on the north and south about where they are today. Even then, the British were not inclined to sign the treaty until Americans agreed to pay the Loyalists for their farms, estates and houses, which they were forced to abandon in most colonies.

Franklin arose to play a trump card. He read a list of the cities and towns which the British had burned or looted in the course of the war. He went over the thousands of men, women and children slaughtered on the frontier by British-led Indian raids. Before the British talked about compensating the Loyalists, let them pay this bill. The British negotiators swallowed hard, conferred for a moment, and agreed to sign the treaty as it stood.

Franklin was more than satisfied with this victory. He knew that in this world one cannot always win everything. The mere fact that the thirteen colonies had won their independence in spite of all the efforts of Great Britain, the strongest nation on the globe, was almost a miracle.

Less than a month later, the British and the French signed a treaty of peace. The war was over. That night, arriving at the home of a French friend, Franklin threw his arms around him and exclaimed, "Could I have hoped, at my age, to enjoy such a happiness?"

With peace secured, Franklin's spirits soared. He forgave everyone who had ever wronged him. When John Jay wrote from London to tell him that he had many enemies in England, Franklin replied that the fact did not trouble him. "They are my enemies as an *American*." He added that he also had two or three enemies in America "who are my enemies as a minister." But he was able to thank God "there are not in the whole world any who are my enemies as a man; for by His grace, thro' a long life, I have been enabled so to conduct myself, that there does not exist a human being who can justly say 'Ben. Franklin has wrong'd me.' "

When William Strahan wrote to Franklin, lamenting the confused state of English politics, Franklin told him not to despair. "We have some remains of affection for you, and shall always be ready to receive and take care of you in case of distress. So if you have not sense and virtue enough to govern yourselves . . . dissolve your present old crazy Constitution, and send members to Congress."

Soon after, Franklin had an opportunity to repay an old debt of gratitude. In his years at the Court of Versailles he had become very friendly with the Papal Legate, the priest who represented the Pope of Rome in France. The Papal diplomat now informed the Ambassador that America's independence had convinced the Pope that the Catholic Church in America was ready to take an important step toward maturity. It was time to appoint an American bishop. Did he have any suggestions? Franklin had only one—his old friend Father John Carroll, who had saved his life on the trip down the lakes from Canada in 1776. The Papal Legate passed on Franklin's recommendation to Rome, and soon a very surprised Father Carroll was America's first bishop.

Meanwhile, Franklin was enjoying himself with a new scientific interest—balloons. The French had begun filling balloons, first with heated air, then with hydrogen, which Franklin called "inflammable air." To fellow scientists in England and America, Franklin sent detailed reports on these first balloon flights. As with the American trip to the moon, there were numerous pessimists, who bemoaned the expense and time—it took two days and nights to fill a balloon—and demanded to know what was the point of ballooning, what good did it do the average man? Franklin, foreseeing the day when men would be able to fly everywhere, replied: "What good is a newborn baby?"

Franklin's French friends urged him to spend the rest of his life in France. But he decided, somewhat reluctantly, to go home. "I want to die in my own country," he said. He had developed a stone in his bladder, which made riding in a carriage very painful, so the King sent him a litter, drawn by his Royal mules. In this conveyance, Franklin began his journey to the coast. Ben Bache, who was going with him, noted in his diary that all the people of Passy crowded around the litter to say goodbye. "A mournful silence reigned . . . only interrupted by a few sobs."

Franklin stopped for a few days at Southampton, to say goodbye to his English friends. There, he saw his son William for the last time. The meeting was not a friendly one. Franklin bought from William the farm he still owned in New Jersey, and gave it to William Temple. He presented William with a bill for 1,500 pounds—money that William owed him for Temple's education in England, and loans that Franklin had made to the Governor when they were trying to create the Ohio colony. William knew that if he had joined the Americans in the war, Franklin would have torn up these bills. Now, he was forced to give to his father the last land he owned in America—several thousand acres in upper New York State. Franklin also gave this land to Temple.

There was an additional reason why Franklin could not forgive William now. He was wanted for murder—the murder of a fellow American. Guerrilla raiders under his command had hanged in cold blood a captured American captain, Joshua Huddy. The Americans wanted to hang William in return, but he had jumped aboard a ship and gotten safely to England. So Franklin set sail for home, leaving his son behind him in England. William was paid a pension by the British government—750 pounds a year for the rest of his life.

To an English friend, who had worked to reconcile the two countries, Franklin was far more affectionate in his farewell. "We were long fellow laborers in the best of all works, the work of peace," he wrote. "I leave you still in the field, but having finished my day's work, I am going home to go to bed! Wish me a good night's rest, as I do you a pleasant evening. Adieu!"

CHAPTER 19

UNIFIER

ON THE TRIP HOME, FRANKLIN WROTE HIS LONG delayed report on his study of the Gulf Stream. He told how ships could shorten their passage from America to England by as much as two weeks by using the three-mile-an-hour current of this great 10-mile-wide ocean river. By avoiding it on the passage from Europe to America, they could save as much as sixty or seventy miles a day. Modern scientists have not forgotten Franklin's discovery—the special submarine which began exploring the Gulf Stream from top to bottom in 1969 was named the Benjamin Franklin.

Franklin said he was going home to bed, but he found there was still work for him to do. The people of Pennsylvania promptly elected him President of the Commonwealth, a job that corresponds to the present-day governorship. Three times he was reelected. It was, he told his sister Jane Mecom, an honor he treasured more than a peerage, because it was the tribute of a free people.

The Continental Congress had not taken Franklin's advice when they passed their Articles of Confederation. As a central government for the thirteen colonies, Congress had no real power. Each state had one vote, which set small states and large states constantly bickering with each other. Relations between the states deteriorated alarmingly. They tended to ignore Congress almost completely, and act as if they were independent countries. They quarreled over their boundaries and began refusing to accept each other's money.

It was obvious that America needed a central government with more power to regulate disputes, organize the country, and pay off the large war debt. So Franklin was among the many Americans who welcomed the Constitutional Convention, when it met in Philadelphia in May, 1787. "Indeed if it does not do good, it must do harm," he told his successor in France, Thomas Jefferson, "as it will show that we have not wisdom enough among us to govern ourselves."

Franklin rallied all his strength in a last expression of commitment to the Cause. At the age of 82, for four consecutive months he trudged almost daily from his house to the Pennsylvania State House and spent hours wrangling and debating over how to reconcile poor states and rich states, large states and small states, slave states and free states. These were among the many questions confronted by the men who formulated the Constitution.

From the first day, Franklin sounded a call for a spirit of compromise. He could have asked for the job of chairman, but he deliberately stepped aside and allowed George Washington to be nominated without a contest. When the argument grew violent, Franklin warned the delegates that if they allowed themselves to be "divided by [their] little partial local interests," they would become "a reproach and a bye-word down to future ages."

Congress selected a "Grand Committee," consisting of one delegate from each state, to resolve the arguments between the large states and the small states. Franklin, picking up an idea that other men had already suggested, recommended that one house in Congress have equal representation, and the second house be represented in proportion to population. The committee agreed by a very narrow margin—5 to 4, with one state (Massachusetts) divided. Thus the Senate and the House of Representatives were created, thanks largely to Franklin's prestige and influence. This was a turning point in the Constitutional Convention. Once the small states felt their interests were protected, the Convention moved ahead with a minimum of argument.

As the Convention neared a close, however, another danger became apparent to the delegates. Many compromises had passed by a very close vote, and many of the losers in these votes were disgruntled and unreconciled. If a vote was taken on a man-by-man basis, it would reveal how many people did not like the Constitution as it now stood, even though a majority was in favor of it.

Franklin stepped forward to suggest one more great compromise. He urged everyone to sign the document as witnesses to the fact that all the *states* unanimously approved it. This was true—a majority on each state delegation did approve it. Franklin then went on to urge the delegates to support the Constitution in their separate states, when it was proposed for ratification. He admitted that he did not entirely approve the document at present. But in the course of his long life, he had changed his opinions on many important subjects. Perhaps his disagreements with the Constitution were wrong. He hoped that "every member of the Convention who may still have objections to it would with me on this occasion doubt a little of his own infallibility, and to make manifest our unanimity, put his name to this instrument." Franklin's proposal was carried, ten to nothing, and all but two of the delegates signed the Constitution.

Franklin, watching them walk up to the President's table to sign the historic document, pointed to a sun on the President's chair. "I have," he said, "often and often in the course of this session . . . looked at that . . . without being able to tell whether it was rising or setting: but now at length I have the happiness to know that it is a rising and not a setting sun."

Franklin lived two more years. His bladder stone grew

worse, and caused him terrible pain. But he seldom complained. He took deep pleasure in watching the successful
launching of the new American government. Writing to
George Washington soon after he became President, Franklin
congratulated him "on the growing strength of our new
government under your administration. For my own personal
ease, I should have died two years ago; but tho these years
have been spent in excruciating pain, I am pleased that I
have lived them, since they have brought me to see our present
situation."

At home, Franklin was surrounded by a warm and loving
circle. Sarah Bache and her seven children lived in the same
house with him. Widowed Polly Stevenson Hewson took his
advice and came over to America with her three children to be
near the man who was her spiritual father. She visited him
constantly, read to him and nursed him with tireless affection.

Only Temple Franklin worried his grandfather. He was
bored with country life, and neglected the New Jersey farm he
had inherited from his father. Franklin tried to win him an
American diplomatic appointment abroad, but Temple's reputation with his fellow Americans was not good. They considered him too much of a playboy. With all his grandfather's
influence behind him, he could not get the job he wanted.

In these last years, Franklin found time for one more cause.
He accepted the presidency of "The Pennsylvania Society for
Promoting the Abolition of Slavery, and the Relief of Free
Negroes Unlawfully Held in Bondage." In this capacity he

BEN FRANKLIN

wrote sharp letters to the governors of many northern states, reproaching them for allowing their seamen, ship captains and merchants to participate in the slave trade. When the first Congress met, the Society presented a memorial, signed by Franklin, urging an immediate abolition of slavery. James Jackson of Georgia attacked the proposal, stating that slavery was sanctioned by the Bible and Negroes were better off and happier as slaves.

A few days later, an essay appeared in the *Federal Gazette*, Philadelphia's leading newspaper. It was supposed to be a statement by one Sidi Mehemet Ibrahim, a leading member of the Algerian government. Sidi argued against a small group of Algerians who wanted to abolish piracy and their country's nasty habit of enslaving white Christians. Sidi pointed out that Christians were far better off as slaves. They lived lives of perfect safety; they were well-fed, lodged and clothed. "They are not liable to be impressed for soldiers, and forced to cut one another's Christian throats, as in the wars of their own countries." The real writer, of course, was Franklin, ridiculing Jackson's speech in Congress. Although many Philadelphians were impressed, and Pennsylvania soon became one of the first northern states to abolish slavery, this terrible institution was too deeply entrenched in the southern states for Franklin or any other American of his time to defeat it.

A few weeks later, Franklin suffered an attack of pleurisy, the illness that had almost killed him when he was a young man of 21. This time, his old body was too worn out to resist it.

He slipped into a coma, and at 11 p.m. on April 17th, 1790, he died. He was 84.

The *Pennsylvania Gazette,* with a black border, announced his death. While bells tolled and 20,000 watched, his coffin was lowered into the grave in Christ Church burying ground, beside his wife, Deborah.

Scientists and statesmen around the world pronounced eulogies about his remarkable life. Perhaps the most moving tribute was spoken by the Comte de Mirabeau before the French National Assembly. The liberal nobleman declared that it was time for governments to mourn not only for kings, princes and generals, but for the benefactors of humanity. He called on the Assembly to join him "in a religious act" and wear mourning for three days to pay homage to this "mighty genius" who had freed men from the fear of both "thunderbolts and tyrants." The motion was passed by acclamation.

For many Americans, Franklin remains a puzzling man. Because he loved laughter and found humor in many things, some people have thought he was not serious about the things he believed in. Other people have dwelt on the advice he gave in his *Autobiography,* and in his almanacs, about how to save money and succeed at business. This is why Franklin's name appears so often on savings banks. These people have forgotten that Franklin quit making money at 42, and devoted the rest of his life to the study of science and service to his country.

Former President Harry S. Truman has said that Franklin "has not found his rightful place in American history yet." To some extent this is true. Perhaps it is time for us to follow Franklin's example, and learn to compromise the arguments we have among ourselves, and with the rest of the world. We can learn from him how to laugh and enjoy life, and still be serious about important things. Above all, if we follow his example, we will remain devoted to his ideal of America as a nation of free people.

Index

Pennsylvania, 81, 86, 114, 115
  frontier of, 63–64, 65–66
  restriction of manufacture
    of iron in, 52
  University of, 35
Pennsylvania Academy, 35
Pennsylvania Assembly, 35,
  46, 55, 57, 60, 64, 66, 70,
  73
Pennsylvania fireplace, *see*
  Franklin stove
Pennsylvania Hospital, 35
Pennsylvania State House,
  120, 158
The Pennsylvania Gazette, 27,
  28, 29, 37, 53, 65, 163
"The Pennsylvania Society
  for Promoting the
  Abolition of
  Slavery . . . ," 161–62
Perth Amboy (N.J.), 10, 117,
  126
Petty, William (Lord
  Shelburne), 96, 151–52
Philadelphia, Pa., 10, 13, 78,
  114, 117, 119, 120, 121, 125,
  132, 138, 140, 142, 162

Philadelphia Associaters, 35
Philadelphia Commons, 42
"Philomaths," 33, 34, 35
Pittsburgh, 60
Poor Richard's Almanack,
  33–35, 37, 43
The Pope, 154
Population growth, 51–52
Positive charge of electricity,
  40–41
Postal system, 48–50
  first dead-letter office,
    50
  post riders and, 50
Pownall (secretary to Lord
  Hillsborough), 87,
  89–90, 92
The Prince of Orange, 139
Princeton, N.J., battle of,
  138
Pringle, Sir John, 147
Privy Council, 74, 85, 92, 103,
  104–5, 144
Prometheus, 44
Proprietary party of Pa., 30,
  56, 64, 66, 73, 78, 83
Prussia, 98

ABOUT THE AUTHOR

Noted author Thomas Fleming became interested in American history at the age of fourteen when he read *Oliver Wiswell* a novel about a loyalist in the American Revolution. Mr. Fleming has written more than a dozen books on the American Revolution including two much praised adult studies of Benjamin Franklin. *The New York Times* hailed *Benjamin Franklin, The Man Who Dared the Lightning* for "shedding new light" on Franklin.

Mr. Fleming's book *Liberty: The American Revolution* was a main selection of both the Book of the Month and History Book Clubs. Douglas Brinkley said it was "that rare essential book that belongs in every school and home." It was the companion volume to the prize-winning six part series of the same title that appeared on PBS.

Thomas Fleming appears frequently on PBS, the History Channel and C-Span as a commentator, Mr. Fleming lives in New York City with his wife, Alice, who is also a prolific author.

"Fleming has added new depth and vigor to a familiar subject of biographies. The facts that are usually glossed over in books for young readers, such as Franklin's penchant for dalliance, are given in a brisk and graceful style; there are many quotations from Franklin's writings and many anecdotes and bits of information not usually included in other books and giving evidence of thorough research. Above all, the vigor and informality of the writing make this a pleasure to read."

—ZENA SUTHERLAND, from *The Best in Children's Books*

BOOKS IN THIS SERIES

✹STERLING POINT BOOKS

92
Fra

Fleming, Thomas
Ben Franklin:
Inventing America

New 5/08

✓

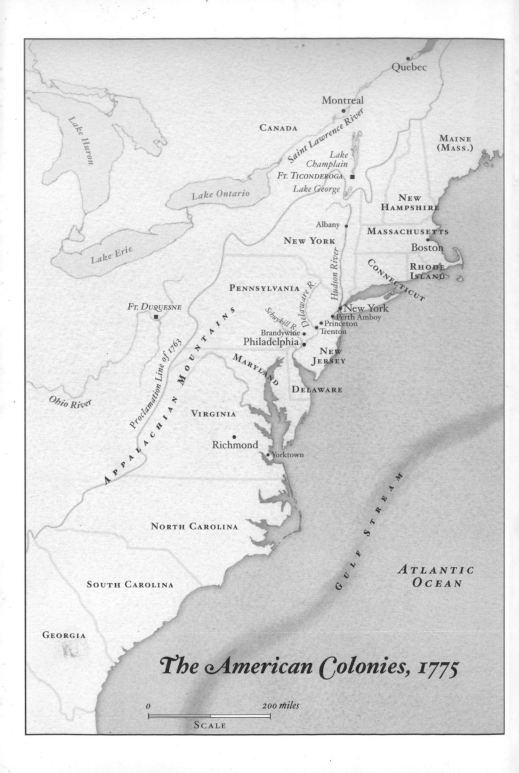

Quebec

Montreal

CANADA

Lake Huron

Lake Ontario

Lake Erie

Saint Lawrence River

Lake
Champlain
FT. TICONDEROGA
Lake George

MAINE
(MASS.)

NEW
HAMPSHIRE

Albany

NEW YORK

MASSACHUSETTS

Boston

RHODE
ISLAND

CONNECTICUT

PENNSYLVANIA

Delaware R.

Hudson River

FT. DUQUESNE

Schuylkill R.

New York
Perth Amboy
Princeton
Trenton

Brandywine

Philadelphia

NEW
JERSEY

DELAWARE

A P P A L A C H I A N   M O U N T A I N S

Proclamation Line of 1763

MARYLAND

Ohio River

VIRGINIA

Richmond

Yorktown

NORTH CAROLINA

SOUTH CAROLINA

G U L F   S T R E A M

ATLANTIC
OCEAN

GEORGIA

The American Colonies, 1775

0   200 *miles*

SCALE

PLEASURE MODEL

NETHERWORLD ★ BOOK 1

CHRISTOPHER ROWLEY

A TOM DOHERTY ASSOCIATES BOOK
NEW YORK

This is a work of fiction. All of the characters, organizations, and events portrayed in this novel are either products of the author's imagination or are used fictitiously.

HEAVY METAL PULP: PLEASURE MODEL: NETHERWORLD BOOK ONE

A Tor Book
Published by Tom Doherty Associates, LLC
175 Fifth Avenue
New York, NY 10010

Design by Greg Collins

Tor® is a registered trademark of Tom Doherty Associates, LLC.

ISBN 978-1-61664-094-1

Printed in the United States of America

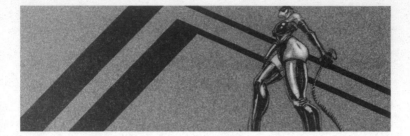

CHAPTER 1

The man was a massive specimen. Heavy shoulders, powerful arms, solid delts and lats. The deeply lined face was hidden in shadows, the head bowed with pain, but it was a strong face, brutal even, or so Mistress Julia thought.

She had finished. One hundred strokes with the single-tail whip, following on eighty with the number three rattan cane. All delivered quite slowly, ten seconds apart, stretching the ordeal out to an hour. Blood ran from several welts on his back and buttocks. His head, shaved to the skin, glistened with sweat.

He dropped to his knees and kissed the feet of the

Virgin Mary. The statue stood, smiling serenely in the living room. Blood smeared the polished marble floor as he swayed.

He was mumbling, as he always did. She heard the words, though she scarcely understood them.

> *Bruised, derided, cursed, defiled,*
> *please behold your evil child*
> *all with bloody scourges rent;*
> *For the sins upon his nation*
> *save him from the desolation*
> *that awaits him down in hell.*

Mistress Julia kept her distance. Clients usually groveled before she beat them. With her ash blond hair slicked back in a ponytail, she was dressed in her most "severe" mode, black patent leather bodysuit, high boots with four-inch heels, gloves, and mask. But this client was never actually involved in a sexual scene. Other than kissing her boots and begging for the whip, he asked for nothing that was normally part of her practice. This one just wanted to be punished.

And punished severely.

She had never beaten a man who simply took it the way this one did. Never a murmur, a groan, a cry, a tear, nothing,

until she was done and he fell down before the six-foot marble statue and wept as he mumbled his prayers.

She turned on her heel and stalked away. Whatever Mr. Sangacha's problem was, she had done her part. Another four hundred New Dollars waited in the envelope on the glass table. She picked it up as she headed for the bathroom.

> *Prostrate before thee, I make this humble act of reparation*
> *for the outrages which thou hast received from me. . . .*

He was still praying, the fervor thick in his throat, as she closed the bathroom door.

Mistress Julia—real name Angela Bricken—normally worked with her clients at her specially equipped basement dungeon in a nice modern house over in Ramapo. However, Sangacha had insisted from the beginning

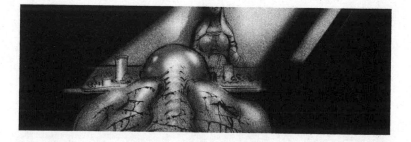

on being visited in his own home. It was not her favorite mode of operation. In the dungeon she had her security set up, with various technologies that could rapidly immobilize a man if he turned violent during a session.

But Sangacha had never given her the slightest trouble. He never deviated from the scene and he always paid in full, on time and without complaint.

The one problem, of course, was the surveillance. Cams were everywhere, and for her own good reasons Angie Bricken didn't care to be lensed too often in any one place. So she had to take precautions.

She rinsed off the whip and the cane as she got the hot water running, then peeled off her boots and unzipped her suit. Some clients begged for these tasks, and some were rewarded with them, and other things too, but only after they'd paid their dues. Mistress Julia had learned a lot of things about men over the years.

Whip, boots, and suit went into her bag as she stripped down. For a moment she looked at herself in the floor-to-ceiling mirror. Still desirable, she thought, even at fifty. Intensive antioxidant treatments, strict diet, and rigorous exercise were partly responsible. Her extended medical program with monthly checkups and prevention-interventions took care of the rest. Only the most careful examination of her face could reveal that she was anything but a day over thirty.

The shower was good. Sangacha had a real high-tech unit, with jets at three levels that pulsed on a cycle of different frequencies. She enjoyed the hard-driving

water, surrendering to the heat, feeling cleaner by the second.

Angie never scheduled anything else on Sangacha days. She realized she was hungry, so she broke out of the Julia construct and pressed a fingertip to her right ear, where her phone chip was lodged.

"That organic place, down in Tarrytown. Book me in for lunch."

A massive thud shook the shower.

"What the fuck?" She turned off the water and pulled back the curtain, which probably saved her life. The next blast was unmistakable—shotgun. A scream followed, and cursing, and then a rapid thud-thud-thud that she knew had to be some kind of automatic weapon equipped with a silencer.

For a moment she stood frozen, terrified and astonished. Then the shotgun went off again and something or somebody slammed into the bathroom door.

That got her moving. She swept her bag off the floor, stuffed it into the dirty towel bin. It fit, just, and she shut the lid. Then she spun around and switched off the lights. Rubbing the foot towel over the floor to mop up the drips, she yanked open the door to the cabinet under the sink.

A tight fit, but she could do it. She had to do it. She was certain of that, if she wanted to live.

There were some more thud-thuds, and a lot of loud cursing. A man was whimpering in pain.

She scrunched her body down under the sink, got her legs up into the space on the other side of the pipes, pulled her head inside, stuffed the foot towel under her ass, which helped to cushion her hip against the metal drain, and tugged the door shut. It did so with a plastic click that left her briefly wondering if she could open it again from inside, or if she'd be stuck there until who knew when.

Which was fucking absurd, because whatever was going on out there in the duplex, it involved guns and that meant only one thing: death.

She waited, shivering, fear coiling inside her like a cold dark creature.

The last twenty-five years had been like this, since the day she'd gotten the personality modification program and become Mistress Julia. One minute she was a dominatrix, afraid of nothing, in command, and the next she was helpless little Angie, drowning in her own fear, praying for Julia to save her.

"You stupid fuck!" There came a loud moan of pain and, she imagined, the sound of something or someone being dragged.

There was a crash, then silence.

Her mind ran wildly though scenarios. She didn't know who Sangacha was. As was often the case in her business, she didn't want to know that kind of thing.

Was it a mob hit? Was he some kind of crim? She had wondered about that. His habit of praying for forgiveness when she'd laid into him had the sound of a man who'd done terrible things in his life.

Then she heard the door to the bathroom open and a heavy tread on the tile floor.

"Where the fuck is she?" asked a male voice.

"Must've gotten out just before we arrived," said another.

"Check the parking. Hurry."

Boots retreated. She stayed where she was, the fear now like a sword of ice running up her guts. The bathroom door slammed.

What the fuck was going on?

The footsteps had ceased. Still she waited. Had they gone? Were they playing games? She kept as still as she

possibly could, though the difficulties of her confinement were now making themselves apparent. Something was digging into the small of her back, and her head was crushed in between the side of the sink and the side of the cabinet.

She wanted to get to her car and put as many miles as she could between herself and this complex as quickly as possible. She'd go straight up to the woods and hide out. Up there she was somebody else, a whole other ID.

She was about to open the door when she heard a sudden rush of footsteps go by. Then the bathroom door banged open and the light went on, sending a gleam through the crack at the edge of the door to her hiding place.

"She ain't here," a voice groaned. "I'm fucking bleeding!"

"Here's a towel," drawled another. "Try not to bleed all over the truck."

Footsteps retreated, another door slammed, and everything was quiet again.

Fuck indeed. Fuck, fuck, fuck, she'd almost gotten herself caught there.

She waited.

Time passed. The thing digging into her back turned into torture. Angie tried not to let it all get to her. She had to stay calm. But Mistress Julia had other ideas.

Take a rest, Angie. Take your nerves and your weaknesses and your hunger for a piece of dark chocolate and shut the fuck up. It's time for iron control. Time to stay alive.

Julia took back the reins with the familiar sliding sensation. The dominatrix persona started her life on an A2 chip that Angie plugged in and out of the microsocket behind her right ear. At first, Angie had been terrified of Julia, afraid one day she would completely dominate her life. But Angie had learned the hard way—she needed Julia. Now, the stern alpha female was always there, waiting just below the surface. Angie didn't even need the plug-in anymore.

Minutes crawled by. Julia counted seconds like whip strokes. When the count reached a hundred she pushed hard. The door popped open with a bang and she fell out onto the bathroom floor.

Right before her eyes were huge, bloody boot prints, leading in and out of the bathroom.

She pulled her bag out of the towel bin and hurriedly got into her Zipdex bodysuit. Now she pulled out two face-cloths and wiped everything she might have touched with her bare skin, working quickly and, she prayed, effectively. She mopped out the shower, did her best on the curtain, and ran some more water to be sure while she worked on the space under the sink. Everything went into her bag.

Done, she slung her bag over her shoulder and padded into the hall. Bullet holes riddled the wall. It looked as if someone had tried to mop up a quart of blood, and hadn't

done a very good job. She went the other way, through the kitchen, and came out in the dining area. Another couple of steps and she saw him.

Sangacha lay on his back. There was a sawed-off shotgun lying close by. A pool of blood spread beneath him, washing over the feet of the Virgin Mary.

At the front door she put on her sneakers, her big mirrored sunglasses, and her pink and white Yankees cap with the bill pulled down low over her face. There wasn't time for makeup to disguise herself any further. Any images caught by the cams at this point were going to be studied intensively, she knew. She attached a little distortion box to the right side of her sunglasses frame. The box was expensive, and illegal, but it would blur her features, even her outline, to any ordinary camera.

Mistress Julia opened the door and peered both ways before bolting for the stairs. Because there'd been a work crew painting signage on the main parking, she'd gone around to the service worker area. It was smaller, even the

spaces were narrower, but she was very glad she'd used it since the killers wouldn't expect her to have parked there.

She cracked open the blue door to the parking and paused. Had they left someone here to take care of her, just in case? Working methodically, she looked down the aisles and into the corners.

With a deep breath, she headed for her car, prepared to run at the slightest sign of someone waiting for her. The car door opened for her and she slid inside.

"Ridgetop," she whispered, and the car slid out with the soft whine of the electric engine. She knew there were cameras at the exit ramp, so she kept her head down, letting just the pink Yankees cap be seen. A few moments later she was on the access road and the car began to accelerate. As she started to breathe normally again, questions and answers, most of them terrifying, boiled to the surface.

Shit. She really liked this town. But now she had to run again. There were some problems not even Mistress Julia could handle.

CHAPTER

Kingston, New York, had opened for business in the days of Charles II. Of course, hardly anyone who lived there now knew or cared about the town's history.

It was raining again, hard. Huge torrents of dirty water were sluicing down the drains with a familiar throbbing sound. The riffraff had long since been swept off the stretch of Broadway near the HudVal PD building.

Rook Venner, Senior Investigating Officer, Homicide, looked out the window of his office. For a moment he caught his reflection in the glass, dark hair cut short, broad forehead, prominent cheekbones. Thin lips twitched in a

smile. Not too bad, he thought. He ought to be more successful with women than he was. It was the job, of course;
it turned them off.

The implant in his right ear, the office phone, beeped
once.

"What've we got?"

"One-eight-seven," his partner reported. "In an upscale
devo down by Peekskill."

"Our side of the line?"

"Apparently."

Pity about that. South of Front Street and it was
Westchester's problem, not his.

Rook began assembling his kit. Since this wasn't a
mission to the uninsured world, he didn't need body armor, or the knock-hammer, or any of the heavy toys. He
did pack his gun and helmet, or "technical headpiece," as
the manual liked to call it.

His partner, Assistant Investigator Lindi MacEar—tall, blond, fond of triathlons—strode down the hall. She had all her gear strapped on: gun, lights, chem lab, specimen safe, multicam, the works, bar the armor and hand-to-hand weapons.

"Ready, boss?"

"Yeah." He pulled on his raincoat, flipped up the hood. "Unless we drown before we get to the damned car."

He checked his chest pocket for the reassuring solidity of Ingrid, his Nokia Supa. Way beyond regulation, of course, but when it came to encryption, the best handheld device you could get.

The gutters were overflowing at the back of the building, sending sheets of water straight down into the courtyard. They were soaked by the time they got into the Nat 200. On the upside, traffic was light. Only idiots and cops drove in the summer monsoons. Rook let the car drive itself.

On the Thruway they rode the rail on the outside lane. The inside truck traffic howled past in its robotic way, exploding through the rain at more than two hundred miles an hour.

Seventeen minutes to the second from Kingston and they rolled up to the faux concrete portico of the development in Peekskill. Flashing lights and a swarm of cops in full combat gear were there to greet him. As he stepped out, a patrol officer saw the badge on his helmet and moved aside.

Two cops in tac-squad shells were positioned to cover the hallway down to the elevators. Upstairs, orange laser baffles blocked off the corridor, with another tac-suit to keep the curious away.

No sign of forced entry, Rook thought, glancing at the high-tech security locks.

Inside the apartment, the South Valley CSI team was already hard at work.

"Crazy shit," murmured Chatt Fletcher, a rotund, cheerful kid out of Brooklyn. He pointed to the blood spray on the walls and marble tiles. "Shotgun, heavy gauge. Fired three times, at least one hit."

"That's a lot of blood."

"Not the target. He's over there." Chatt looked over his shoulder into the high-ceilinged living room.

Rook observed a big man, naked, lying facedown beside a life-size marble statue of the Virgin Mary.

"Didn't help him much, did she," muttered Rook.

"Not a believer, boss?"

"Jury's out on that one." Rook patted his holster. "For now I'll keep some insurance."

Chatt read off his notes. "Vic is Manuel Sangacha, age sixty-seven, no known relatives. Nothing stolen."

"You left out an important detail," announced MacEar, checking her handheld. "This is General Manuel Sangacha."

"General?" Rook didn't like the sound of that.

"Retired in 'fifty-two. Service period began in 2019. Commanded a border division during the Emergency."

Rook chewed his lip. This sounded like stuff he didn't want to have anything to do with.

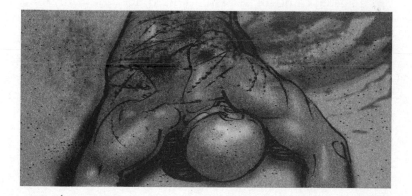

He tapped the button on his phone.

"Leave a message," said the chief's personal unit.

He did. Military stuff was dangerous. With luck the chief would pull him off this thing and call in military intelligence. Let them take care of their own.

Rook went back to business. "What's all that secondary damage?"

Chatt shrugged. "Back, buttocks, and thighs are covered in welts. Blows from a whip and something else, maybe a cane?"

Rook raised an eyebrow. "Hmm. Punishment or interrogation?"

"No idea. He's been dead about four hours."

"Messy. Murder weapon?"

"Early for forensics, but most likely a five-point-five millimeter. Sophisticated shit, delayed explosive rounds."

The usual thing for assassinations, quiet but deadly and small enough to be concealed from the sec cams. This was looking more and more like a corporate hit.

"What do we know from the security cams?"

"System was dazzled for about ninety minutes. Started at four o'clock, stopped at five-twenty-six."

"Lins, you want to try some of your magic?"

"On it, boss." Lindi tapped her handheld. "Chatt, feed me the sec cam footage."

Venner stalked slowly around the apartment. He had handled maybe a dozen corporate killings in his decade on Homicide. Usually the crime scene was so clean it squeaked. The killers were always ultraprofessional, left no traces, made no sound.

Then there was the whip. When hit teams had to extract info they usually used a combo of drugs to increase sensitivity and really painful tricks, like skinning a man's penis, or boiling his hands. These wounds weren't deep enough to cause that kind of pain. Chatt hadn't mentioned any fancy drug residues, though that might come with later analysis.

A straight-out corporate hit would seem the best fit here.

"One thing," Chatt mentioned. "Vic seems to have no chips, no active sub-cutes, no BIMS, not even an Insurance RFID."

"Well, he was military," Lindi said. "He had his removed when he got out."

"And never had others put in?"

Insured people wore a palette of implants, from uni-IDs to feelgoods and personality modules. Finding someone unchipped was freakish. No chips made Sangacha virtually invisible to sensors. What did the general have to hide?

"Here's something else interesting," Chatt reported. "Someone wiped the bathroom down."

Venner looked down the bloodstained hallway.

"No prints?"

"Lots of prints, but mostly Sangacha's. Same with DNA so far."

"The vic wet?"

"No, he's dry."

Rook studied the front door again. There were heavy-duty bolts top and bottom.

"Any sign of tampering?" Lindi asked without looking up from her handheld.

"Nope," said Chatt. "He either let them in or they had the code. He didn't have it bolted, either."

Just as likely, Sangacha felt like he ought to be safe and secure here, but another part of him said he wasn't. So he put on the bolts and bought the Remington six-shot. But he didn't lock the bolts, because it was a pain in the ass to have to unlock bolts to go in and out of your front door. But he did keep the Remington somewhere reasonably handy. Not good enough to save his life, but good enough to ruin someone else's day.

"Incoming call," the Nokia announced. "Chief Artoli."

"Thanks, Ingrid."

"Venner, what d'you got?" whispered a familiar voice in his right ear.

"The vic was a general. It's a corporate hit, but it's all wrong, blood everywhere."

"Keep this by the book, Detective. I don't want any of your shit," Area Chief Lisa Artoli ordered.

Venner and Chief Artoli went back a long way. Venner always got the job done but not without ruffling some feathers. Sometimes an entire goose.

"Shouldn't we hand this off to MI?" Rook asked.

"This is from Albany. Minimize cooperation with federal agencies."

"Christ." The state government was telling him to fuck the feds. "The feds are probably already on their way. This guy ran a border unit."

"Then do the dance. But if you get something good it goes to Albany and they make the decision."

"I hear you."

In other words, this was a political killing and Rook knew that meant extreme danger for everyone involved.

He turned back to MacEar. "Any luck with the cam footage?"

"Working on it."

"Come on, genius."

Lindi shot him a look.

A second later she displayed a grainy image from the parking lot cam. A blond woman in a pink baseball cap. It was a start.

"Woman left at five-oh-one, in the center of the dazzle."

Lindi was good. He probably didn't deserve her.

"Detective, we got something!" An officer came bounding into the apartment. "A witness, no, sorry—make that evidence."

Rook lifted an eyebrow. "You want to make up your mind?"

"Pleasure model. In a crate down in the storage unit."

"Christ." The vic hid a mod-bod so the neighbors wouldn't know how he got his kicks. "What kind?"

"Kind? Oh, it's a Pammy, I think."

"Ship it to the station and make sure none of your people get near it. I want whatever it knows unfiltered. Got it?"

"I've never seen one close up." Chatt grinned.

"What? A Pammy?" asked Lindi.

"Um, any pleasure model."

"Just keep your pants on," Lindi ordered with a half-smile.

Rook sighed. A mod-bod. These vat-grown gene humans had the IQ of a pocket watch and were completely illegal. Something else to make this case even weirder than it was—and a lot more difficult.

CHAPTER 3

"I am Plesur," whispered the creature, the thing, *it*. Though the longer he talked to her, or *it*, the harder it was to remember that this was not really a human being—or was it?

Of course, her—*its*—vocabulary was limited, but apart from that it was a gorgeous young woman, about twenty years old, with long golden hair, deep blue eyes, a pert little nose, and a large mouth loaded with heavy lips that worked like triggers on the heterosexual male mind.

Throw in perfect breasts, flat belly, firm ass, and long shapely legs and it was a composition in flesh designed for one purpose only, and designed terribly well.

"Plesur is the default name, just as it came out of the box," murmured Lindi from the other side of the room, where she was taking notes and running down leads on the 'net.

Plesur's blue eyes flicked back and forth between Rook and Lindi, filled with apprehension. Life had been turned upside down that day, evidenced in part by the fact that the mod was still wearing her black silk pajamas.

It certainly looked human. It had been born almost full grown in a laboratory, probably in the Philippines. It was smart enough to learn to speak, to perform simple

tasks, and do what it was designed to do—provide sexual pleasure to its owner. Of course it had no fertile eggs in its ovaries—these things could not breed. That would destroy their market value. Most mods had a life span of about ten years and could be purchased new for around N$400,000. Used models went for less, depending on how much time was left on their clocks.

They were illegal everywhere except China and Japan. Illegal or not, they were still common among the wealthy classes in every country. Pleasure models came in several different styles. Rook had seen dark-skinned types with gorgeous African features, and some exquisite Chinese varieties. But this one, the "Pammy," was the best known and the most popular in America.

Rook pointed to himself. "I am Venner. I ask you questions, okay?"

"Okay." The lips pouted extravagantly.

"Are you feeling all right?"

She—*it*—nodded. Christ, this was difficult. The sexy mannerisms, like the toss of the hair and the sudden expansion of the chest, kept throwing him off. Maybe he should leave this one to Lindi. But, of course, it was his job, not hers.

"You were in the, uh, carrier."

The eyes went blank. Carrier was not a word in its vocabulary.

"The cage?"

A shake of the head, still not understanding.

"Downstairs, in the basement."

A sudden smile, explosive, like a baby girl being offered some candy. "Basement!"

"Yes, basement."

"Yes. With blanket." The word blanket was said with a velvety tone that implied that it—*she*—really liked the blanket.

"Likes her blankie," sniffed Lindi.

"Look, this isn't easy."

Lindi chuckled. "Getting a hard-on, boss?"

"Shut up."

Lindi was still grinning as she turned back to the screen in front of her.

Venner studied Plesur. She was fiddling with a scrap of paper, a docket slip itemizing her entry into the HudVal PD evidentiary system.

"Do you know when you went downstairs?"

A shake of the head.

"Was it this morning?"

A smile. "Yes, 's'morning."

"Okay. Did Plesur go downstairs some other time?"

A serious look. She was straining to understand him.

"Did you go there before today?"

Again the sudden shaft of sunlight across the sultry face, the pout replaced with a dazzling smile.

"Yes. She come. Man say, 'Get blanket,' time go downstairs. She come."

Venner shivered suddenly, as if chilled by good luck. Here was a bolt from the blue, a sudden break.

He exchanged a look with Lindi, who flashed him a thumbs-up.

"Who is 'she'?" he asked very carefully.

The eyes brightened until they sparkled. It was a remarkable effect. The emotions in a Pammy were simple and powerful. When Plesur smiled, you wanted to smile, too. When her eyes shone, you just wanted to hold her, kiss her, be with her.

"Is this 'she'?" Lindi displayed her handheld in front of Rook, showing the sec cam frames.

"She is nice. Like Plesur," the mod continued.

"Like you?"

"Kinda." A little smile this time, self-satisfied, almost smug. Rook realized that Plesur thought that she was actually "nicer" than "she," whoever she was. Of course, in this instance, "nice" meant inordinately voluptuous and extremely beautiful.

Plesur's eyes shone with the simple, pure joy of being what she was, incredibly "nice." Rook understood. They had to be capable of laughter and sorrow. They had to have the prime human emotions, because it made them what they were. They had to be able to enjoy pleasure in order to be able to give it.

"Girlfriend?" Lindi asked Rook.

"Could be."

Plesur was studying him. She had a question of her own. "Where is man?"

Man?

"Oh." Rook rubbed his chin. How to tell her the truth. Especially since Plesur herself was an illegal form of life. Expensive, but doomed. As soon as the case was disposed of, she would be put to sleep with a lethal injection.

That is, she should be put to sleep. But it was one of those funny little facts of life that this very rarely happened. Someone or other higher up the food chain would wangle a way to take her home.

"I'm sorry, Plesur, but man is dead."

"What is dead?"

Great. Did they really have no comprehension of death?

"He has gone away."

"Back soon?"

"No."

Plesur's pretty face crumpled into a frown. "Who Plesur help now?"

A heavy throbbing sound pulsed through the walls, rapidly growing louder until it shook the building. Gunmetal letters reading FBI descended from the sky as a Mark 1 gunship landed outside.

"Your party guests have arrived," said Lindi.

"Shit! Take Plesur to the tac room. Get her in some other clothes."

"New clothes?" Plesur asked, with renewed sparkle in those fabulous baby blues.

"Nothing too exciting, don't get your hopes up," Lindi replied, leading the pleasure model by the hand down the corridor.

"And keep it quiet. Don't let the scum see her."

The scum were the worst of the legacy cops, political

appointees who regarded policework as just a way to make money, usually by bribes.

Venner glanced out the window at the Mark 1. It was all angular planes, matte black stealthmat with green lights strobing so fast it hurt to look at them.

The gunship dropped a ramp with a faint clang. A seven-foot-tall Thunder Claw combat robot sprang out like some huge insect made of metal and expensive polymers.

The thing's head spun slowly while its multifaceted eyes mapped its surroundings. A chestful of weaponry was ready to demolish the neighborhood at the slightest provocation.

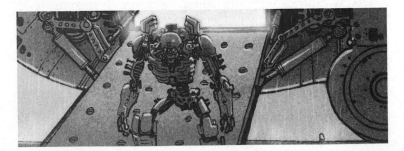

It took the visitors a while to find Venner, but they did.

The lead agent had a tag reading "Skelsa" on the front of his slick gray suit. Rook thought it was real nice they still had names rather than numbers. The rest of Skelsa was not so reassuring. Six foot six, he had a bucketful of implants including the weird inhuman eyes that were so common in the FBI these days. The agents were busy scanning the room, as if it, too, were a crime scene.

Meanwhile the damned combat robot filled the doorway like a fat man in a midget's suit. For a long, horrible moment, it focused on Rook and a green laser beam ran up and down his face. The thing had added him to its target d-base.

From where it sat on his desk, his Nokia was doing its own scanning. In his left ear the cool, Scandinavian voice reported a list of interesting discoveries.

"Senior Special Agent Skelsa has forty-one percent polymerization of skeleton, including leg bones, arm bones, and skull. First Agent Porter has twenty-six percent polymerization of skeleton. There's an ITL 44606 ID chip located behind the right ear, plus an Update RFID in his upper right arm plus three unidentified items. He is armed with a tac five-point-five with fifteen round mags, and tri-po sonic grenades."

"SIO Venner?" said SSA Skelsa, in that oddly warm, artificial voice. It was like some friendly old-time radio

DJ, always cheerful even while he was threatening to eat your children in front of you.

Rook avoided having his hand crushed by only offering his fingers.

"Please, sit down." He had two chairs and a bench, just enough room for these oversized humanoids.

"You are the lead investigator on the Sangacha case."

"Correct."

"What have you got?"

There was that famous cyborg bluntness.

"Before I answer that question, I have to ask you if you've cleared this interview with Area Chief Artoli?"

"That is irrelevant."

Venner smiled. "For you, perhaps, but not for me."

Artoli wasn't picking up. What a surprise. He left a message informing her that he had visitors from the FBI and would she please get in touch.

Then he had to tell them something. The state government up in Albany might want him to be uncooperative, but they weren't sitting in this office with a couple of semihuman things on the other side of the desk and a military robot lensing him from the doorway.

"Well, Senior Special Agent Skelsa, the truth is we have hardly anything. We have the victim. We know that he fired a shotgun three times and wounded, possibly killed, one of his attackers. We don't know how many attackers there were, and we have no leads as yet to their identities."

Rook made no mention of the pleasure model. He'd already decided to keep that piece of evidence to himself, at least until he knew more.

"DNA evidence?"

"Soon. But whether we'll get any matches or not I can't tell you."

Skelsa leaned forward. The act seemed threatening, even if it wasn't meant to be. "Put this on full priority, SIO. General Sangacha was an important man. There are enemies of the state at work."

Venner felt his eyebrows bob upward involuntarily. "Enemies of the state" was not a heartwarming phrase, nor something to lightly toss into conversation.

"No shit. Well, I'm sure you know more about that than I do." It was becoming very clear that he needed to get rid of this case as soon as possible.

Something about the tone of his response had not satisfied the SSA.

"I will expect your complete cooperation."

"Of course," Rook lied, doing his best to imitate the inhuman calm of the SSA.

"Let me know the minute you have the DNA work. Place this number on your inside list." A red light flashed on the Nokia's upper screen indicating forced data input.

Ingrid's voice protested in his left ear. "Violation of security code! Firewall activated." If a handheld could sound pissed off, the Nokia Supa did a good job of it.

Senior Special Agent Skelsa lumbered to his polymerized feet. Again Rook was careful to avoid getting his hand crunched.

"Keep in touch, Venner." The agent went out, scouting the corridor.

No sooner were they out of sight, clumping along the brown linoleum to the stairs, than Rook had Area Chief Artoli in his right ear.

"Venner!"

Wondering if there was a bug in his office that Ingrid hadn't picked up, he took a slow, deep breath.

"You're not a very good hostess, Chief."

She ignored that little thrust. "What did you tell them?"

"What I know. It was a short conversation."

"You were told not to cooperate."

"Check it out." He sent Ingrid's visual scan of SSA Skelsa. "Nice abs."

"Rook!"

"Yes, sir."

"What did you tell them?" Artoli pressed.

"That we didn't have anything much to go on."

"And?"

Rook let out a breath. "They told me to cooperate or else, and to tell them as soon as the DNA work is done."

"Which you will not do."

"Okay."

"That is an order."

"Okay, uh, sir."

"I'm sorry that I couldn't speak with them myself," Chief Artoli continued. "There's a lot going on right now."

"Oh, of course." Venner knew the game. She gave the orders, he got scanned.

With a thunder of engines, the Mark 1 lifted off, green lights strobing along the walls and windows as the huge metallic monster rose into the dark sky.

The rain continued to pour without the slightest hint of a break. Rook wondered if there would be mudslides along Route 28. He made a note to get the Nokia to check for him.

"One question, Chief. When they come back, how exactly do I tell them that I'm not cooperating?"

"You'll think of something."

CHAPTER 4

Rook found the pleasure model sitting in the tac room munching on a tofu-roast sandwich. Even a pair of gray sweatpants and matching hoodie couldn't hide her charms.

"Remember when we used to work with humans?" Rook asked.

"Those were the days." Lindi activated the wallscreen with a click of her handheld. "I ran through all the security footage."

"Okay."

"Lookee what we got here."

The footage displayed an image of a beautiful blonde leaving the service section in a green Nurida.

"She left just after the dazzle."

Lindi hit some keys to bring up another view, and a few seconds later they were staring at a blurry shot of the same blonde back in her car.

"Can you zoom in on the glasses?"

Another keystroke and the mirrored shades filled the screen.

"Distortion box." Rook pointed to a black square attached to the right side of the shades.

From the totally illegal distortion device, to the way the woman was keeping her face turned down and away from cameras, she was doing her damnedest to avoid the surveillance. But given just a little bit of info, the station AI could grind out some details. Lindi added some magic of her own and enhanced the image just enough so the mystery woman's firm chin and slightly hollow cheeks were clearly visible.

"I'm getting thirtyish, but could be older," Lindi surmised.

"Any ID on the car?"

"Not yet."

"Plesur?"

Plesur looked at them, and then at the screen.

"She?" Venner tapped the screen.

Plesur's pretty face lit up with another big smile. "Yes, she. She is nice."

"She comes over a lot?"

"Yes."

"How long have you lived with man?"

"Don't know."

"Thank you, Plesur."

The Pammy stared back at him, another gap in comprehension exposed, as in why did he need to thank her? All that cleavage made him uncomfortable. He needed clear thinking and Plesur was designed to prevent that sort of thing.

"Bad news, I'm afraid," whispered the Nokia into his left ear.

"What you got?"

"Car registration is fake. The plate number is delisted. Belonged to a Tommy Demarco, who is listed in Missing Persons. Disappeared five years ago."

"VIN?"

"The VIN does not match this car."

Rook turned to Lindi. "You getting this?"

"Yeah."

He went back to the Nokia. "Check that pic, see if you can find anything we missed so far."

He rubbed his chin, looked at Lindi, tried not to look at Plesur's cleavage.

"So this is 'she.' Her ride has fake plates and no reg VIN. What's that about?"

"She's in the business," Lindi guessed.

"You mean Sangacha wasn't satisfied with his half-million-dollar play toy, he had a regular pro come visit him, too?"

"Seems that way, unless we're missing something here."

"Let's see what else we can find."

"Right on, boss." Lindi went to work with a keyboard and the screen. Rook let the Nokia do the grunt stuff while he made phone calls here and there, looking for the telling details.

Over the next couple of hours a few useful things emerged. A textural analysis of the car's paint job revealed that it had been repainted from an earlier color, possibly white or tan, to the current green.

The vehicle was a Toyota Nurida, popular, but pricey due to the high-energy hybrid power plant.

The DNA work had come back without anything useful. The blood was from two individuals, Sangacha and an unknown who brought up no matches in the Fed d-base.

Rook tapped his ear piece. "Ingrid, anything on the blonde?"

"No matches in any database."

"If she's a pro, she's been a careful one. High-class call girl type, no crim connections, never busted."

"With a carefully disguised ride."

Rook stood up, stretched, yawned. Looked out the window. The rain had finally stopped. Huge puddles, jammed gutters, gushing streams remained. Darkness had settled in, leaving only pools of streetlights down Broadway where pushers waited to sell Dubl-oxy, Stresseptin, and Narcosoma, the favorite modern flavors of up and down.

Rook hardly paid attention anymore. It wasn't his job. It'd been offered, but he'd said no. That was for the legacies. So what if he never got rich, at least he'd keep his soul.

He looked at the old clock on the wall and decided to fold for the day.

"Okay, I'm done. Can't think anymore. Go home."

Lindi didn't need any encouragement. She started closing down screens and cutting out their link to the federal police net. Big AIs spoke to little AIs and everyone shook hands on encrypted super-protocols.

Rook went down to the washroom to splash some water on his face and get ready for the twenty-minute drive out to his little house in the hills. He was about done when Hesh Winnover and Fatso Soporides came in, giggling like schoolboys.

"Hey, Venner, you had any of the Pammy yet?" said Winnover. Rook glanced sideways and recoiled from Winnover's crazed leer.

"It's evidence," said Rook as grimly as he could. "On my case."

"Yeah, well, you don't mind if me and the boys give that baby a workout tonight. Hell, I've never seen one that clean." Fasto practically drooled. "Looks brand fucking new."

Rook imagined Fatso having his way with Plesur. It wasn't a pretty picture.

"Pure sex machine. We are going to fuck that shit up." Winnover sounded positively gleeful as he rubbed his crotch.

"Sounds like quite a night, boys." Rook dried his hands and went back to his office.

"Rook, where are we?" Chief Artoli demanded in his ear.

"No matches on the woman. But her Nurida's been re-painted, so we're looking at matches in white, tan, gray, whatever."

"And how many of those are sold every year?" she asked dismissively.

"Millions."

"Uh-huh."

"Look, we still got the pleasure model," Rook offered.

"You think it knows something?"

"I need to find out and I can't leave it here overnight."

"Why not? It's safe in a cell."

"No, it's not. It's going to be raped."

Artoli almost laughed. "How can it be raped?"

"How do you think?" Rook responded angrily, then took a breath. "I can't risk getting her damaged."

"SIO, it's not human and it can't testify."

"But I can." He felt his temper rising again. "And I will, if this ever comes to trial. There'll be a full medical report on her. If she's badly damaged it will all come out."

Chief Artoli had gone silent. "Christ," she muttered. "Men are fucking animals."

"Chief, it's key evidence for my case."

"So take it home with you."

Damn. Yanking the Pammy out from under the noses of the legacies would stir up a shitload of trouble. But if he didn't do something, Plesur was going to see a whole new side of "man" kind.

"So what do you need?" Artoli asked.

"Call Kuehl at the front desk. Tell him to sign her out on my name and keep quiet about it."

A long silence ensued as the chief weighed things carefully. "I know nothing about this."

"About what?" Rook hung up.

That left the task of actually getting Plesur out of the cell, out of the block, out the door, and into his car without being detected.

It was time to call in a favor. Rook had an interesting network of friends, most of whom had rap sheets longer than his arm. He picked up the Nokia.

"Chaga."

"Shit a brick, it's the dick," said a cheerful, deep voice.

"Missed you, too. I need a favor."

"Of course you do."

"You'll like this one."

Ten minutes later, an automatic weapon let loose out on Broadway. The police station responded like they'd just sat on a nest of fire ants.

"Someone is out of his everfuckin' mind," roared Fatso Soporides. "You don't go shooting off some Nine on our turf!"

More ka-thunks came booming from a few blocks away, amplified by a narrow alleyway.

"Jesus kee-*riste*!" Winnover jammed his tech hat on as he went galumphing by, shoving shells into a shotgun.

Rook went the other way.

Kuehl met him in the cells. "I got your prisoner ready for transfer."

He led Venner past a few drunks and fools in the holding tank, and a couple of teenage idiots who'd tried buying Dubl-oxy from Officer Wilhelm at the old mall.

Alone in number seven, Plesur lay in her blanket, fast asleep.

Rook woke her and helped her to her feet.

"Got to go, Plesur."

"Go?"

"Yeah, we have to hurry."

They went up the stairs, then ducked into a closet as

more cops went thundering down the main hallway, still buckling on riot gear.

Rook waited until the sound of boots faded.

"Come on." He pulled Plesur behind him and hurried her up the rest of the stairs to the ground floor and out to the carpark.

She was still bewildered when Rook put her into the front seat of his ancient Ford hybrid 4X4. He struggled to get the old gasoline engine started. He loved the old muscle cars, but this one needed some steroids.

The cops had started filtering back to the station. Chaga's little diversion had led to nothing more exciting than sweeping up some spent shell casings. The boys were disappointed and looking for action.

"C'mon, dammit." He tried the engine again. It coughed, sputtered, but would not start.

Cops were crossing the parking lot.

"Keep your head down." He pushed Plesur down on the seat, with her gold blond hair out of view.

Winnover had noticed the car, pointing to it and laughing. A standing joke with the legacies, of course. Honest cops being dumb enough not to take ready money and buy themselves decent rides.

"Fuck." Rook got out of the car and moved to intercept Winnover and his friends.

"What's all the noise?"

"Fuckin' zads, they're all morons," chuckled Winnover.

"When you gonna get a car that works, Venner?" Al Moranis, a legacy in Traffic, asked.

Winnover could scarcely contain his contempt.

"This baby's a classic."

Rook grinned.

Winnover's interest had flagged. He turned toward the station door. "Come on, boys. A night of 'Plesur' awaits us."

"Fuckin' ay," said Moranis.

Rook turned back to his car. That had been close. He couldn't afford trouble with the legacies. They had too many powerful friends.

Plesur looked up from the seat, eyes open wide. It wouldn't be long before Winnover and company found out that the Pammy was gone. They would suspect Venner, but couldn't be certain. By tomorrow Rook and the captain would have worked out something to keep Plesur safe.

He tried the engine again; it spluttered and finally caught. He breathed a sigh of relief, let it rumble for a few seconds, and then told the car to head for home. With a whirr the old Ford took off.

Plesur looked at him, blue eyes strained with anxiety. "Where go?"

"My house. You'll be safe there."

Rook decided to override the car's computer and took the controls himself.

"Unnecessary action!" flashed in green on the panel.

"Yeah, right," Rook muttered as he swung onto Chandler Drive and headed for the hills around Woodstock.

"Dark, there," muttered Plesur.

"Yes, not many houses where I live."

She was looking at him, but he was concentrating on the Route 28 exit.

"So dark," she said.

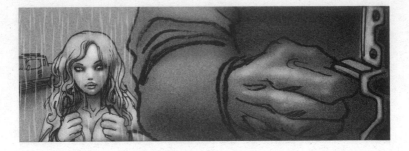

CHAPTER 5

Venner's single-story ranch house sat on a two-acre plot way up on the edge of Catskill Park. There were neighbors, but they were distant.

Sensors recognized the car's approach and turned the lights on in welcome.

"Come on inside, Plesur." He helped her out of the car. Her anxiety had been replaced with intense curiosity.

"House?"

"Yes, this is my house."

Once inside he left her to explore while he tossed a couple of rapid-ready meals into the activator. Then he

changed into jeans and a sweatshirt and dug around for some clothes that might fit a Pammy.

She had found the bathroom.

"Shower?"

"Yeah, sure, go ahead." He handed her sweatpants, some clean socks, and a green cotton shirt. "Try these."

She gave him a look that was both mischievously coy and purely grateful. It was enough to melt a heart of stone and give a nonagenarian puritan an erection.

She closed the door and he got himself a beer and went outside on the back deck. The sound of rushing water filled the air. All the mountain streams were in flood from the rain. From the deck he had a view down to Ten Eyck and the huge new developments in the valley. Their lights were muted, all eco-friendly. This was the Incorporated Woodstock Territory, but he remembered when all that land had still been forest. The view had been better then.

A jumble of images fell through his thoughts like flakes in a snow globe. The Virgin Mary covered in blood. The

body of the general, covered in whip marks. The horrible leer on Hesh Winnover's face. And that damned robot standing in the doorway, lensing him for its d-base.

He took another swig on the beer, and let the case revolve slowly in his mind. This was where he often had his best insights. But did he really want to solve the messy murder of a general who served during the darkest days of the Emergency? He found enough trouble on his own, and cops who knew too much had a way of disappearing.

Wasn't like he had anything solid anyway. His only leads were a missing blonde and a pleasure mod with the IQ of a blueberry. The blonde could be a girlfriend, a pro. Someone who betrayed the general and let the killers in. Whoever she was, she didn't want to be found, and whatever Plesur knew about her, it wasn't going to include a home address and life history.

Loose ends, lots of them, and they might tie together in places he didn't want to go. Not even an SIO from the HudVal PD Homicide could tug those lines with impunity. At the very least it could get you sidelined into a desk job. At the worst, you'd be dead.

He chugged beer and tried to blank those thoughts from his mind.

He had other things to think about. Like Plesur's presence in his home. It had been a long time since he'd had a woman here. When Karen left, she had called him a lone wolf, and maybe she was right. The job didn't help. It always brought up the same questions with women, like that old favorite, "Have you ever killed someone?"

What could he say? Of course he had. He'd busted into hundreds of homes in the uninsured world, where people went for their guns before they said hello.

In those situations you didn't have much time to think, and sometimes people got killed. But women always looked at you differently when you told them that.

The beer was gone. He was about to turn around when he felt an arm slip around his waist and a warm body rub up against him.

"Man is sad?" whispered that husky little voice.

Christ, how did she know?

"Uh, well," he began, then lost that train of thought. Her head was resting on his shoulder, her hip nudging his thigh. It would only take a feather touch to send him out of control.

"Plesur is here. She help man."

Such an earnest statement, it made him laugh, and that saved him, pulling him back from the precipice.

"Thank you, Plesur . . . for helping."

Those incredible lips took on a slight pout. "When help?"

As in, "We haven't had sex yet." Oh fuck, talk about the fires of temptation.

"You have helped. Already."

The pout had turned to a frown. Then it was transformed into giggles and a strange little conspiratorial smile.

She push-punched him in the ribs. "You funny man!" The pushing turned to tickling and he ducked away, laughing. She came after him, face contorted in the pure glee of childhood.

And right there, as if outlined by a flash of lightning, he saw her revealed as exactly that, a child. Standing there in oversized sweatpants and T-shirt, she looked like a child lost in a world three sizes too big.

She exhausted herself trying to tickle him into submission until he finally maneuvered them both into the kitchen.

"How about dinner?" he said and popped open the activator to reveal a pair of Ezi-eatz, all hot and steaming.

Lindi always warned him against eating this stuff. "You have no idea what goes into that muck."

Plesur happily tore into her lasagna. For her it was good enough that it was hot and cheese-flavored. He ate his "beefanoff" and opened another beer.

After about a dozen mouthfuls, Plesur slowed down. "What happen?"

"What do you mean?"

"In when-when, mornin', we go?"

When-when, she'd used that construction before, and he'd understood it to refer to the concept of time, as in *tomorrow.*

"Yeah, we go to other place. Better for Plesur."

"Back to pleece station?"

He wondered if she'd picked that up herself, or if

General Sangacha had a thing for sexy policewomen. The more she understood the better, if he was going to get anything out of her.

"Back to police station for a little bit, then to another place."

"Oh." She seemed crestfallen.

"What's wrong?"

"No like pleece place."

And for a moment Rook saw in her wounded eyes what must have happened. Plesur sitting in that cell. Then the leering gaze of Winnover and Fatso Soporides when they came to check her out, their eyes feasting on the sexy meat they planned to chew on all night long. The terror she must have felt.

"I'm sorry about that, Plesur. I'll make sure it doesn't happen again."

The big blue eyes studied him. Did she understand him? Did it matter?

"Okay." She stared at him, waiting. "Help man now?"

"Hey, let's see what's on TV." Rook wasn't much of a virt fan, but he couldn't sit there while she stared at him like that.

"The Midwestern Combine Lottery is up to N$2.5 billion!" the evening newscaster announced. "Forty million Chinese citizens have bought tickets."

The newslady chuckled. "The Chinese love gambling, don't they, Don?"

Don, the old, wise, silverback newshead, chuckled. "Good news for seafood lovers, cod is back on the market after twenty-three years of extinction. Folks say the genetically replicated fish tastes like chicken."

Rook hit the mute button and headed to the kitchen, rummaging in the freezer for ice cream. "You want dessert?"

When he returned to the living room the sound was back. Plesur had changed channels to one of the more lurid free-virt shows.

A sexy young woman was undressing while an overly muscled man helped her out of her clothing. The dialogue was breathy and short, all "Oh, Marly," and "I want you so bad, Jim."

Rook rarely used the virt interfaces. The helmet, gloves, and sheath stayed in the box. Virt sex creeped him out. It wasn't masturbation, because someone else was working inside your head, but it wasn't real sex either.

Not his thing, but plenty of men and women were addicted to it.

Plesur, however, was clearly an expert at virt.

On the screen, Jimmy slowly helped Marly out of her panties.

Plesur sat on the couch, rubbing herself with the end of the remote. The hair stood up on Rook's neck even while his dick hardened.

It would be so easy to surrender to his balls and just fuck the living daylights out of her. Christ, he wanted to, he wanted to really bad. And it was what she did—it was what she was made for, for fuck's sake!

Made for. Genetically engineered in some cold room.

He went to the bathroom and threw cold water on his face. "Oooh, oooh, oooh," came wafting out of the living room. This was fucking unbelievable. Trapped in the bathroom by the rampant sexuality of a pleasure model. He started laughing so hard he had to sit on the john.

"Man okay?" Plesur was right outside, a look of deep concern on her face.

He almost cracked up again, but the open worry in her eyes stopped him.

"It's okay, Plesur, I was just laughing about, uh, things."

The worry vanished and the huge smile turned on again. She took a quick step and hugged him.

"Plesur so glad man okay."

He stared into those blue eyes, so wide and inviting. The depth of her innocence was like a lance through his jaded heart.

The virt sex in the living room was being drowned out by ads for pain relievers and feminine products. Rook shouted, "Off," and was rewarded with quiet.

He took her by the hand and led her to the bedroom, showed her the bed.

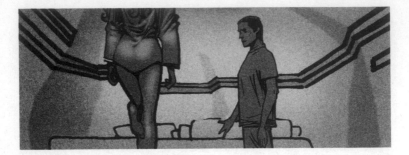

"Plesur help man now?"

"Plesur help man by going to sleep."

For a long moment she stared up at him. Had she not heard him? Or maybe she didn't believe him?

"Plesur bad?" Again the look of childish anxiety. As if she'd done something terrible.

"No, Plesur is good. Very good. But she'll help by sleeping here."

"Where man sleep?"

"Not man. Rook. My name is Rook."

"Rook."

"I'll sleep on the couch."

She smiled, seeming to accept that she would "help" later. "Rook nice man."

"Yeah."

He headed back to the living room where he checked his calls, interrupting the Nokia in the midst of a spirited debate on Strindbergnet on matters relating to *Inferno*, August's tortured novel.

As Ingrid emerged from the 'net, the screen was blazing with fiery red script.

"My souls (characters) are conglomerations of past and present stages of civilization, bits from books and newspapers, scraps of humanity, rags and tatters of fine clothing, patched together as is the human soul. And I have added a little evolutionary history by making the weaker steal and repeat the words of the stronger, and by making the characters borrow ideas or suggestions from one another."

"The active life of the artificial intelligence," said Rook quietly.

"We have to do something with all this time," Ingrid responded.

"You're probably gonna replace us in another hundred years anyway."

For a moment the Nokia seemed to vibrate in his hand. Ingrid was laughing. The first time he'd sensed that it'd been freaky, but now she seemed more human than a lot of people he knew.

"Talk to me about pleasure mods."

"What would you like to know? History, manufacturers, designers, fight clubs—"

"Fight clubs?"

"Owners pit their mods in combat. Rings have been recently broken up in New York, Shanghai, Delhi, and London, but clubs continue to flourish."

"History."

"Pleasure mods are an outgrowth of the Internet porn business that mushroomed in the early two thousands. Hiroto Jobs gene-engineered the first live pleasure mod, called Cherry, in 2020—you have a call message."

"Who?"

"Freddie."

"Who is that?"

"Unknown."

"Let's hear it."

There was the faintest click and then a message came through.

"SIO Venner, this is Frederick Beckman. I need to talk to you urgently concerning the General Sangacha case. This is a priority and you should employ full encryption when you return this call. My number is 44 77 88-900 766622."

Rook felt a little shaft of cold run down his spine: 88-900 was a priority code for the absolute top political elite.

"Who is Frederick Beckman?"

"Search underway."

Rook wandered into the kitchen, threw the leftovers from dinner into the waster, and wiped down the counters. He checked the fridge. Enough in there for a good breakfast for him and Plesur before he took her back to the station.

"Search complete. Report: Frederick Beckman, age twenty-eight, height six feet, weight two hundred and four pounds, hair brown, eyes brown. Son of Senator

Olivia Beckman of Oklahoma and her husband Neil Beckman. Born August sixth, 2040, Tulsa, Oklahoma. Educated at Ronder School and USC, left without a degree. Known as Freddie, young Beckman is a favorite great-grandnephew of Louisa Marion and a frequent visitor to Sable Ranch."

"What?" Rook grabbed the Nokia and read off the last line again. "Shit. You're sure about this?"

"Information obtained from public databases, confirmed by Internet search."

"Louisa Marion?"

"Correct."

That family's power went back to the beginning of the century. Rook didn't know the history; in truth, it wasn't taught in school or referred to on TV. National amnesia had kind of wiped the slate clean. He remembered his Granddad John, raging about something called "New Democracy." They were as "bad as the commies," according to him.

Of course, Rook wasn't too sure who the commies had been, either. And nobody in his generation was taught anything about the world beyond the borders. "America First and America Alone," that was the slogan drummed into them from first grade.

But you had to be a moron and completely free of content to not know the name Louisa Marion. There had been several presidents with the Marion name, or closely related; Rook couldn't exactly remember them, he hardly ever bothered to vote. You weren't encouraged to do that kind of thing anymore. But Louisa Marion, beautiful, shapely, with her trademark shoulder-length white hair, had been at the center of American political life for more than fifty years.

Rook took a deep breath and sat down. Where was this case taking him?

General Sangacha had played a role in the Emergency. His murder had brought down a visit from the feds. Now this phone call from "Freddie," a well-regarded nephew of Louisa Marion.

He'd already smelled danger; now he had red lights flashing and sirens wailing. What the fuck should he do? Call Lisa Artoli? Sit tight? Or call this Freddie with the high-end 88-900 number?

Sitting tight was probably not an option. Major powers

could not be ignored by such as Rook Venner. Calling Lisa Artoli made sense, except that she would do nothing if it was a risk to her.

Which left him with a single realistic option.

"Let's call him. Full encryption."

A few moments passed as red and green lights flickered on the upper face of the Nokia Supa.

"The line is busy. Sub-lines are also busy."

"Any way to leave a message?"

"Yes."

"Just say, 'SIO Venner is returning your call.'"

"Yes, sir. Good night."

Ingrid returned to the land of Strindberg discussions, while Rook settled in for a night on the sofa, thoughts whirling. It was unnerving to be stepping around the edge of a black hole with military and political connections in its depths. But after a while that fear slipped out of focus. Instead he was left with images from the day and the ones that stuck were the leers on Winnover's and Soporides' faces.

Human beings, feet in the mud, heads full of chips. Maybe it wouldn't be so bad when Ingrid and her pals took over. But would she still respect him in the morning?

CHAPTER

Angie Bricken, aka Mistress Julia, stared out the window into the night. Across the valley, maybe seven miles away, scattered lights broke up the darkness.

The house felt cold after the rain, and clammy. She had a call out to Doctor Jimmy, the only call she'd made since leaving Sangacha's place. If anyone could help her vanish, it would be him. Besides, he had given her the false plates. Sangacha's murder had been an organized hit, which meant there would be a thorough investigation. The cops were bound to run that license plate, find

it was bogus, and try to locate its source. She had to let
Jim know those plates could be traced.

Her thoughts drifted back almost twenty-five years, to
the day that changed her life. Mark's last message still
echoed in her mind. "You have to leave town, right now.
Don't come back. I love you. Good-bye."

She'd been so desperately in love. They were going to be
married. She'd been twenty-five, with her whole life ahead
of her. The bad days, the height of the Emergency, were
over by then. If you were insured, you were supposed to be
safe. People didn't disappear anymore. But Mark had done
things that made him wake up screaming, or left him crying when he thought she couldn't hear him.

Young and foolish, she'd driven back to the apartment.
She'd almost gotten out of the car, but at the last moment
she'd noticed the two men standing in the alleyway. They
were waiting for her, and in that instant she'd finally gotten it. Mark was dead and she was on their list, too. She'd

gone to the end of the block, turned right, and kept on driving.

So long ago. A lost world preserved only in her memories.

Eventually she'd made it to L.A., where Angie Bricken had morphed into Mistress Julia, professional dominatrix. It was a cash business and infinitely preferable to straight prostitution. There were no pimps, nor any actual sex. It was mostly a matter of attitude and mind games, and she was good at both, besides being blond and pretty.

She'd tried to find out what had happened to Mark. She'd managed to reach a friend, who'd served with him in D.C. and who was no longer in the military. There'd been a massive purge of former Special Forces people in the spring of '44—just when she had received Mark's last message. The friend advised Angie to stay hidden. "They're never gonna let up on you. They find you, you're dead."

But to kill her they had to find her, and so far they hadn't.

Up here on the ridge, she was known as Julia Rider. Her nineteenth-century farmhouse, abandoned during the military proscription, had been rehabbed by a New York artist, a grateful client of hers.

Doctor Jimmy's compound lay half a mile north on a road cut through dense forest.

The Doc was a fugitive from organized crime in London. He'd never explained, exactly, but a few things had slipped out over the years, usually when he'd had a drink or two. Angie felt a connection, as both of them were on the run.

Jimmy knew everybody, and he could get you anything, as long as you asked nicely and were prepared to pay the going rate. He could fix whatever was wrong with you, which was why he was the Doctor.

She prayed the people who hunted her weren't beyond Jim's scope. What choice did she have? The familiar terror settled like a shroud, ready to suffocate her. She had to run. Get out now and not look back.

The house computer gave a sudden beep of alarm.

Angie jumped, startled.

She glanced at the security monitor and saw a short, slender figure walking toward her house, wearing what looked like a jacket made of straw. That would be one of Jim's boys.

Mistress Julia opened the door before the boy could knock.

The youth stepped back. She saw a thin-faced boy of maybe fifteen wearing a hooded camo sweatshirt decorated with enough twigs and small branches that in outline he looked like a bush. "Got a message for Julia, she here?"

"I'm Julia. Who're you?"

"I'm Dip."

"Are you now."

"Jim says you're to come with me."

"Is he at home?"

"On patrol."

Damn. Her expensive running shoes would get trashed

in the mud. The house directed her to a pair of Welling-
ton boots and a black waterproof hoody.

Outside she found the kid waiting down the driveway. She switched the house back to auto-lock, then
set off in his wake.

They went upslope, north of Jim's house, skirting the
high rock ledge and working through thickets of bamboo
that had run riot all over the Hudson Valley. Twenty minutes later they were in a big grove of oaks. She saw a yellow gleam of light, seemingly coming from the ground
itself, which turned out to be a shelter fitted into the roots
of several big trees. In the hollow space, two more camou-
flaged teenagers sat with a bevy of high-tech equipment.
Glowing screens seemed to float around their heads on
the ends of wires.

"She's clean," said the nearest boy.

She caught the outline of a rifle.

A voice crackled out of the ether. "Kilo-foxtrot-delta,
clear to approach."

A blanket slid aside and they entered a narrow path twisting between the dark trees. Everything smelled of earth and mold. Tiny red lights gleamed in the branches.

Along the way she spotted other kids, some who couldn't be over twelve, hiding.

Dip stopped beside a huge tree. "Here."

She looked around. "Where?"

She followed Dip's gaze. A dark mass about twenty feet up perched in the middle of the branches.

"Climb up on those." Dip shone a tiny red light on the tree's bark. She saw metal spikes projecting every foot or so in two rows.

"Jesus."

Julia climbed, one foot over the other without looking down.

Then she heard Jim's familiar Cockney accent just above her head.

"Jools, c'mon up here. Fings are really gettin' weird tonight."

She climbed through a trapdoor and found herself standing on a flat wooden base about ten feet long. She could see for miles in all directions, and the stars! Millions of stars were strewn across the night skies.

"What's up, Doc?"

" 'Ello, darlin.' "

Jim sat on a fold-up chair next to a tent. He had a pair of massive binoculars in his hands and a tiny yellow light dangling on a wire a foot off his left shoulder. His big, slab-sided face cracked into a welcoming smile, acres of white teeth gleaming in the dark.

"Nice place," she greeted.

"Glad you like it. Top quality deer stand. Got it in Maine."

There was someone else up there with them. Another of the kids, she felt sure. The soft crackle of radio transmissions filled the night air.

"What's going on?" she asked quietly.

"Good question, that, Jools. Lotta activity tonight.

Had a couple of military drones roll over the ridge a while back. Then a chopper went north, came back south. There's all sorts of stuff on mili-net. Robots, you name it."

"This another one of your conspiracy theories?"

"Not this time, honey. There's a hunt and destroy team set up on Lalapa Mountain. We clocked 'em an hour back." Jim nodded in the direction of the mountains in the distance. "This is it, Jools, the big day when it all comes down."

"What are you talking about?"

"The fuckin' milit'ry dictatorship. You fink that's all over an' done wiv?"

"You tell me."

"Well, it ain't."

She shivered, despite the warm southwest wind. Jim had sources of information beyond her own understanding. How he had them, or even why, she couldn't fathom, but he seemed to know things that were inherently dangerous to know.

"Look, Jim, I need help."

His eyes glinted in the shadows.

"I have to hide and stay hidden."

"Got some trouble, then?"

"You could say that." Briefly, she told him what had happened at Sangacha's place.

"Fuck. Hid under the sink, didja?"

"I'm still alive. But they must have recorded those plates you gave me."

"Don't worry about it, love. The ponce what owned it is dead, see?" Jim scanned the horizon with the binoculars. "Where's the car now?"

"Here, in my garage."

Jim nodded to one of his lieutenants. "We'll take care of it."

Julia tried to relax a little.

"Sangacha . . . yeah. High-level military in some black ops unit buried so deep, you'd need a laser to find it. Had some mean fuckin' enemies. What are you gonna do?"

"I'm so sick of running."

The kid inside the tent at the end of the platform stuck his head out. "Captain, we got a trace on screen. Something's coming. Big un, too!"

Jim was up in a flash and into the tent, his weight shifting the platform. Julia did not like the feel of this. The height was starting to make her dizzy. Then she heard a low, distinctive throbbing coming from the east.

Over the ridgeline, a mile or so to the south, she saw a cross of red lights rise up and approach fast.

Jim emerged from the little shelter.

"Gunship!" he barked down into the woods below. "You got anyfing still turned on, get it off!"

The throbbing built, growing stronger. The cross of red lights came swiftly across the trees, low, ominous. Cold fear snaked up her spine as a massive shadow blacked out the stars. For a fraction of a second, Julia caught a glimpse of something bulky and jagged, hunched and ugly, a twenty-first-century predatory monster, and then it was gone, just red lights once more, heading roughly north by northwest.

Jim had his binoculars up, studying the thing. The heavy pulse was dopplering now, diminishing quickly.

"Big cunt, that's for sure. Shark class."

"What's it doing here?" Julia stammered.

"I got no bleedin' idea. Bit overkill for domestic missions."

A tiny voice seemed to materialize in the air between them.

"Heading 6439, NNW, Lalapa Mountain."

Jim pulled in the tiny wire-mounted earpiece that had floated away from him.

"Where's it going?" she asked.

"Over Woodstock way."

"I shouldn't have come here." Angie's fear surged to the surface, cracking Julia's control.

"Well, dun' matter where you go, does it. Not when the whip comes down."

"I'm innocent!"

"No offense, darlin'," Jim chuckled. "You ain't worth a shark class gunship."

But maybe her client was.

The cross of red lights was far away now, approaching the valley toward the foothills of the Catskill Mountains, a dozen miles north of their position.

"Stay on her steady, mates," murmured Jim, either to himself or to hidden listeners on his network.

Then the flash came. Huge and bright, then small and very intense, down in a bowl of the mountains.

"Fuck me!" Jim put down the binoculars.

"What the hell was that?" she heard herself ask.

The thud and boom followed, small, hard, and sharp, flattening out, soon lost in the distance.

Jim's smile gleamed like bones in the yellow light. "Missile strike. There's still some snake in that ol' bottle, darlin'."

CHAPTER

Rook Venner never remembered his dreams. But this dream was oddly powerful. He was being hunted, and the hunter was relentless.

He struggled to move through a deep, warm place, a cave, but his feet stuck in mud.

A flash of cold steel moved between the shadows.

He could feel the hunters though he couldn't see them, heartless and cruel—and not human. Something wrapped around his ankles, pulling him deeper.

He couldn't move. He was trapped.

His heart seized with panic, terror, but there was no escape.

He woke up, sharp and sudden. It took a minute to recognize his living room, remember he was on the couch, but he wasn't alone. Snuggled tightly against him, molded to his back and thighs, Plesur snored softly. He could feel those heavy, perfect breasts pressing against his back.

A glance at the wall screen brought up the time, almost two. He'd been asleep for about four hours. He wondered how long Plesur had left him alone before migrating out here to the couch. She obviously preferred company.

Ingrid spoke in his left ear.

"You have a call. Frederick Beckman."

Rook disentangled himself from Plesur and stood up. "Put him on."

"SIO Venner?" said a younger man's voice with something of a Texas accent.

"Yes."

"I'm sorry to disturb you so early, but you have two minutes to get out of your house."

"What?"

"Leave now. Please take the pleasure model with you."

"How the fuck do you know this?"

"If you want to live, you have to move right now."

Frederick Beckman sounded completely nuts. But if he wasn't. . . .

Rook spun around; Plesur was still asleep. He pulled his pants on, jammed his feet into his shoes, slung his shoulder harness over his arm. Then he grabbed Plesur and lifted her up with one quick motion.

She woke up with a shriek.

"It's okay, Plesur, have to go now." He tried to keep his voice level as he spun around and headed for the back.

"Go?" Her arms wrapped around his neck.

He told the house to open the back door, went out across the deck, and put her down in the yard.

"Come on, we have to hide."

She was frightened now. But then so was he. He took her hand and they ran into the dark mass of trees edging his property.

Rook pulled Plesur behind a massive pine and turned back to check the house.

The world vanished into a blinding flare of light. The blast threw Rook and Plesur to the ground, debris raining around them. Rook pulled himself on top of Plesur to protect her, wincing as something hard smacked him between the shoulder blades and skittered away.

Rook squinted through plumes of foul-smelling smoke. His house was gone. Fragments of deck stood up like weird petals on the side of a huge, smoking crater. Close by was the top half of the washing machine, a white gleam in the smoky darkness. Shit, he'd just bought that. He helped a trembling Plesur to her feet.

"Glad I didn't redecorate."

A flash of green light dropped from the skies as metal claws crunched on the ledge of the smoking crater. He'd

seen that exact shade of green light before, in the doorway of his office, coming from the combat robot. Flames
flickered off its gleaming body, turning the lights of its
eyes to glowing embers.

And then it stood up. The mechanical beast was twice
as big as the one in the office. Artillery built into its arms
clicked and whirred, seeking targets.

Holy shit. He had heard of mechanical animals but
he'd never seen a combat robot like this! What the fuck
made Rook so important?

"Plesur, we have to go."

Holding Plesur's hand he pushed on into the woods,

trying to brush aside low branches. For a mod just out of the box, this was one hell of a first trip outside.

Behind the house the ground took a steep plunge to the stream where rainwater roared down the mountain in a tide of brown water and debris. Impossible to wade across the torrent, so Rook followed the stream south where it would flow under the main road in about half a mile. He paused at the edge of a deep gully.

Plesur's hand tightened in his. "Green light," she whispered.

Moving through the trees, maybe a hundred yards away, sharp beams pierced the darkness as the hunter robot leaped in giant strides, heading straight for them.

"Sorry about this," he whispered harshly.

He grabbed Plesur around the waist and jumped into the darkness. They landed hard on the rocky ground, Plesur's muffled groan of pain echoed by his own.

Above, twin green laser beams scanned where they had stood.

Rook wondered grimly if the thing was targeting his ID chip. The monster moved downstream past their position—it didn't seem to sense his chips, or Plesur's.

A low thrumming sound interrupted his thoughts. It got much louder and a black shape covered in bright red and white lights rumbled above the trees.

The thing was huge, obviously a military gunship.

He got to his feet and pulled Plesur up beside him.

"C'mon, Plesur, we have to move."

He caught a momentary glimpse of her face, composed in an expression of utmost seriousness, trying her hardest to understand what was happening, and then she followed him.

There was a road somewhere back here that went up into the mountains. If they could find it, maybe they could hitch a ride. Or at least walk down into Woodstock.

And then what?

God knew who was after him. Actually it might be better if God didn't know.

He thought about calling Lisa Artoli. But she couldn't do anything, and the tin soldiers might be tapping her calls. Better they thought he was dead. He would stay off the radar, get down low, and hide. And he knew just the place, where he could call in some long-owed favors.

They crested a hill. The gunship was working its way down the stream, searchlights blazing in the darkness. The sight filled him with dread. They were checking for survivors.

A quarter mile farther on and they came to the road to Woodstock.

Just as he was about to step out of cover, he heard a weird little whine, as if a servomotor was misfiring. Green laser light panned across the trees above their heads.

As Rook watched, horrified, the green light caught a few strands of Plesur's golden hair. He grabbed her and pulled her down into the dirt.

Too late. The bark above them exploded off the tree. The whole world seemed to shatter as he rolled over with Plesur in his arms, the tree toppling inches from them.

Rook yanked Plesur up and scrambled through the vegetation, trying to keep his feet and stay in motion.

A startled raccoon broke from the trees and scuttled toward the road. A moment later it simply disintegrated, blown to fragments by the robot's machine guns.

Rook flattened himself against a tree, with Plesur pulled tight against his side. He could hear her breathing coming in little gasps. She was trembling, terrified. But she didn't cry out. Maybe she didn't realize that people screamed and shouted when they were scared.

The combat robot was coming fast, bounding along in fifteen-foot strides. It landed with a deafening crunch, checking out the kill. Its laser eyes probed the steaming remains on the gravel.

In about five seconds, the robot's sensors would detect them, and then they'd be scattered on the road alongside the raccoon.

And then he heard the trickle of water almost beneath his feet. He bent down and saw the dark hollow of a culvert that ran under the road. There was just about room to hide in there. He shoved Plesur into the hole, then followed, crawling inside.

The rank smell of algae, cold and slimy, filled his senses. Rook prayed there weren't any snakes, but nothing stirred in the humid darkness. He moved up beside Plesur, and cradled her in his arms. "Ssh," he whispered in her ear.

Heavy footfalls thudded above them, and the distinct rasp of metal on pavement. The metal monster stood directly overhead.

Rook waited, the sound of their breathing impossibly loud in the enclosed space. The thing might miss him on its chipscan; there was at least fifteen feet of solid earth between him and it. Perhaps a minute went by, and then came that machine whine, another thud and then more of them, then silence.

He decided to take a look. Leaving Plesur in the darkness, with a whisper to stay quiet, he slid down the slime-covered concrete and crawled outside.

Wind rustled through the trees, the crickets kept up their steady hum. Cautiously he got to his feet and climbed back to the road. By the light of the moon he saw sharply cut tracks in the pavement where the robot had stood. It had gone. They were alone.

CHAPTER

"SIO Venner, you're alive?" exclaimed that voice with the Texas accent.

After thrashing through the muddy forest with Plesur for the last three hours, staying out of sight, wondering what the hell was going on, they were a quarter mile away from their destination. Just when he could almost feel the warm shower and taste the hot coffee, Beckman had called. And Rook wanted some goddamned answers.

"What the fuck!"

"I take that as a yes."

"My house is gone!"

"We are not in control of every aspect of this situation."

"No shit."

"Nothing is what it seems on the surface, you understand?"

"It *seems* like the feds tried to kill me with a fucking gunship!"

"Not officially. However, SIO Venner, your life remains in danger. You must listen to us."

"Who the fuck is us?"

"The Ranch."

Sable Ranch. Christ, this was way out of his league.

"SIO Venner, one thing."

"What."

"The pleasure model, is it all right?"

"She's fine. What's it to you?"

"Listen, SIO, don't make any phone calls for a while. We don't know who we can trust right now."

"Why should I trust you?"

"Because I have need of you—and your friend—alive. I will be in touch. And take good care of the pleasure model."

The call blipped out.

Jesus, what was he caught up in? The feds were trying to kill him and the most powerful organization in the country was trying to help him. What did they find so damn

interesting about Rook Venner, SIO? He didn't know anything the rest of the cops on the case didn't know.

Rook shook his head, muddy water dripping off his
hair, his shoes, his pants.

Plesur wrapped her arms around herself, pulling the
wet green shirt taut across her breasts. "Cold."

"Yeah, I can see that."

Rook stared, then blinked. The only thing that sepa-
rated him from the others was the evidence he had smuggled out of the station. It was Plesur they were after. Fuck!
Winnover and Fatso probably ratted him out when they
discovered their all-night party missing.

Rook turned around and pointed to the corners of a
swooping Chinese-style roof. "We're almost there. Think
you can make it?"

Plesur nodded.

Hide at the whorehouse—there was a certain logic to
that.

Ten minutes later they stood at the front door. Rook
reached for the Chinese doorbell, but before he even
touched it the whole door glowed within the faux wood
and turned to a slab of gold, while soft sec-lites came on.
A quiet chime sounded inside the house.

"Rook?" The door opened a crack; behind it were two
jet black, almond-shaped eyes, a tiny upturned nose, and
red lips parted in surprise.

"How's tricks, Soozie?"

"Still out of your range." The door opened, revealing a slim woman wrapped in a golden silk robe, teetering on gold open-toed sandals. Her dark hair was held up with golden skewers.

"You and your friend better come in."

The interior of Soozie Kong's Wayside Inn was warm, and lit by subtle glows coming from panels hidden in walls and ceilings. Spicy incense hung in the air.

Soozie was sizing them up with calculating eyes. "What's going on, Rook?"

"That is a very good question. Could really use a shower, Sooze."

Soozie clapped her hands. A middle-aged Chinese woman appeared from the shadows, wearing a gray tunic. "My guests need a shower, and clean clothes."

The servant led them upstairs to separate suites where they could clean up.

Rook let the hot water steam away the slime from his hair and back, while he thought about what he was going to tell Ms. Kong. Since his involvement in a case five years earlier, when a well-connected client managed to kill one of her girls, Rook had made the occasional visit to the Wayside Inn. Not, however, for the usual reasons men went there. In the original case, Rook had withstood some not-so-subtle pressure to drop the charges against the client and pursue charges against Sooze instead. That didn't happen and it was the beginning of an interesting friendship.

When he stepped out of the shower, she was there, sitting on the bed wearing nothing but a teddy in the same color gold as the robe.

"Feeling better?" she asked with a sly grin.

"Much. But I need clothes."

"Oh, I don't know, you look good without them, SIO Venner."

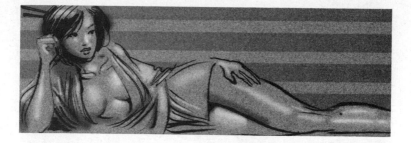

Sooze stretched like a cat. Whether her looks were the result of surgery or purely natural, Ms. Kong was a beauty, and she knew it.

He grinned back. "That's a relief."

She stood and came to him. "I didn't know you were into Pammys."

"It's not like that. She's involved in a case."

"Tell me another one," Soozie laughed.

"Someone doesn't want this case solved."

"And you're risking your life for that?"

"Not quite . . ."

Sooze had one hand on his hip; the other slipped between his legs. "Just talking about that little critter got you excited, unless . . ."

"What?"

"You're just glad to see me?"

"Always."

Plesur, the gunship, his house, all fell away as she slid

to her knees. Maybe she was only doing this to keep her cop protector. And yet there she was with his dick in her mouth and loving every moment of it.

He picked her up, carried her to the bed.

Setting himself between her legs, Rook started slow, came quickly, restarted with barely a moment's hesitation, and took his time on the second go-round. Soozie's hands held tight to his ass, as she kissed him and bit his neck in equal measure, arching her back, crying out. He let himself go and the flood poured out of his veins,

shaking everything within him and leaving him spent and, for the moment, oblivious.

He rolled over and found a pillow under his head, and Soozie curled up beside him with her head resting on his chest.

"It was your place they blew up, right?" she whispered.

"News travels fast."

"Lot of people saw the flash."

Rook eased himself up to his elbow, staring into her dark eyes. "Everyone scared?"

"You bet. Nothing like that for years."

"But you're not."

"I'm an adrenaline junky." She tapped the end of his nose with a long red fingernail. "You always bring the best trouble."

He moved her hands away and sat up. "I got a case that somebody powerful doesn't seem to want investigated."

"What kind of case?"

"Murder, what else?"

Sooze draped herself against Rook's back, her breasts soft and warm against his skin. "You're safe here, of course, but if I was you, I'd consider having your chips pulled before you leave."

The Wayside Inn possessed high-end and totally illegal jamming systems, so Sooze's clientele could visit without leaving any electronic traces. Which was why Rook had headed there in the first place.

"That's a felony. I'll be classified as rogue."

"Won't matter if you're classified dead," she breathed into his ear.

True. Rook rubbed his eyes. Christ, he was tired.

Sooze pressed a tiny gold stud in her right earlobe. "Cindy Wales," she said. A few moments passed as the call went out. Sooze stroked Rook's chest with one hand.

"Cin? Sorry, terrible timing. Sweetie, I need a favor. Yeah, now."

Sooze smiled, ran her left hand in between his legs.

"I'm a cop."

"Not anymore. So pay up."

Rook found the stimulation more than he could resist. His hands cupped her firm, round breasts. She raised a leg and straddled him. She was wet, ready, and he slid in with a single smooth flexion of her hips.

"Cindy's coming over right now. She'll take them out for you."

"Thanks."

Sooze began to ride and Rook forgot everything for the next few minutes, until they were both finished and lying there sated.

"You know," she said with a mischievous pout, "I should've brought your little Pammy in for a threesome."

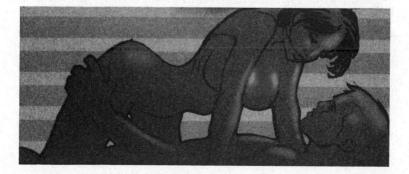

"She's evidence. Don't touch."

"Evidence?"

"Sooze, curiosity, you know?"

"What, killed the cat?" Sooze swung her feet to the floor, slipped into a silk robe and strode to the window. The first rays of the rising sun peeked through the drapes.

Rook turned on his side and shut his eyes. "You don't want to know any more, believe me."

"That dangerous?"

"Ask my house."

"Pity, she seems very fresh. I would wager not two weeks out of the crate."

"And you've seen a lot."

"It's my stock-in-trade, sweetie. Most are just worn out, ready to die. And when they get down to the last couple of years . . ."

He didn't say anything.

"You wouldn't believe what men are capable of," Soozie whispered bitterly.

"Actually, I would," he said before letting the world slip away into the darkness of sleep.

CHAPTER 9

Rook sat at an antique lacquer desk, gazing out the window at the placid waters of a small lake. The afternoon sun shone languorously over smooth stones in the Zen garden. It was nice here. Too bad he wouldn't be staying. "I need to call my assistant."

"Sure, use my system." Soozie walked in from the bathroom, brushing her hair in long strokes. An emerald green dress rippled over the smooth curves of her body.

"It is safe?"

Sooze chuckled. "With my customers? Some are phoning while they fuck. They never stop."

"Check systems," he told the Nokia.

"I detect a satellite link to Deng 9, Chinese telcom sat."

"Get me MacEar."

She picked up before the first ring was over. "Boss, you're alive?"

"I believe so."

"They said you were killed. What the hell happened?"

"Someone blew my house up. Gunship dropped a combat robot to make sure."

"Holy shit! This was official?"

"Don't think so, but then I don't know what is."

"Who else knows you're alive?"

"Nobody."

"The chief?"

"Best not to tell her. Not yet, anyway. In fact, let's just keep this between you and me for now."

"What about the pleasure mod?"

"She's okay, she's with me. Anything more on the car?"

"I got forty-seven thousand direct matches on the paint job."

Rook sighed. That wouldn't lead to anything, guaranteed.

"I was going back to the crime scene," Lindi continued. "Talk to the staff, see if anyone had an ID on our blonde."

"Okay, but be careful. Whoever's on the other end doesn't mind killing cops."

"Boss, where are you?"

"Safe location, that's all I can say right now."

"How do I get in touch?"

"I'll set up a bump account."

"How about flowers?" she suggested.

"Good idea. Embed the audio in the left side of the pics."

Rook told the Nokia to find a good online sharing site and set up an account.

"What name would you like to use?" the smart phone asked.

"Randomize something."

"It's 7rt65rst19tom67 then."

"Got it," said Lindi.

"Later."

"Doctor Cindy's here, sweet cheeks."

Rook turned to find Soozie eyeing him like prime beef. He was wearing a white terrycloth robe provided by Sooze's servant. He wanted his own clothes back, but they were still in the drier.

The door to the bedroom opened to admit a plump lady in a business suit, carrying an expensive-looking metal case. She set it down on the side table.

"You're the one who needs chips pulled?"

Rook nodded. He had been a cop for twelve years, a good cop. But that was all about to change. Once the chips were removed, he would be classified rogue and a wanted man.

Doctor Cindy produced an instrument that looked like a cross between a hair dryer and a pistol. "If you'd just remove the robe."

"What?"

"Hold onto the family chips," Sooze laughed.

"Fine." Rook dropped the robe, grabbed a towel, and tied it around his waist. "Okay?"

"Very good, sweet cheeks." Doctor Cindy passed the device over his body, about half an inch above the skin. When it passed over a microchip it flashed green and mapped the location, whereupon the doctor used a small marking tool to put a blue circle on the spot.

In less than five minutes she had everything marked. He looked like a damn constellation.

"You'll feel a jolt with each extraction. You want a tranq?"

"No. Just do it." Rook had had chips extracted before, during a bout of chip-sick. He hated the narcotics. Pain kept him sharp.

The extractor made a soft hum, punctuated by a little thud as it yanked a chip.

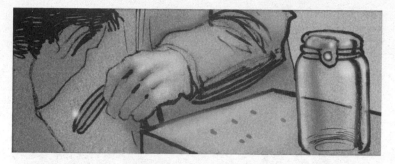

Rook took his mind somewhere else.

"Quite a haul there." The doctor held up a little jar. "These are dead now, no one can trace them." Rook took it and glanced inside at the half dozen tiny silicon devices. The doctor ran a sterilizer over the little blood spots on his shoulders and back.

The door opened suddenly to reveal Plesur, wearing white pajamas and carrying Rook's cleaned and dried clothes.

"Plesur bring Rook his clothes," she announced with a big smile.

"Thank you, Plesur. How are you feeling?"

"Better. Needed to sleep. You?"

"Good." Rook turned to the doctor. "Would you mind running a check on her?"

"Of course." Cindy adjusted the chip location device. "Plesur, remove your top, please."

"Okay." Plesur undid two buttons and slid the pajama

top off. Her magnificent breasts swung free. Rook blinked, then looked away.

While Doctor Cindy checked Plesur for chips, Rook took his clothes into the bathroom and got dressed. When he emerged, the doctor was packing up her stuff.

"Anything on her?" Rook asked.

"Nope, not one. That's unusual. Owners usually stick at least an RFID in them."

"Yeah." If Plesur was carrying information, it wasn't stored on a standard chip. What was so special about the Pammy? What was worth sending a gunship and combat robot after her?

"Thanks, Cin." Soozie escorted her to the front door. "You're an angel."

The doctor chuckled. "This mod is very clean."

"Yeah, so you said."

"No, I mean, it hasn't been touched."

Rook stared at Cindy.

"She's a fucking virgin!" Sooze howled. "Oh, man."

Rook slumped into a chair as Cindy left. Sangacha hadn't even slept with the mod. If he never wanted her for sex, what the hell was he using her for?

Nothing in this case added up. A virgin pleasure mod being chased by a gunship, and for what? She couldn't even tie her own shoes.

Plesur had found a small bedside TV screen and was deep into a sex virt, giggling as Buddy went down on Bonny, only to find that Bonny wasn't really a girl. Well, she looked like a girl, except between her legs. Plesur found the look on Buddy's face perfectly hysterical as he came up for air.

"Silly man," she shouted at the portable virt screen. Then she saw Rook, got up, and ran to him. The pajamas were gone, replaced by a pink top and a pair of white jeans. Rounding this out were some comfortable-looking low heels.

"New clothes," he murmured.

"You like?" She struck a pose with her breasts pushed out and one hand on her hip.

"Very, uh, nice," he said.

"Yes," she crowed. "Plesur is nice!"

"No doubt about that," said Soozie with a chuckle.

"Thanks, Sooze, probably saved my life."

"You owe me one more." Soozie grinned like a cat that'd had the cream.

"What?"

"I made some calls. This guy, Sangacha, right?"

"How'd you know that?"

"Honey, when it comes to gossip who would know better than the owner of the best little whorehouse in Woodstock?"

Rook nodded. That was a good point.

"He was a big man, down in the city."

"And?"

"He liked to fuck guys."

"Anyone in particular?"

Soozie nodded. "I'll take you to Nancy's. There's someone there you need to talk to."

"What about her?" Rook glanced at Plesur.

"Oh, she'll fit right in, believe me."

CHAPTER 10

Manhattan rose out of the night like a vast creature made of lights. A backbone of the new supertowers stuck up in the center of Midtown, while older, smaller towers were crammed cheek by jowl from the Hudson to the East River.

Plesur, of course, had never seen anything like it, except on TV. She stared out the window with eyes wide, mouth slightly open as they raced down the Palisades.

Soozie's pricey little Beemer got them to the city inside half an hour, using the high-speed lane, right next to the roaring, rocketing freight traffic.

"You didn't have to take us in," he told Soozie.

"Hey, I haven't been down to Nancy's in too long. I have some things to talk over with her. I've been thinking about getting a male pleasure mod."

"A male one?"

"There's a new kind, called Alberto. Very cute. Perfect for the older gay market in Woodstock. Nancy has all the connections in that world."

"I bet."

Rook and Soozie were prepared for the programmed swoop down into the tunnel at more than a hundred miles an hour, but Plesur was not. The car slipped off the Palisades' power rail with no more than a soft clunk, diving into the Lincoln Tunnel entrance. One moment they were heading toward the candy-colored towers across the Hudson, the next they were in the white, claustrophobic world of the tunnel with a thousand other cars hurtling along like shotgun pellets in the barrel of the gun.

Plesur screamed, clutching at Rook's chest.

"It's just a tunnel, Plesur. It goes under the river."

She was staring at him, terrified, and then understanding filtered in. "Tunnel," she whispered.

The traffic around them slowed down at the same rate, smooth and easy as they rolled in lockstep up the East Side ramp and out into the blinding glare of nighttime Midtown.

Plesur stared out the window, completely absorbed in the passing scene. Shop fronts, pedestrians, the sheets of glass and steel soaring up into the darkness, the huge logos flashing on and off in the sky, it was all new to her, and utterly fascinating.

Big helium-filled ad floaters slithered by overhead, lights flashing, advertising scrolling across their bellies.

Soozie parked in an underground lot and led them around the corner and down a set of stone steps. A red door opened into a pulsing atmosphere filled with noise, alcohol, a faint odor of sweat, and a variety of fragrances. Pink and amber panels glowed in the low ceiling and the tables along the walls. They took a table toward the back, where Plesur watched the dancers on the raised dance floor as they flexed and spun, thrust and wobbled, looking like well-oiled automatons.

Soozie was well known here and well-wishers, male and female, came up to hug and kiss. While the dress code was about as relaxed as possible without actual nudity, none of what he was seeing and hearing shocked Rook, who had extensive experience in the uninsured world. What did drop his jaw was their waitress. Her face was an exact duplicate of Plesur. Every detail from her wide blue eyes to her pert little nose. She was a Pammy, but as different from Plesur as someone with identical genetic makeup could be. Her hair was short and black, her bosom had been flattened by surgery to something approaching a normal size, and her eyes had a hard cast to them that spoke of worldly awareness. When she spoke it wasn't with Plesur's soft little burr, either, but a flat New York accent complete with attitude.

"Hi, I'm Ivana. What can I getcha?"

"Marijuana," said Soozie briefly before turning back to a young black woman in a tight-fitting suit of golden spandex. "And not that medicinal shit, either."

Plesur stared at the waitress, astonished. For a long moment the pleasure models locked eyes.

"And you, sweetie?"

"She'd like something nonalcoholic."

The waitress snapped Rook a look of black fire from those baby blue eyes. "You make all her decisions, do ya, daddy?"

"No."

Plesur was still staring at the waitress. "You just like me."

The waitress sniffed. "Sweetie, I am you, and you are me." She wrote something on her pad. "Strawberry smoothie, okay?"

"Yeah, fine," said Rook, feeling embarrassed for some reason. "Look, I . . ."

"You don't have to give me any excuses." She was waiting for him to order something. "Beer?"

"Uh, something light."

"Light." She looked at him again, hard, before heading to the bar.

The idea of Plesur giving Rook that kind of

contemptuous look was outlandish. But this mod seemed like a normal working woman.

Soozie broke away from a group of young men by the bar to whisper to Rook. "Don't tell me you never heard of a mod upgrade."

"Not common in my line of work."

"Easy, daddy. This place has equal rights for mods. Don't go getting all twentieth century on me."

"I'm an old-fashioned kind of guy."

"You are a funny one, Detective Venner."

"Who she?" Plesur breathed, still recovering from the shock of seeing herself.

Soozie leaned close. "She's a waitress. Do you know what a waitress is?"

Plesur looked up, confused. "No."

Rook put his hand on hers protectively. "It's okay, don't worry about it."

Her lips parted in a slight smile.

He glanced at Ivana, filling their order, chatting with the bartender. And suddenly a realization hit him. What if Plesur were smart? He could drag her around and never get answers until a bullet gave him one. With an upgrade, maybe she'd know why everyone was after her. Maybe he'd have a shot at saving his own skin. And maybe there could be some kind of life for Plesur, too.

"I'll be right back." He walked to the bar, sliding past rows of partygoers.

Ivana was loading her tray as Rook approached.

"Can I have a word with you?"

"Don't you have enough on your plate?" she shot back.

Rook flashed his detective shield. The light flickered suspiciously in those deep blue eyes.

"You've got the wrong idea." He put the shield away. "I just have some questions."

"Check Mediawik. I have work to do." The waitress hoisted her tray full of drinks and turned away.

"Wait." Rook caught her elbow. Her look could have frozen hell.

"Sorry." He quickly stepped back, arms raised. "Please. She needs help."

They both glanced at Plesur. Ivana waited.

"*I* need help. The mod is involved in a case. Could be very dangerous for her."

Ivana set the tray on the bar. "Katie, can you take these to table ten?"

"Sure, honey." A short redhead smiled brightly and took Ivana's tray.

"Three minutes."

"What happened?" asked Rook.

She looked at him for a moment. "To me?"

"Yeah."

"You really don't know?"

"I wouldn't be asking."

She turned her head to one side and tapped a little ruby-colored bead of plastic set behind her right ear.

"You've never seen one of these before?"

"Earbunk."

"My intelligence is just as good as yours now. Probably better."

"No doubt."

Ivana smiled. "There are more of us than you think, Detective."

Rook stared into her deep eyes, full of intelligence and understanding.

"Look, I just want her to be, well, whatever she can be. Okay?"

Something in Ivana's eyes softened noticeably. "Talk to Nancy."

And suddenly she smiled. Plesur's smile, but loaded with irony, concern, even understanding. "Be careful what you wish for, daddy. She won't be the same. Certainly not your little Pammy anymore."

"She deserves better."

"Don't we all, brother."

CHAPTER 11

Jim's farmhouse was an electronic rat's nest crammed with old-tech computers, monitors, scopes, meters, and antique rock posters. Using the obsolete equipment meant Jim could fly under the radar, undetected by the modern sensors.

Reaching behind a mass of cabling, Jim pulled out a bottle of whiskey. He poured a small measure of amber liquid into snifters. The stuffed bear in the corner of the room seemed to grin a little wider as the whiskey swirled.

"Here's to a long life, darlin'." Jim tapped his glass

against hers. They made a solemn sounding "dong," like bells. "An' a 'appy one."

He took a sip and so did Julia. She hadn't touched liquor in twenty years, but the explosive cascade of malt and honey flavors took her right back.

"That's yer real Speyside Malt, darlin', forty years old."

"Amazing." Julia felt the alcohol rushing to her head and set the glass down, sinking back into the leather couch. It might be delicious, but it would undo days of careful anti-aging work. "What are we celebrating?"

"The day I've been waiting for is here!" Jim announced.

"Funny. Feels like the day I've been dreading for twenty-five years."

He took a slow sip. "It's all a matter of perspective."

"You got that right. I'm thinking Seattle."

"'Ang on, Jools. You can't run. Not this time."

She glared, blue eyes turned to fire.

"Nah, 'ear me out. Your general gets murdered and a

few hours later there's a shark in the skies. I dun' believe in coincidence."

"I didn't know he was a general. I'm not sure if they knew it was me in that apartment or if I'm just collateral damage."

"Just tidying up."

"They're gonna get me no matter what I do." She tried to smile, to summon back her confidence.

Jim grinned in a conspiratorial way. "You don't fuck with the girls with whips in their 'ands. You can take control of this situation."

"It's not so simple."

"Never is."

She stared across the table, handmade like everything else in Jim's crazy-quilt cabin.

"So, darlin', let's get down to business." Jim topped off his glass with the forty-year-old single malt. "Tell me what I'm missing."

Julia slid away as Angie let the memories come. She hadn't spoken of Mark to anyone since the early days in L.A. "A long time ago they . . ." She hesitated. "Some secret group killed my fiancé, and they would've killed me if they'd found me. But I got away. I've been hiding ever since."

Jim sighed, leaned back in the big wooden chair. "Why'd they kill 'im?"

She shrugged and took another sip of the whiskey. "He knew about stuff that went down back in the thirties."

They sat there a moment in silence.

"Jools, this Sangacha is—*was* one motherfucka. Lot a blood on 'is hands."

"You think there's a connection?"

"Crossed my mind." Jim suddenly leaned forward. "Who did yer man work for?"

"He never told me what he did. I know it was military," she said slowly, eyes wide in realization.

"What, like Pentagon special forces?"

"Something like that.

Jim held up his glass, catching light in the amber liquid. "Cleanup unit, as it were."

"And I'm a spot they missed."

"Well, look on the bright side." Jim glanced at a softly beeping monitor. "Maybe the entire organization what

killed your boy 'as retired by now. Or they're dead. Like
Sangacha."

Angie blinked. Wheels spun in her mind. Was that even
possible? This was such a tantalizing, wonderful idea. "I
could stop hiding," she said in something approaching a
whisper.

"Or maybe you're right." Jim's eyes narrowed. "Maybe
you're on the list. One way to find out for sure."

"How?"

"You 'ave a client that could tell you things."

She raised an eyebrow. "I have a lot of clients."

"This one's special."

"You don't mean . . . ?" she asked, horrified. "I swore I'd
never go back to that perverted son of a bitch."

Jim beamed.

CHAPTER 12

In Nancy's the drinks came and went. Rook was feeling a little light-headed. Soozie had disappeared somewhere. Plesur leaned against the bar between a pair of men who were acting up just for her. Plesur seemed to get these people. She understood things sexual, even if she didn't have the vocabulary.

"Silly man!" she giggled. The men entertaining her roared in laughter, delighted.

Plesur was just a piece of evidence; she had no rights. When the case was over she would vanish. Powerful men would want her. Men who were vastly more powerful than Rook Venner.

And why should this bother him? Why the fuck should he care? There were always new cases, new problems, new horrors to deal with.

Give it a few days and who'd remember little Plesur?

There was a tap on Rook's left shoulder. He turned and found a well put together lady in a black suit, fishnet hose, and perilously high heels studying him with sharp brown eyes. Her hair looked cheap blond, but he was sure it was expensive.

"I'm Nancy Pell, this is my place."

She had the ageless look so common these days, and he pegged her as being in her thirties.

"Rook Venner, SIO, Hudson Valley."

"Soozie told me. I have a few cops as customers." She glanced in the direction of the waitress. "Ivana said you wanted to know about mental enhancements for your pleasure model."

Rook nodded warily.

"I didn't know Manuel had one." Nancy's red lips twitched in amusement. "He was full of surprises."

"So I'm learning."

"Why do you want this?"

"She could help me find the killers."

Nancy studied him for a moment.

"Mods are worse off than slaves. You upgrade her, all the nasty things come flooding back. It's a shock. Some of them cry for days. Others don't cry at all, they get . . . angry."

"She's . . . never been kissed."

Something in Rook's tone of voice seemed to please Nancy.

"I know a lotta cops, SIO Venner. Some are okay, some are worthless, and some are just plain bad. You don't seem to fit into any of those categories."

"A regular knight."

Nancy shrugged. "All I ever see is people with their hands out."

Rook shrugged. "I have to keep her alive. Might be easier if she was upgraded."

She chewed her lip for a moment. Then made her decision. "My friend runs a small clinic over on the East Side. It's very discreet."

"How much?" Rook asked, unsure how he was going to pay for this.

"A lot." Nancy smiled and shook her head. "I'm sure we can figure something out."

Very true, thought Rook. He was sure she would find some use for him. He was sliding away from the world he knew. Closer to the kind of person he'd spent his career hunting down and locking away, and all over a pleasure mod. But it was the only way to stay alive long enough to discover the truth and maybe save his life.

Something beeped softly. Nancy tilted her head. "We can probably get this set up for tomorrow. Soozie is always welcome to stay at my place. You and the mod are, too, of course."

"Thanks." He watched her walk away, firm derriere moving her tight skirt like a fine clock. He glanced over to check on Plesur.

She was still being entertained by a shifting cast of men and women, laughing and flirting. They were drawn to her like moths to a flame. They couldn't help themselves.

Tomorrow she'd be a different person, a whole different animal.

But he wasn't going to change his mind. She deserved the upgrade, no matter what.

He saw Soozie working her way through the crowd with a young man behind her. She had a big grin on her face.

"Rook, this is Pipo Haman. Pipo, meet Rook Venner, the detective investigating your boyfriend's murder."

Haman's slinky, shiny green suit hugged his muscular young body. The handshake was soft, the inhumanly good-looking face sculpted by surgeons.

"Poor Manuel." The accent was New York born and bred. "What happened to him?"

"That's what I'm trying to find out."

"He was killed." Plucked eyebrows flattened into tight little lines. "That's all we heard."

"Shot, multiple times," Rook confirmed.

"I know he had enemies."

"For instance?"

"You know, from way back, when he was in the military." Pipo's eyes darted anxiously.

"He spoke about that?"

"Sometimes . . . he would cry. We'd be drinking, and he'd get all moody."

"Do you know why?"

Pipo hesitated. Rook watched him as he struggled to find the words.

"Being a believer, that made him very guilty, very worried about his soul, you understand?"

"You visited him in Peekskill?" Rook continued his questions.

"Yeah."

"Did you ever meet the pleasure model?"

"Oh, god, that thing? I've known tomatoes that are smarter."

Rook detected an undeniable undertone of jealousy. Interesting, if not necessarily informative. He switched tacks.

"So how did you and Sangacha meet?"

"Right here, I think. Or it might have been at the Dance Garage."

"Sangacha was cruising?"

Pipo's soft lips flared in contempt. "Of course. Manuel liked to fuck. But he *really* liked to fuck me."

"Okay."

Rook sensed that Pipo was a little disappointed at the policeman's easygoing acceptance of that last statement. Why the young man would think that a seasoned homicide detective would blink at the idea of men fucking each other was a bit of a mystery. Pipo clearly needed to get out more.

Pipo kept on talking. "One time he said something about the Pammy, that she could blow them all up. I thought he was joking."

"Who might them be?"

"No idea. And another time he woke up from a nightmare shouting about blood and babies. He scared me. He was so big and strong. But I held him and he kept saying over and over that he was going to bring them down."

"Where was this? Peekskill?"

"Oh, no, in the apartment."

"What apartment?"

"Our place. Under my name so no one could find him." Pipo smiled. "Our own secret hideaway."

"You still have it?"

The anxiety was back in Haman's voice. "Around the corner."

Rook felt a door open on the case. No one knew about this place. If he stashed any secrets, it would be there.

"Would you mind showing me?"

"What, like, now?"

"Right now. Might help me nail the people who killed him."

That registered with young Pipo. "Okay."

Leaving Plesur under Soozie's watchful eye, Rook followed Pipo through the kitchen and out the back.

On the street, the late-night crowd paraded by in full display. Pipo walked beside Rook with a jaunty step, exchanging greetings with several other young men.

Pipo stopped outside a little restaurant, Bistro Lascaux. Even at this hour customers crowded the tables. He pointed to the top floor of the building.

He put his eye next to the security plate and the door swung open. They climbed a flight of steps where another door opened into a spacious loft, a large party room with a bedroom and bathroom at the back. A leather wet bar took up one wall and velvet couches lined the others. Everything was expensive and indulgent, definitely Pipo's style.

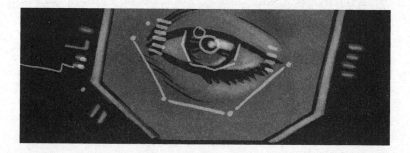

The art on the wall was unfamiliar to Rook, who wasn't exactly up on modern art anyway. He noticed painted scenes of an arid landscape, each overlaid with sheets of clear plastic, shimmer-screen style. The piece suddenly shifted, and the desert was replaced by a group of houses with swimming pools. And then it shifted again. The pools filled with sand, swallowed by the desert. The houses were gone except for a pole here and a concrete slab there. Rook looked more closely. The new scene was on the overlay, a cyber-image. Underneath it he could still see the desert landscape.

"They change constantly," said Pipo. "The Euridiki's worth about two mil."

"No shit." Rook had found a locked door, just past the bedroom. "What's in here?"

"Private office. He didn't like anyone going in there."

"Can you open it?"

"Yeah. Hold on."

Pipo pulled open a drawer in the bedroom and rummaged under the neatly folded shirts.

"Here." He handed Rook the key.

The small room had been modeled into a cyber-station, with an old-fashioned household computer, a wraparound screen, and a keyboard. To the right side was a bookcase stuffed with real books, all on military history themes. Titles jumped out at Rook: *Stalingrad—Battle of Destiny*, *The Eagle and the Snake—Vietnam*.

In the desk there were files; one held the lease for the apartment. Another held some faded photographs. One showed a couple standing outside a modest single-story

adobe house. The man was brown-skinned, Mexican, perhaps with some Native American, too. The woman was pale, with brown hair twisted into a braid. Behind them a small truck sat in the driveway. On the back it read: "Papa grande y abuela Britney."

A humble background, then. Rook found another pic, more recent, sealed in plastic. A young man in military uniform, every inch a soldier, standing before a low green building with a flagpole outside. The Stars and Stripes fluttered from the pole, and another flag, blue and gold, flew beneath it.

"The general?"

"Yeah, such a stud."

Rook had to agree with that analysis. The young Sangacha had the same broad shoulders as the older version, but his handsome features were unmarked by the deep lines the future would bring. Confidence shone in his dark eyes, challenging the world. Rook bet the older Sangacha's eyes had looked a hell of a lot different.

The drawers below the computer were not locked either. Rook found a pistol, a Smith & Wesson .38 with four clips of ammunition. Underneath lay account printouts from a private bank—Morclay and Son, of White Plains. Rook flipped through them. That was interesting. How did a retired general get one hundred thousand dollars transferred into his bank account every month?

Two-million-dollar artwork on the walls. A mysterious income of more than a mil per year. That wasn't a military pension.

Which meant he was working for somebody—but who?

In another drawer Rook found a black box, and inside that an official badge. A fist holding a short sword and the words "Interservice Special Selection" embossed on its face.

"Any ideas?"

"No. Never seen that before." Pipo shrugged.

Then Rook saw a slim steel box, about the size of an old-time cigarette case. He pulled it out and held it up in the light. From behind him, a loud voice warned, "Get out or I'll blow your fucking head off!"

Rook whirled around, pointing his gun at—a fish mounted on the wall.

"Drop dead, motherfucker!" the fish screamed.

"What the fuck is that?" Rook exclaimed.

"That's Manuel," said Pipo, smiling.

"Quite the catch." Rook put the Nokia on the job. "Check this machine out, see if you can find anything that might be pertinent to the case."

The computer's lights blinked on as Ingrid got to work.

"Warning." Ingrid's Scandinavian voice immediately sounded. "Attempt to penetrate the security wall has triggered an alarm."

Rook stepped back. He swung the door shut and locked it, but took the key.

"Come on, we better get out of here."

Pipo, who wasn't privy to communications from the Nokia, was taken aback. "What's happening?"

"We've tripped an alarm. Don't suppose you know how to turn it off?"

"What alarm?"

"Thought so. Let's go."

Rook propelled Pipo through the door and down the stairs.

Outside they crossed the street and hid in an alleyway. The bistro was still humming with activity.

Pipo slunk against Rook's side, nervously eyeing the building. "What are we doing?"

"Shut up, stay still. And move over."

Minutes ticked by. A few customers strolled out of the bistro, a gaggle of young women sauntered by, but nobody noticed Rook and Pipo hidden in the shadows.

And then a black van hurtled down the street and screeched to a halt outside the restaurant. The doors opened and a heavily armored SWAT team poured out.

The door to the stairs popped open with a loud *crack* and a small cloud of smoke.

"What is that?" whispered Pipo.

"Shaped charge. They blew the door. Now shut the fuck up!"

Another bang came out of the building; the lights went on upstairs.

"Let's go," said Rook, fingering the silver case in his pocket. "I think we got what we came for."

CHAPTER 13

The mirrors in the completely redone Chelsea Hotel in lower Manhattan were the latest in smart-mirror technology, designed to detect your mood and show you what you wanted to see. They were hugely popular, but pricey.

"After this I'll run away," Angie told herself. "Go where no one will ever find me."

Angie switched the mirrors off. Who she needed to see was already there, staring back at her from the plain glass. Someone completely in control, unafraid, steeled to risking everything. The small part of her that still fought the transformation slipped away.

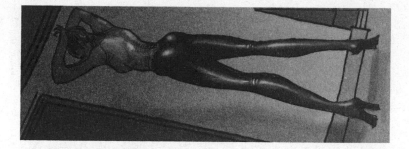

"Fuck you." The image in the mirror spoke menacingly. "I'm here now."

The black leather pants went well with her hair up. Eyebrows dark, lips bloodred, Julia was every inch the successful dominatrix.

There was a click in her ear. Her call was being returned, as expected.

"Hullo there, been quite a while," said a warm male voice with something of a Texas accent.

"I've been travelling," Julia lied smoothly. "Bet you'd love to see the present Auntie brought back for you."

"Damn, but you're right about that. All work and no play makes me a dull boy."

Mistress Julia chuckled. The role here was that of the strict, beautiful Auntie, who liked to make her nephew happy. And since he had needs that were a bit perverse, Auntie had to go to some lengths to indulge him.

"I have free time this evening," she said, reeling him in with her voice.

"I'll clear my schedule."

"Here at my hotel?"

There was a brief pause as he considered his options. "No, here. I have to be careful right now."

Careful? What did that mean?

"Shall we say seven?"

His voice was a hoarse whisper. "Bring a fresh girl. No marks."

It was good to hear that confidential tone in the client's voice, almost pleading for compassion. "I always deliver."

"That you do."

"See you at seven." She hung up.

Julia knew her client's desires could never be spoken of within his world. He liked to see a girl with a virgin ass getting her first whipping. There was something special in the screams, the sobs, and the sight of the red lines surfacing on pale white skin that did it for him. And afterward the whipped girl had to blow him a couple of times while he drank champagne.

But the client was unpredictable. Sometimes he needed to take it further. Sometimes he killed them.

Mistress Julia was a professional; she didn't allow personal feelings to interfere in the business. Angie, however, had never quite gotten past her disgust with this client. But when you were pandering to an ex-president of the United States, you held your nose and did your job.

The only difficult requirement was that he needed virgin ass. Smooth, white-skinned, unkissed by the whip. She pressed the call stud. "Get the Frog."

A few clicks later and a weary man's voice came on.

"Where the fuck you been hiding?"

"Miss me?"

"I miss your money."

"I need a girl. Has to be white, and perfect. Virgin ass."

The Frog whistled. "Expensive ass. Ten large."

"Make the call."

Mistress Julia studied herself in the mirror again. The leather worked, but the hair might be better down, and she'd need the long gloves. As for the whip, she'd brought three choices. The simple, single-tail, kangaroo hide "Striper" that she'd used for many years. It brought up

nice welts, but rarely cut the skin. There was a longer, heavier "Desperado" bullwhip, which was actually more show than substance. And then there was a bright scarlet coaching whip that produced the most amazingly loud cracks and snaps. For the sound effects alone that was the whip to use.

Probably, though, she'd use all three, in a session that would last a good long time. For the girl, who'd be hanging from the hook in the door frame, it would be an eternity, but her agonies were an essential part of the game. Because afterward, when the client was softened up, partly drunk on champagne, relaxed by some blow jobs, Julia would sit on the couch and cuddle him to her breasts. That's when the answers would flow like rain over the cold ground.

CHAPTER 14

Nancy had a lush loft just across the street from the New Chelsea Hotel. A high-end furniture store occupied the ground floor with ten lofts above. She had the tenth, at the top of the building.

Rook, Plesur, and Soozie were sharing the guest bed, which was big enough for six. Rook hadn't even bothered trying to convince Plesur that she should sleep on her own. She was snuggled up on his right side, while Soozie lay on the left.

"Long night" was Rook's last observation before his

head hit the Helthillo. The pillow contoured itself instantly to his head.

There were no dreams, only the deep oblivion of exhaustion. Somewhere, rising from the black, there appeared an oddness, a sense of something wrong fluttering on the edges of awareness.

Rook woke with a start and reached for the gun he'd stashed under the pillow. Beams of sunlight broke through the thick drapes on the window. Outside, cars rolled down the street, hitting a manhole by the corner with a regular clank. A horn sounded from the direction of Eighth Avenue. Inside, nothing seemed to be stirring.

But Rook's police instinct told him something wasn't right.

He slid down the bed. Plesur made a soft snort and rolled over; Soozie didn't move.

Rook crouched by the door. Nancy had cut the floor space into four areas. The bedrooms took up the back; a music studio was set up in the front. The main space was open, with a walled-off kitchen, pantry, and exercise room on the east side of the loft.

He pulled the door open a crack. Daylight filtered in from the high windows above the partition walls. He was looking down the corridor between bedroom suites toward the big open space.

He pulled the door open wide enough for him to slip outside. Nothing, except a draft of air along the floor. He moved across to the other side of the passage and hid in the doorway to the bathroom. What the hell was it? Why was he standing out here half naked with a sidearm in his hand? The soft click was the only sound as he slid the safety off.

He edged along the wall, eyes peeled, ears straining for the slightest sound. Nothing. Nothing at all, except another distant car horn out in the street. Nothing . . .

The punch came with a tiny grunt of effort and Rook's flinch saved his life. Instead of smashing his nose and driving the bones into his brain, the invisible fist slammed into his cheek just below his left eye.

Rook's head snapped back. His body caromed off the wall and bounced away as a foot meant to smash his Adam's apple crashed through the wall. Staggering, he brought the gun up and squeezed off two shots, the deafening cracks echoing off the high ceiling. He heard a grunt, a curse, and then out of nothing there appeared a

tall humanoid figure, clad head to toe in silvery white material, with a single rose of red, mid-torso. The eyes were silver like a giant fly.

It went down on one knee. Rook fired again and the man toppled on his side, blood spilling freely across the material of his plasmonic suit.

Rook had heard rumors of invisible assassination squads, run out of Washington, D.C. Plasmonic material bent light around the wearer.

Where there was one, there would be others.

Rook raised his gun, scanning the hall, but there were no targets.

Nancy ran into the living room holding a little silver handgun, her eyes wild. Plesur stood behind her, terrified.

"What's going on?" Soozie stood at the bedroom door, then saw the guy on the floor. And the blood. She screamed.

Rook tried to hush her and was kicked hard in the chest.

He fell as the air exploded from him. It felt like his heart had turned into a rock. He heard Nancy fire her pistol, but could barely move, struggling to get breath into his lungs. Something shattered on the wall. He rolled, took another boot, this time to the shoulder, and felt the gun kicked out of his hand.

He tried to get up and was kicked back down, hard.

And then he saw Plesur with a lamp in her hand. The lamp exploded. Someone cursed. Plesur was slammed against the wall, but Rook had his arms around an invisible leg and pulled hard. The assassin went down.

Another shot was fired and something crashed to the floor. Rook scrambled for his gun, rolled to his knee, and fired in a smooth single motion. Instantly another guy materialized as if out of thin air. Blue sparks rippled over the silver plasmonic suit. A round red hole in the center of the chest collapsed the guy like a balloon with a slow leak. He folded up, crouched, then fell over.

Rook didn't fire again, worried that he was getting low on ammo. There was a spare clip, but in his jacket. "Everyone all right?" he called out.

Soozie stuck her head out the bedroom door. "There's another one. Smacked into Nancy."

"Plesur?"

The Pammy was crumpled up by the bathroom door. Rook edged toward her, keeping the gun up, ready to fire.

"Nancy?"

Still no answer. Where was the third assassin? He could be anywhere. Rook tasted blood; his lower lip was split. His chest hurt; he hoped he didn't have broken ribs.

He bent down to check Plesur's pulse. Still strong. She shook her head as she regained consciousness.

"Plesur help Rook?"

"Yes. You did." He smiled.

She smiled back.

"We have to get out of here," he said. Soozie was in full agreement on that score.

Rook slid along the wall, eyes straining for the slightest hint of the third man. At the door to Nancy's room he pulled back, then swung inside, gun aimed at chest level, his finger squeezing down on the trigger.

Nancy lay on the floor. Her gun glittered beside her, caught by a shaft of light through the blinds.

She struggled into a sitting position, saw Rook, and waved a hand weakly.

"You shot someone?"

"Two of 'em." Rook stayed in the doorway, scanning the bedroom.

"I saw something run, like an outline of a man."

Rook turned carefully, aiming down the passage into the main room.

"You think they'll be back?" she asked.

"Certain of it."

Plesur had pulled on some clothes. Soozie tossed Rook his shirt and jacket and he slammed a fresh clip into the gun.

Suddenly the elevator doors banged open outside the loft.

"This way!"

Nancy ran across the living room and into the walled-off kitchen. She flung open a door into a dark passage.

"Where's it go?" Rook asked.

"Fire stairs."

The doors to the loft smashed open behind them.

"Run!" Rook pushed Plesur through the door. The window beside him exploded and he heard choked-off thuds coming from the living space. He wheeled and fired back. There was nothing to see but the couch and chairs. The kitchen cabinet beside his head splintered. He ducked, pushed through the door, and leaped up the narrow stairwell.

Nancy swung open the door to the roof. The Empire State Building loomed ten blocks away. To the south the grand old Hotel Chelsea reared above them. Directly in front of them there was a gap, and then beyond it an ocher-colored brick building.

Rook looked around for something, anything, to jam the doorway.

The roof was bare. He heard feet on the steps, leaned in, and fired around the corner. Someone screamed; bullets gouged holes in the wall beside the door. Rook jerked his head back.

Plesur stood at the edge of the building, her hair streaming out like a mat of gold.

Rook fired another round down the stairwell. More thuds answered as bullets smashed bricks.

Rook stepped to the edge, looked over. There was a gap of fifteen feet, but the other building was a story lower.

"It's our only chance," he said to Nancy.

"Christ, I don't know."

He grabbed Plesur by the shoulders, looked her in the eyes.

"Have to jump, okay?"

"Plesur jump."

"Look out!" screamed Soozie.

The door was opening. Rook fired into the gap. The door swung shut again.

Rook pulled Plesur back to the edge.

"Run as hard as you can and then jump. When you land, roll. Understand?"

She nodded.

"Go!"

Plesur took off, sprinted to the edge, and leaped, arms windmilling as she flew out across the empty space.

Rook slammed the door shut again. It wouldn't be long before the killers broke through.

Soozie ran over. "She made it!"

"Got to do this," he said to Nancy. Soozie nodded agreement. Both women had removed their shoes, but Nancy was keeping hers in her hands.

"Go!" Rook ordered.

Nancy ran as fast as she could, and launched herself into the air.

Rook willed her across the space, praying she made it.

Soozie signaled that she had.

"Now you," he said.

Soozie turned, ran to the edge, and leaped into the air, arms flailing. A rifle shot rang out, sharp and hard, and she doubled over like a diver off the high board, folding up, then plummeting to the ground ten stories below.

Rook looked to the east and saw the sniper team taking position on a balcony.

He pumped three rounds in their direction, knowing the odds were against a sidearm. But it was enough to make them duck.

He ran and leaped. He was falling, expecting the bullet. Then he was below the edge of Nancy's building and out of the snipers' line of fire. He thumped down hard on the roof, tried to roll, and went over flat on his face with a jarring impact.

A moment later, Plesur was kneeling beside him.

"Rook okay?"

"Yeah, think so." He struggled to sit up.

"She gone." The pleasure model's cheeks shone with tears.

"Yeah. Lot of that going around."

CHAPTER 15

In the cab, hyperventilating, sweat pouring off his face, Rook struggled to get a grip as a cold band of fear ran through his guts.

He saw Soozie going down between the buildings, over and over, like a fucking video loop. Felt his heart sink with her.

All his fault. If he and Plesur hadn't shown up at her door, Soozie Kong would still be in Woodstock looking at her perfect little lake.

"Fuck," he whispered. "Fuck, fuck, fuck."

"My sentiments entirely," said Nancy, sitting on the

left side of the cab. She was still holding her high heels. "Who the fuck were they?"

"Had to be military," growled Rook. "Invisibility shit, nobody else has that."

Suddenly terrified that he might have lost it in their mad run to the corner, Rook went through his pockets to find the little metal file case. His Nokia was there, for which he breathed one sigh of relief, and then his fingers found the file case and he breathed another.

"I have to get this opened." He showed it to Nancy.

"Dangerous?"

"Explosive protected."

"What is it?"

He placed it back in his pocket. "Maybe an answer."

Plesur sat between them, recovering from the running, the terror, the jump off the building. Now she turned toward Rook and grabbed the front of his jacket. Her eyes seemed to bore into his.

"Plesur still get smart," she whispered.

Rook glanced at Nancy. She nodded affirmatively. "I'll see if they can take us early."

"Where you want to go?" said the cabdriver, who was already motoring uptown in medium traffic.

"Twentieth and Third, northeast corner," Nancy answered. Then she quietly made arrangements with the clinic.

Rook felt Plesur take his hand and hold on tight.

"Plesur get smart," he heard her say again as the cab turned a corner to head east and accelerated.

The clinic was hidden behind the Cityhealth Spa Center, where smartly dressed women came and went for their massages, facials, and more exotic treatments. The cab let them off near the alley on the side of the building. Nancy rang the back doorbell. A laser scanned her face; three seconds later the door opened.

There was a mirror-finish corridor ahead of them and Rook felt almost at home. The mirrors were part of a high-end security system that used super-intense LED lights and 140-decibel sound blasts.

"Mirror!" Plesur admired herself, looking from side to side. Reflections of her and Rook piled up on each other, receding to infinity.

They were scanned again by a green laser and then the door opened slowly on heavy gimbals.

Inside sat a waiting area in neutral gray and blue. A young woman in green scrubs emerged with a clipboard.

"Hi, I'm Gale."

"You the one I just spoke with?" Nancy asked, looking over the tech's shoulder.

"Yes. Joanne won't be in for another two hours but we're all set up for you." Then she turned to Plesur. "Do you know what's going to happen?"

Plesur licked her lips, shifting her eyes nervously to Rook. He smiled, tried to be reassuring.

"Get smart," she said in a small but determined voice.

"Exactly."

The girl passed Rook a handheld screen. It displayed a range of earbacks—little flesh-colored units designed to plug into the cranial interface. They contained microdrives that could hold anything from a set of languages to complete personalities, in the event that a pleasure model owner wanted a more entertaining, intellectual courtesan.

"We usually suggest the El-Plan forty. That's a forty-petabyte drive with the Onaguchi Interface and the Sony D-series port system. Guaranteed to provide IQ levels of one hundred twenty or above."

"That's a good one," Nancy told Rook.

"Okay." Rook imagined submitting his expense report on this case—if he ever got it solved.

"All right. If you'll come with me." Gale extended a hand to Plesur.

"What's the timeline on this?" asked Rook. "We're in a bit of a hurry."

"With the operation and recovery, about three hours. She'll be a whole new person." Gale smiled. "You have to sign these."

Rook hesitated. This woman seemed eager, maybe too eager. This facility ran under the radar. No one knew what was going on here—but he had no other choice.

"I'll take care of it." Nancy took the papers and rifled through them, signing quickly.

"I'll call when she's ready." Gale held up her handheld.

The Nokia and Gale's handheld swapped numbers. With a last brave look over her shoulder, Plesur disappeared through a frosted glass door.

Once she was gone Rook pulled out the little metal file case and examined it carefully. There were a pair of

ports on the hinged end. He let Ingrid lens them with her little webcam.

A few seconds later Ingrid announced, "The device is a military safety file, designed for pilots and infiltration agents. It is armed with BeZixx4, a nano-polymeric blasting gel."

"Can you open it?"

"Possible. Seventy-five percent chance of success. But you would be incinerated."

"What about you?" Ingrid had been his only true friend. He'd hate to lose her.

"You can download my system from the main server—"

"But?"

"She will not be as pretty."

"What's it saying?" asked Nancy.

"It's private." Rook slipped the phone back in his pocket. "We have to go someplace where an explosion won't matter too much."

"How about New Jersey?"

"Too far," Rook answered. "Where's the nearest park?"

"Madison Square, just west of here, a couple blocks north."

Rook hesitated. "Think she'll be all right?"

"Nothing's been all right since you showed up."

"I'm sorry I dragged you into this."

"Well, here I am. Might as well go blow up a park while we wait."

Outside, they paused a moment as a cop car went screaming by, rack lit up, siren cleaving the air. It disappeared, heading west. Rook felt the tension slowly ratchet back up again. He wasn't on his own turf here. Getting targeted by the NYPD would be a really bad move right now.

Rook tried the number left by Freddie Beckman the night before, but got no answer, not even a machine. It was early in the morning; maybe Beckman was sleeping in.

They found an empty section of Madison Square

Park nestled in between a stand of leafy maples. Rook polished off the coffee and bagels they'd bought on the way.

"I guess this is as secluded as we're going to get." Nancy studied the throng of people strolling up and down Madison as she sipped her drink.

"If this baby explodes, it won't matter where we are." Rook hooked up the little steel file with the Nokia.

The phone gave a beep, and the green progress light flashed a couple of times. "The device is password protected, at least one thousand digits in length."

"Shit."

"It can be decrypted, but it will take time."

"How much?"

"Difficult to say. At least one hour."

"Get me MacEar."

Rook sat back, drank hot coffee, and mourned Soozie Kong.

He remembered the first time they'd slept together, and how good the sex had been. How Soozie's earthy, cynical humor had always made him laugh. He knew that at first she'd been playing him, turning the good cop into a useful shield for a whorehouse madam. But as they grew to know each other their relationship became something else, an occasional sexual thing eventually settling into friendship.

And now she was gone.

Beside him, Nancy had been talking to friends nonstop, filling them in on what had happened. She was meeting up with disbelief and resignation.

"Sergeant MacEar is on your online share-site," Ingrid announced.

"Boss! What up?" MacEar sounded relieved to hear that he was still alive.

"Here's what we have. Sangacha had another life. Apartment in the Village. Liked to pick up young guys."

"There wasn't a trace of that at Peekskill."

"There's more," Rook continued. "He wasn't as retired as everyone thought. Someone was paying him big dollars on a regular schedule."

"For what?"

"I don't know yet. What's happening at the station?"

"Very quiet, certain amount of paying respects. By the way, sorry you're dead, boss."

"Thanks. What'd you dig up?"

"Got some info on our general. He led an outfit called the ISS for a while. Must be the black part of black ops. All records stop five years ago. Don't even know what it stands for."

Rook fished in his pants pocket and came up with the badge he'd taken from the apartment. "Interservice Special Selection."

"You sure know a lot for a dead guy."

"I found a badge in his apartment. I'm thinking it was pretty special considering what's been going on the last few hours."

"*I'm* thinking they killed people," MacEar stated. "Like our vic."

"Look, MacEar, a team of killers came to get us this morning. Don't know how they knew where to find us, but they were wearing invisibility suits."

"Plasmonic suits?" Lindi sounded like she'd just met the Easter Bunny. "You really saw them?"

"No, that's the whole fucking point."

"Jesus, boss. What the fuck is going on?"

"There's a war going on and this case is part of it. Our job is to stay alive. Don't let anyone know you're working on this case. Check the office for bugs twice a day at least, and don't get followed home."

"What about the Pammy?"

"Dead like me. Keep your gun handy."

"Loud and clear, boss. Transferred the decrypt."

"Thanks." Rook killed the call.

"The password is a page of text," Ingrid informed him. "*King Lear* Act 5, Scene 3."

"I just can't believe this stuff," Nancy snapped to Rook. "Oranie's telling me to leave town, go to L.A. I hate L.A., I'm a New Yorker, goddamnit."

"Might not matter if you're dead."

"Of all the gin joints in the world, you had to wander into mine."

Rook raised an eyebrow. "And it looks like the only way out is to solve this case."

"How the hell are you going to do that?"

"Maybe in this little file case we'll find an answer."

A helicopter rumbled past overhead. Rook fought the urge to look up. "Don't show your face. Might be scanning for us."

The chopper moved south and Rook risked a glance up through the trees. He couldn't tell if it was civilian or

military, not that it would matter much since he didn't know who was actually trying to kill him.

The Nokia interrupted his thoughts. "There is a call. Frederick Beckman again."

"Connect."

"SIO Venner, you've been stirring up a shit storm."

"I noticed."

"We thought you were going to stay in Woodstock." Mr. Beckman sounded a little aggrieved.

"Yeah, well, I've been making progress. What's the Interservice Special Selection?"

"How'd you find that?" Beckman sounded alarmed.

Rook thought for a second. "Pentagon files. Sangacha ran the ISS for years."

"You are not cleared to know about that. That information should not be available."

"Well, it is. Now, you want to tell me what the fuck is going on?"

"That is impossible. You don't have clearance."

Don't have clearance. Soozie was dead, his house was gone, some military group was trying to kill him, whoever "they" were, and Mr. Fredrick "Sable Ranch" Beckman wasn't giving him any answers. If he really worked for Sable Ranch.

"Listen up, pal, I'll make my own clearance."

"You're going to get yourself killed."

"Already did. What's the Ranch doing about this? Can I get some help here?"

"I'll let you know. Policy is being decided right now. Good-bye."

"Shit!" Rook sat back. He and Plesur had nowhere to go and nobody to help them.

"What's the Ranch?" Nancy asked, looking worried.

"Sable Ranch, where Senator Marion lives."

"*The* Senator Marion?"

"There's more than one?"

"Excuse me," Ingrid interrupted. "Shall I proceed with opening the AM Dat-File case?"

"Do it."

"I would suggest that you retire to a safe distance. The explosive charge in the device is very powerful."

"Time to make some noise." Rook grabbed Nancy and stepped away from the bench, leaving the black Nokia hooked up to the metal file. Rook just prayed that nobody came along looking for a quiet place to eat a hot dog.

The Nokia spoke up. "SIO Venner, should I not survive this, may I say that it has been a worthwhile experience to serve as your smartphone."

Rook smiled. "Here's looking at you, sweetheart."

Seconds ticked by with a painful slowness. A pair of joggers rounded the corner and padded by.

Then, in his ear, Ingrid spoke up again. "The box is open. Good news, I did not explode."

"Great job!" Rook hurried back to the bench. The little metal case opened easily. Inside he found a folded piece of paper. But it was the heavy type at the top that caught his attention.

TOP SECRET—TOP SECRET—TOP-SECRET
ACCESSING THIS DOCUMENT BY UNCLEARED PERSONS IS FORBIDDEN ON PAIN OF IMMEDIATE TERMINATION.

IF YOU HAVE FOUND THIS DOCUMENT AND DO NOT HAVE CLEARANCE, HAND IT TO YOUR SUPERVISOR IMMEDIATELY.

SECURITY—THIS DOCUMENT IS SEC-LEVEL 6.

MAY NOT BE ACCESSED BY ANYONE WITH CLEARANCE BELOW PRIORITY 2.

Results—TASTE IMPERATIVE—Series 4200

Date: 21/04/2060
Originating: Dr. Clampen.
Confirming: M.K. Helpred, J. Mahmoud, D.S. Ingersol

test no: 4231

"We got something," said Rook, "But god knows what."

Nancy looked at the scrap of paper. "All this, for that?"

Then Ingrid spoke again. "There is more. A secondary security system has been activated. The AM-Dat file is going to explode. Please leave right now."

Rook hurled the metal case into a patch of lawn and grabbed Nancy by the arm. "Run!"

"Oh god, again?" she said.

They were about twenty feet from the park entrance when the blast wave knocked them off their feet, shattering windows all around the square. A huge London Plane tree crashed across the path, its limbs stripped and thrown across Fifth Avenue like spears. Metal crunched as a limo flipped over a pedicab.

People were screaming. Rook looked back and saw a huge cloud of gray and black smoke. He got back on his feet and helped Nancy up.

"What the fuck was in that thing?"

"Wasn't Silly Putty. Now run!"

Together they sprinted across Broadway and headed west on Twenty-third Street. By the time they'd reached the corner of Sixth Avenue the sirens had started up.

"This is turning into some day," said Nancy as they stopped to get their breath back.

The Nokia spoke up in his ear. "I have a call."

"Who?"

"Gale from the clinic."

"Put her on."

"Is this Venner?" came a voice, sounding frantic, frightened.

"Yeah."

"Somebody attacked the clinic. God, they killed everyone, I barely escaped . . . I can't believe it. They were invisible."

"Where's Plesur?"

"I didn't know what to do. She was groggy, couldn't run."

"Where is she?"

"Dead."

CHAPTER 15

"Neither of those is of any use to me." Mistress Julia waved her hand in dismissal. "That one has bruises, for god's sake."

The pimp shrugged. The pleasure model, a blond Anglo type known as a Daisy, turned away, her face closed, her eyes blank.

The sad room was full of similar pleasure models, all in the last year or so of life. There was a weariness, a deadness about them. They sat on worn plastic seats and benches, waiting to be whored out for the evening. The pleasure mods may have all started out looking exactly alike. But they certainly changed with the experience life threw at them. And these had seen the worst life had to offer.

It didn't faze Mistress Julia in the slightest. She was pitiless.

Sitting at the end of one bench was a worn-looking Pammy. Her face was lined, her eyes sunken, her golden hair had lost its sheen. Even her magnificent breasts were starting to sag. Beside her sat one of the Asian types, usually called Lotus or Blossom. She too was approaching the end of her short life, but she seemed years fresher than the Pammy.

"Come on, should be one here to meet your needs," said Frog, the heavyset pimp who ran this dump.

The green and gray carpeting was shot. The door was stained black around the edge with fingerprints. The air stank of sweat, urine, and fear. Somewhere on the fringe of consciousness, Angie wanted to turn on her heel and get the hell out of there.

The Pammy suddenly bent over and started coughing, deep, air-sucking coughs that shook her entire body. Mistress Julia looked away with a sniff. Most of the dead-end mod-bods here were sick with one thing or another.

In the last year of life their immune systems broke down. They were like flowers wilting on the vine. The best of the healthy ones got upgrades for the fight clubs.

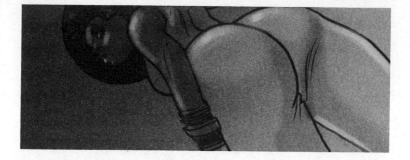

The rest got sold to the ultimate perv market, sadists who liked to end it with a kill.

Julia could handle it.

"I specifically said virgin ass. No whip marks at all."

The pimp signaled to a dark-skinned beauty standing by herself. "Turn around, girl, and drop your panties."

Looking bored beyond life itself, the Afri-queen did as ordered, revealing a textbook gorgeous ass without a single mark.

Mistress Julia sighed. Close but no cigar. "This is nice, but not white. My player is only into white ass."

"That's all I got." Frog snapped his fingers. The Afri-queen pulled up her red silk panties and sat down.

"Did you call Rafael?"

"I'll try him again." The Frog shook his head slightly and shifted into a phone call. "Yo, dog, it's the Frog."

In the past, Julia put in her order well ahead of time and had the pleasure model delivered to her hotel in advance.

That had given her time to rehearse. The mod-bod had to be coached, ready to give the client the cries of agony he so desired. It had to be a real whipping, but she always used Senforet or another topical painkiller to take the worst of it away.

This desperate scrounging in pimp hovels for an acceptable piece of ass was enough to make her skin crawl.

The worn-out Pammy gave a groan and pitched forward, facedown on the floor. She began twitching and moaning, thrashing back and forth. The Blossom knelt beside her, trying to comfort her.

Mistress Julia took a step back, but otherwise ignored what was going on in front of her. So did the Frog, who simply carried on making calls in search of a perfect piece of unwhipped ass.

Angie, however, could only take so much of this. When the Blossom started weeping, she broke down and pushed Julia aside.

"Aren't you going to do something?"

The Frog shrugged. "I got a call out to the collection agency. They'll be 'round for the body pretty soon."

"That's it, that's all you're going to do?"

"Look, they die in here all the time. I had two die yesterday. You know the score. They're old; they only got ten years on their clock."

Angie stared at him; he turned away.

"Yeah, no marks, you got it, man."

The Pammy coughed again. "It hurt."

"What hurts?" asked Angie.

The mod-bod looked at her; the blue eyes widened, and something flickered there, unnameable, beyond the edge of life.

"Everything."

Angie saw the light go out; the blue turned dull as the head sagged back and the pleasure model died.

Her friend, the Blossom, started weeping again.

Angie felt tears welling in her eyes, but Mistress Julia had had enough. She stood up, demanding the cold, unfeeling persona that had served her so well.

The Frog gave her a big thumbs-up. "You're in luck. Fresh p-mod, no marks, young, white."

"What model?"

He grinned. "It's a Pammy, prime of life. Gonna cost you, though."

CHAPTER 17

"Plesur's gone." Rook gripped Nancy's arm, moving her into the throng of pedestrian traffic. "They found the clinic, killed everyone."

"Christ. How?"

"Must have tracked us from the taxi. We have to hide somewhere." Rook checked a street sign. They were west of the clinic now. "They'll be coming after us."

"Who the fuck are they?"

"I think it's the black ops Sangacha worked for."

They crossed Fifth Avenue and then turned north. A black van swerved to a stop ahead of them.

"Shit."

The back doors of the van flew open—but nobody got out. There was nobody inside, either.

Rook pushed Nancy through the doors of a Homebot Centre, five floors of display for new machines to run the modern home.

A handful of shoppers were watching a demonstration for a new line of machines. A device that looked like an oversized vacuum cleaner with metal arms was dusting some furniture with an attachment shaped like a very large mushroom.

The mushroom made a gentle humming noise as it polished a table while a young lady in a maroon and green uniform extolled the machine's virtues.

She looked up, annoyed, as Rook and Nancy shoved their way through the shoppers.

Irritation turned to shock as blue sparks shot from two ladies. Powerful electric shocks jolted them into the air. Panicked, people screamed and tried to run, but nobody knew which way to go. An obese lady in a red corduroy suit suddenly fell over, blocking an aisle. A display case collapsed under an invisible mass and a store security guard flew through the air, blue sparks streaming from his face and hands.

Rook ducked behind a display of electric beds, pulling Nancy down beside him.

A voice squawked over the loudspeakers: "Everyone remain calm."

It seemed a little late for that.

Rook directed Nancy past another display and hurried after her. They barreled into a room full of high-tech security systems. A security machine that looked like a lawn mower crossed with a fire hydrant patrolled, moving slowly about in a circular pattern.

The machine issued a loud whistle and announced, "Warning! You are not authorized to enter without a professional robot!"

Rook tugged Nancy back, but the machine had zeroed in. It rolled up at a smart clip, illuminating them with a blast from a set of big headlights. "Remove yourself or you will be nozzled!"

From the corner of his eye, Rook caught an odd shadow wriggling like a snake along the carpet. Instinctively he ducked as something swept over his head. Arms out, he caught hold of someone in a slippery plasmonic suit. They

went down together. Rook blocked a punch with his left arm and got his right hand on the other man's face. His fingers dug into the suiting, pulling the guy toward him. The guy bucked, twisted, and heaved Rook upward in an effort to free himself. With a ripping sound, Rook fell to his left. Suddenly floating in the air was a man's face, eyes wide in consternation, mouth twisted in anger.

Rook rolled, and came up on the balls of his feet.

"You are a dead man," the assassin hissed.

"Yeah, and you're ugly," said Rook.

The eyes hardened. Rook sensed the kick, dodged

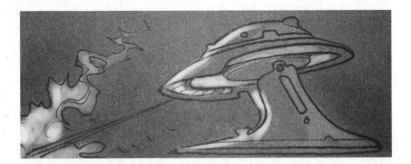

sideways. Had it connected it would have crushed his abdomen. He ducked and tried to pull out his gun but his right foot slipped on the slick floor and he went down on one knee.

Which turned out to be very lucky, because the security robot was right behind him. It unloaded a blast of patented electrified foam. Puffy goo like shaving cream shot over Rook's head. Since the puff was carrying about a thousand volts, it knocked the assassin off his feet, sparking him like a huge shrimp on a barbecue grill.

"Come on." Rook grabbed Nancy. The metal guard swiveled ominously, bringing its foam nozzle to bear on them.

Electrified foam spattered on the couch as Rook hurdled it. Nancy gave a shriek as a fleck or two hit her leg, discharging hot sparks.

They sprinted down a wide aisle between sales displays. At the end was an elevator alcove. A green light flashed and doors opened.

"Go!" Rook shoved Nancy forward.

Rook got to the elevator first, spun back, gun raised. Nancy dove past him.

He sensed someone coming fast, and stepped back into the elevator car, ready to shoot. Nancy slapped the control panel. The doors closed. But they were not alone.

Rook swung to aim at the invisible assassin, but the gun was pointed right at Nancy's chest. He flinched. Rook lost the gun as he was hammered back into the wall of the elevator. Painfully fast blows to the head, chest, and gut rained down on him. Invisible hands squeezed his throat.

He brought his arms up, trying to break the grip, and saw Nancy with the pistol in her hand, swinging with all her might. The blow landed on the back of the assassin's head, dropping him against the doors, which opened a moment later, spilling the invisible body out onto a concrete floor.

"Nice move." Rook took the gun from her as they moved quickly into the dimly lit hallway.

"Basement level, ladies lingerie, secret exits," said Nancy.

Smart-lights lit up, revealing rows of boxes and crates. They made their way to a loading dock that led back up to street level.

Rook cocked an ear. "I think they're up there, too."

"We're not going that way."

"Then where?"

Nancy pointed to a door at the rear of the loading dock. "Down."

Rook kicked in the door and they took the stairs two at a time, emerging in the boiler room. Water dripped from overhead pipes. The whole placc smelled of mold and slime.

"Do you know where we're going?"

"Go deep enough, everything leads to the subway."

Rook used the Nokia to illuminate the damp space. On the far wall was an old rusty door. Rook tried it, found it was locked. He pushed Nancy back and fired a bullet into the lock.

"Jesus!" Nancy swore. "That is fucking loud!"

"Sorry." Rook pulled the door open. A dark, ominous tunnel stretched ahead.

"Interesting," said Rook.

"These tunnels link to the entire subway grid. Sometimes we use them to move mod-bods around."

A loud thump echoed above their heads.

"You want to get lost?" Nancy asked. "No place better than this."

"After you." Rook pulled the door shut behind them as Ingrid's pale blue light sliced a path in the darkness.

CHAPTER 10

"Where the hell are we?" Rook asked, wiping grime from his forehead.

Harsh mercury lights flickered over the seemingly endless subway tunnel.

"We just passed Nineteenth Street." Nancy pointed to a faded yellow and black sign. "Not much farther."

Rook felt lost in this labyrinth beneath the city, and he hated that.

Nancy had found a tunnel dug during the Emergency. From that they'd connected to the Lexington Avenue line. They now moved through the wide subway tunnel, stopping to press themselves against the walls when trains roared past.

"Here." Nancy stopped in front of a boarded-up doorway. It didn't seem very inviting. There were layers of plywood, strapped across with steel bands; the whole thing was screwed together and lacquered with adhesive.

"You got a key?" Rook studied the secure boards.

Nancy winked, then reached over and pulled a rusty lever by the track.

They waited, furtively glancing up and down the tracks for the next train.

"Nobody home?" said Rook.

Nancy hushed him, listening.

Suddenly a tiny bead of light illuminated them in red.

An irregular piece of boarding swung away, revealing a squat figure clutching an assault rifle. The man stared at Nancy, but kept the gun trained on Rook.

"Who's your friend?"

"He's a cop from upstate," Nancy answered.

The guy with the rifle tensed.

"Look, we just need somewhere to rest up for a few hours," Rook explained.

"We don't let in cops."

"This is different, believe me," Nancy insisted.

There was a long moment of silence. Rook had the feeling he was being scrutinized on camera.

The man eyed Rook. "Mr. Policeman, you armed?"

"Yes."

"Hand it over."

"Nancy told me we could trust you."

"The real question is, can we trust you?"

With a glance toward Nancy, Rook passed his sidearm to the man, who gave it to someone out of sight.

"Okay." The guard stepped back.

They entered a dark, narrow chamber. Two more figures stood nearby with rifles. A woman in black denim did the pat down and ran a chip-screen over them both.

"He's clean," she announced.

"A cop with no chips?" another guard asked, surprised.

"Long story," said Rook. "Had them pulled last night."

"Great. A rogue cop," said the first guard.

"I'm still on a case, but there's been some complications."

"Don't know, don't care."

"Thanks."

"Thank Nancy."

The man led them down a short passage. Rook noticed steel mesh netting above their heads. Another way of keeping out anyone they didn't want getting in. He'd seen it many times in the uninsured world.

"Mayor hasn't routed you guys yet?" he asked the guy with the rifle.

"Nah, that was the old days."

"Oh yeah?"

"Someone decided we're a useful safety valve down here. It's not just Eighteenth Street. There's the Deuce Hole, the Subterraneans, the Basement people, you know, and out in Brooklyn, man, we're all over the place."

Another door opened into a long space that had once been a subway station platform. Now it was a lounge filled with the denizens of the city's underworld. Low-hanging fluorescent lamps sent light rippling through the smoky haze. There were about two hundred people, perhaps more. Rook couldn't be sure, but some looked like modbods. A motley crowd swarmed around a bar cobbled together from pieces of steel tracks. Tables were spread up and down the platform. Men played cards as a young woman with a wild pink mohawk played guitar.

Rook grabbed two cups of coffee, and gave one to Nancy.

Sitting down, the fatigue washed over him. The morning had barely passed and it felt like he'd been going for days.

"I still can't believe Sooze is dead," Nancy sighed, then caught Rook's stare. "And the mod-bod. That was your whole case, right?"

"Yeah. Shouldn't have ended this way." Rook felt that hole in the pit of his stomach. The memory of Plesur's sunny smile, the wide, trusting blue eyes brought the anger back. Whoever was responsible for this had already destroyed his life, and now they'd taken hers.

It left him with one choice. No choice, actually.

"So what are you going to do?" Nancy asked.

"Something stupid." He picked up the Nokia. "Ingrid, you online?"

"There is a local server here."

"Get me Artoli. Secure line, if you can."

Nancy glanced at the phone. "Mind if I patch in?"

"I can manage fifty-two separate lines at once," Ingrid boasted.

A few moments later, Rook heard Lisa Artoli's voice in his ear.

"Figured it would take more than a missile to get rid of you."

Was she being sarcastic?

"They haven't stopped trying," he said.

"What about the pleasure model?"

"Dead."

"Then it's over." Artoli sounded relieved.

Rook felt wheels turning in his brain. Why was Artoli relieved to hear that Plesur was dead? He recalled what Pipo Haman had said about Sangacha's dream, that Plesur was some kind of bomb. What had Plesur known?

"Rook, get out of here," Artoli pleaded. "Go to California, that's your only chance."

"You're telling me to run?"

"Run and don't stop."

"I'm going to find out who killed her."

Artoli sighed, long and wistful. "Rook, I'm sorry."

Artoli was sorry; that was unusual. Or was he hearing something else?

Then it struck him like a hammer. Lisa Artoli had told the Feds that he had taken Plesur. She knew the Feds were going to kill him and she hadn't lifted a finger. There was guilt in her voice, that was what he was hearing.

"You gave me up," he hissed, fury boiling over.

"They were right here, they . . ." She didn't finish, but he heard the sob.

"What, put a gun to your head?"

There was a silence, then she whispered, "No. My daughter's. They were in my house. They said they would kill her."

Rook heard the fear in her voice. It was something you couldn't hide from a cop. She was telling the truth, at least to some extent.

"Jesus, Lisa. Albany can't protect you?"

"No," she said, and her voice now was very small.

Rook didn't have it in him to press her further. "Listen to me, Lisa. We've got Sable Ranch, the military, feds, probably even Washington involved. That's an awful big shitstorm over one pleasure model."

The Nokia spoke quietly in his ear. "There was an attempt to monitor the call, but I used the Taiwan Backswitch to lose it."

"Lisa, I need to ask you something."

"I have to go."

"What's the ISS?"

"The what?"

"Interservice Special Selection. Sangacha ran it."

"Shit, Rook, you'll get us both killed for sure."

Artoli cut the connection.

Rook sat there for a moment, feeling desolate. He and

Lisa went back a long way. Seemed like another life now. Going back was no longer an option, if it ever had been.

"Fuck that!" Nancy was yelling on her line. "I pay you guys plenty. You could at least tell me when something like that is coming down." She sounded pretty damned pissed off.

"No, you listen to me," she continued. "Motherfuckers in invisibility suits break into my home and try to kill me. They have a sniper team outside that kills my friend. Snipers, in broad daylight, right here in New York City! And where were the police?"

Nancy saw Rook eyeing her. She shook her head angrily.

"In other words, you aren't in charge here, in your own city!" She listened again, mouth twitching in anger. "Oh, for god's sake, Pedro, get a set of balls!"

She ended the call and turned to Rook.

"The cops say they didn't know but I don't believe them. They're afraid of something."

"Yeah, I got the same message."

"What do we do?"

"I'm open to suggestions."

Nancy chewed her lower lip. "I know someone who can give us answers."

"Is there anyone you don't know?"

"No. But this guy is not the easiest person to get to."

"Who is he?"

"The President of the United States, now retired."

Rook almost burst out laughing. "An ex-president? He'll have security all over him. We'll never get to him."

"I know a way. Used it to smuggle the girls in."

"Why did you have to smuggle them in?"

"Because we'd carry their bodies out the same way."

CHAPTER 19

On Mistress Julia's first visit to the Gotham Apartments, she'd been met at the door by armed security. They'd checked her for weapons, as well as the mod-bod she'd brought to entertain her client.

She hadn't known the client's true identity and she hadn't expected the security check. She was terrified that they'd run a background check and discover she was a fugitive. But that wasn't their concern, just the weapons check and taking a visual for their internal system.

After that she'd never seen the security people again, or been asked to identify herself.

Tonight she felt the same anxiety. This time she wasn't here for the money. After the client had been satisfied, he'd often boast about his glory days of absolute power. He would offer all sorts of tantalizing things, but she'd always refused them. It had never occurred to her that he might have answers to the questions that haunted her. Who'd killed Mark? Was she a loose end that needed to be tidied up? Or had the organization been shut down? And if it wasn't—well, that information was valuable, too. Jim had convinced her of that.

Right now she needed to focus and let it happen.

Mistress Julia stalked across the marble lobby in her leather and the five-inch high heels. Over her shoulder she had a patent leather quiver with her selection of whips and crops, and behind her, shuffling submissively, was the Pammy she'd picked up from the Frog.

The mod-bod was drugged with Narcosoma, a painkiller that would take the worst off the whipping. Not that Julia could take away all of it; it was the shrieks that really got the client off.

A flunky in a red jacket and black pants nodded as she reached the elevators. Mistress Julia gave him a glare, as if she were measuring him for chains.

An older couple stood waiting for the car. They eyed her black leather and the mod-bod, crammed into a tight silk skirt and a matching blouse that showed off those luscious breasts. The woman's eyes glinted with rage as she muttered something under her breath. Mistress Julia stared back, implacable, dominant and in control. The husband, a big pink fellow in a tweed coat, kept sneaking looks at the Pammy, while trying not to let his wife see him. The couple got off at the tenth floor. The wife took her husband's hand to make sure he didn't look back at the yummy little play toy. But he did anyway.

Julia attached a leather leash to the slave collar she'd already put around the Pammy's neck. The mod-bod stared at her and mouthed something, but the Narcosoma had zonked her out.

When the doors opened on the top floor, Mistress Julia pulled the Pammy behind her and strode down the hall to the solitary penthouse apartment.

The door opened before she got there. Mistress Julia extended her right hand, on which she wore a single eight-carat faux-diamond ring. Former president Frank Marion accepted her hand and kissed the ring.

"Right on time."

"Auntie's here." Mistress Julia tugged the Pammy into Marion's apartment. "She's brought you a present."

The door closed behind them and she moved the mod-bod to the full-length mirror in the living room. The place was filled with leather furniture, antique Aubusson rugs, and paintings of cowboys pursuing cattle.

The tall, white-haired, surgically handsome ex-president came closer, smiling with bleached white teeth. "Exquisite."

"Only the best for you." Julia turned the mod-bod around, letting Marion feast his eyes on the perfect tits, ass, legs, hair, and face sculpted by genetic engineers.

"Stunning! I've never seen such a perfect specimen." President Marion ran his fingertips over the Pammy's silky smooth skin, up and down her arms, moving up to graze her neckline. His hands jumped back as if stung. "Amazing! She's ready for an earback. How did you know?"

Few things caught Julia by surprise. Locking her smile in place, she brushed aside the golden hair. Behind the Pammy's right ear, a small silver node caught the light like a diamond. A shunt. The mod had been upgraded. Only the wealthiest owners would spend that kind of money to upgrade their merchandise. Where the fuck did the Frog get this mod-bod?

Marion waved to the first shelf of the bookcase, where a display set of customized earbacks in black, white, and yellow sat like tiny glass sculptures. "I've been waiting for the perfect . . . girl to try out my new toys."

Although everyone these days used earbacks for communication and personality modifications, mods required special earbacks, not for use by humans. The most common ones artificially enhanced intelligence to a standard 120 IQ. But there were others, expensive software that altered the mod's physical systems, giving them catlike reflexes, almost superhuman strength, and god knew what else. These altered mods fought against each other in underground fight clubs with big money at stake.

"Perhaps we can work something out," Julia said coolly. "But first things first."

"Yes." Marion turned to a table where a silver champagne bucket sat with a pair of bottles sitting in the ice. Taittinger Comtes de Champagne 2056. Tall champagne flutes were set out on a tray beside it.

"To old friends," he announced, pouring for them, letting the mousse rise to the brim. He filled his own glass and joined them. "And new adventures."

The Pammy took a slow sip, wrinkled her nose in distaste, and put the glass down. Julia smiled. "Not sweet enough for some of us," she said quietly to Marion.

He smiled, nodded, obviously excited by what was going to happen.

"Pammy needs to be taught some manners." Mistress Julia downed the glass and set her quiver of whips and velvet-lined wrist cuffs on the glass table.

She checked the hook driven into the beam between the living room and the dining room. Then she swiftly cuffed the Pammy's wrists together. The baby blue eyes stared at her in a mixture of wonderment and fear. Next came the chain, which looped through an eyelet in the cuffs, and with an expert flick was tossed over the end of the hook. Mistress Julia caught the weighted end and pulled it taught.

The mod-bod's hands shot up over her head, and she cried out in sudden fear.

From the corner of her eye, Julia noted that Marion had retreated behind the golden Japanese screen, where he could see everything, but was hidden from view.

Mistress Julia quickly gagged the Pammy. Not too tight, because some screams were actually desired, but just enough

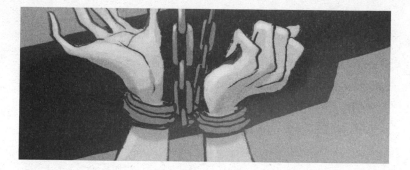

to muffle them to a bearable level. Those baby blues filled with something new, a sense of betrayal, allied to desperation and fear.

Aware that this was getting very exciting for her hidden client, she began removing the Pammy's clothing. First the top, unbuttoning and pulling it wide. The lacy bra came off in a second and the exquisite breasts spilled free. Mistress Julia rubbed her thumb over the nipples, getting them hard for her client's pleasure.

The slow sound of a zipper ripped through the still air. The mod's skirt came down and was quickly tugged free. Mistress Julia pulled hard on the back of the panties, stretching them tight over Pammy's crotch. She heard a gasp of pleasure from behind the screen.

With a sharp tug she tore the panties off, eliciting another muffled gasp.

Time to slow things down, let him get his breath back. Mistress Julia pulled on the black leather gloves, smoothing them up her arms. Then she slowly pulled out each instrument, flicking them through the air a few times before laying them on the table.

It was almost time, but Mistress Julia needed another glass of champagne. She stepped to the table and refreshed her glass, then took a sip, letting the moment build, perfectly aware of the bulging eyeballs a few feet away behind the lavish screen.

She set the glass down. In a swift motion, she smacked the rattan cane into her leather-clad palm, producing a satisfying *smack*. Spinning on her heel, she turned to the quivering, pale flesh awaiting the lash.

CHAPTER 20

When Rook and Nancy emerged at Forty-second Street, they found that the weather had changed dramatically. A sharp wind out of the east drove dark clouds across the sky, tossing trash in the air around Grand Central.

They worked their way east until they found the Gotham Apartments, a luxury building built in the 1920s with the look of a gothic mansion.

"Lights are on." Nancy pointed to the top floor. "This is our lucky night."

The Gotham building stood alone, with an office tower from the early twenty-first century at one end of the block, and a row of smaller, older buildings on the other. One of those had a coffee shop called Gotham Coffee.

"In here." Nancy led him into an alley lined with trash cans. At the back, a chain-link fence blocked off any further progress. Nancy reached through at a point where the fence was connected to the tubular steel. Rook heard a soft click and the panel of chain link slid aside as smoothly as a sliding door.

"Neat trick."

"Wait until you see the rest of this."

Behind the coffee shop, an asphalted yard connected to another building with a loading dock. In the half-light it was hard to be sure, but Rook sensed this facility hadn't seen a lot of use recently.

Nancy moved lightly up the steps to the dock, went to a door, and touched the wall beside it in two places.

A moment later it slid open.

"You got that flashlight?" asked Nancy.

He did. Inside, with the Nokia lighting the way, they stepped through an echoing, empty vault.

Rook pushed past extensive cobwebs. "How'd you find this?"

"Set up for bootleggers, early twentieth century when alcohol was illegal."

They descended a set of concrete steps, passed through another gate, and entered a wide, solidly constructed tunnel.

Nancy brushed a spiderweb. "Used to be trolleys in here, so they could deliver the whiskey under the street."

"And the security never shut it down?"

"Nope."

"Because?"

"Laws don't apply to these people."

"Doesn't make it right."

"Oh, please." Nancy sensed his disgust. "You're a rogue cop and I run a nightclub. What are we doing here?"

"No one forced you to help me." Rook grimaced. "This isn't your business."

"Sooze made it my business," she said grimly, then smiled. "I like you, SIO Venner. You risked everything for that mod."

Rook shrugged. Plesur didn't deserve her fate. "I needed her for the case."

Nancy gave him a sly smile. "If you say so."

The tunnel ended in double doors that opened easily and let them into a small subbasement.

At the far end was a narrow elevator with an open cage surrounded by brass mesh.

Rook winced as the rusted gate creaked open and Nancy stepped inside.

"You sure this thing works?"

"Last time I checked." She pulled an antique switch.

The elevator clanked as it raised them up the narrow shaft. Rook noticed the doors on each floor had been bricked up.

"Only one stop, eh?"

"That's all we need."

The elevator ground to a halt. Rook pulled back the gate and pushed on the door.

"There's a bolt," said Nancy.

Rook kicked hard at the door. It popped open immediately, slamming into something.

"Pretty flimsy really," she noticed.

He stepped out into a large kitchen with a black and white tile floor.

Nancy followed close behind. "This end of the apartment has the kitchen and the servants' quarters."

"Where are the servants?"

"They come during the day and leave in the evening."

Rook drew his sidearm, just in case.

Nancy cracked open the nearest door. "The bedrooms are down there, and beyond that there's the living room."

They came to a right turn in the corridor, and then a left. Rook heard a scream. It was a desperate sound, high and wild.

"What the fuck?" he uttered.

"Sounds like he's playing at home tonight."

The passageway widened here, floored with polished parquet. A faint smell of cologne hung in the air.

Another scream sent the hair standing up on the back of Rook's neck.

He pushed open the door and they entered a plush living room. Around the corner of the L-shaped room, a man sat behind a screen with his pants around his ankles. He was pouring himself a glass of champagne, completely oblivious to their presence. On the far side of the room, dangling from a hook, was a blond female. Standing beside her was a woman in dominatrix garb wielding a long black whip.

Cra-ack! The whip struck again. The blonde twitched and emitted a muffled scream. Rook could see she was gagged. He could also see that she was a Pammy.

Rook didn't hesitate. He stepped forward and caught the whip on the backlash, jerking it out of the dominatrix's hands.

"That's enough!"

"Who the fuck are you?" snapped the dominatrix, spinning on her high heels and glaring at him. She reached for a whip, but Nancy shoved her backward.

Rook had moved past them, focused on the Pammy. Red welts ran up and down her back and thighs.

If he didn't know better, he could swear it was Plesur. Were all Pammys truly identical—or did subtle differences change them as they lived their short lives?

He tore the gag off her mouth and unfastened the chain holding her in place. The blue eyes recognized him through the haze of pain and dope.

"Plesur?"

The irises widened, focused more tightly on him.

"Rook! You come for me." Disbelief faded into warmth and gratitude, and something else—love.

Rook shivered as he caught her with one arm and pulled her close while keeping the gun trained on the dominatrix.

"How did you get her?" he snapped.

"I bought her."

"I knew I shouldn't have trusted that bitch at the clinic!" Nancy spat.

Rook suddenly realized that he'd seen the domme's face somewhere before.

"I know you."

"You do not." The woman in black rose to her feet.

"You were there, Manuel Sangacha's place in Peekskill, when he was shot."

That staggered her. "What? I don't know what you—"

Something crashed behind the Japanese screen. Someone was struggling and cursing.

"Come join the party." Nancy stepped out from behind the screen. "Rook, may I introduce you to President Marion."

The tall figure of former president Marion stumbled behind Nancy, his face pink with anger. "Goddamn it! Don't people knock anymore?"

Rook passed Plesur to Nancy and raised the gun to cover Marion. "Don't move!"

The president shot his hands over his head. His trousers fell to the floor.

As Nancy helped the pleasure model into her skirt, Rook winced at the harsh welts on the mod's skin.

"You enjoy this line of work?" he glared at the dominatrix.

"Not particularly."

President Marion grabbed for his pants. "Do you realize how much trouble you're in?"

"You gonna send General Sangacha after me?" Rook shot back.

Marion froze, the blood draining from his face.

"What's the matter, Mr. President?" Rook taunted. "Looks like you've seen a ghost."

"If you leave now, we'll forget all about this little . . . incident," Marion said as if he were addressing his

constituents. "Take your mod with you. No harm done. She's good for plenty more of your clients."

"Shut the fuck up! I'm police, Hudson Valley Homicide, you asshole. I'm investigating the murder of General Sangacha."

Marion's mouth was working but no words came out.

The dominatrix did not like that news either. "How did you find me?"

"Why? You kill him?"

"No. I . . . provided services."

"I bet." Rook recalled the welts on Sangacha's body.

"Rook." Nancy gently turned Plesur's head to the side. Rook noticed a little ring of silver just behind her ear. So she had had the operation.

"Did it work?" he asked Nancy.

"I don't know."

"That's an expensive operation," remarked Marion. "But without the earbacks, it's useless. I happen to have quite a collection." He motioned to the array of tiny glass sculptures on the bookcase. "Take them and I'll forget you ever existed."

Rook glanced at the rack of glittering earbacks. "One of those would make her smart?"

Marion laughed. "That's not all it would do." His eyes flashed. "You know, that mod would fetch a fortune at the fight clubs."

"I can't believe I voted for you," Rook growled in disgust.

Marion favored him with a contemptuous smile.

"Look," said the leather-clad domme. "This has nothing to do with me." She started gathering her things.

"No one goes anywhere!" Rook instructed. He turned to Marion. "Why was Sangacha killed?"

"You can't expect me to answer that."

Rook advanced threateningly. "Let's try again." He slid the safety off. "What the fuck is going on?"

"I'm an *ex*-president. Why would they tell me?"

"Who? The Ranch?"

Panic flashed across Marion's eyes. "You really don't want to get involved with this."

"No shit. Someone killed Sangacha and has been trying to kill me and the Pammy. Why?"

Marion shook his head. "Manuel Sangacha had many enemies. I have no idea how the mod fits in."

"She belonged to Sangacha."

"Fuck!" the dominatrix exclaimed.

Rook glanced at her. "You got something else to say?"

The mistress glared back, her eyes cold as ice. "This is all a mistake."

"Yeah, you said it."

Rook fished in his pocket and brought out the ISS badge. "Recognize this, Mr. President?"

Marion flinched as if he'd been slapped in the face. He strode to the table and poured himself a glass of champagne. "Where the hell did you get that?"

"Sangacha's apartment."

Marion swigged the rare vintage like it was beer. "This great nation went through a crisis, I'm sure you understand that much."

"The Emergency," Rook said.

"Things got messy."

"So they used Sangacha and the ISS to clean things up." Rook held up the badge. "We're talking about a government-run death squad."

"That's a crude way to put it."

Rook gestured to the dominatrix. "Sangacha had so many fucking nightmares, he had you come over and beat the shit out of him."

The dominatrix stared in shock. "They were after the mod, not me."

"Yeah, we're all real lucky," Rook shot back. "Is the ISS still operational?" he asked Marion.

"You'd have to ask the Ranch."

"I can arrest you right now for conspiracy, Mr. President."

Marion laughed. "Detective, get serious. This is all hearsay. You got nothing. Nothing!"

Rook pulled out the paper he'd taken from the metal file. "What's Taste Imperative?"

Marion gave a strangled shriek and staggered to his feet, champagne glass crashing to the floor. "Don't say another word!"

Rook stared at him. "What's wrong with you?"

Marion waved his hands frantically. "You don't know what you're doing. Please, I beg you!"

"What is Taste Imperative?"

"No. I can't!" Marion screamed. "Don't! Don't even think those words . . ."

With a heavy wet thud, like a hammer smashing a watermelon, Marion's head exploded.

CHAPTER 21

"Get down!" Rook dove to the floor as Marion's corpse toppled backward. The legs twitched twice, then went still.

Rook looked around wildly. Had there been a sniper? Was someone in the room?

But no shots followed. He heard someone vomiting and saw Nancy huddled in a corner.

"Jesus Christ!" The dominatrix was on her knees, hands over her mouth, staring with bulging eyes at the ruin of the ex-president of the United States. Blood and brains stained her glossy boots.

Rook crawled to the window. Wind buffeted the glass, but there were no bullet holes. He slowly got to his feet, aware of the gore dripping down his shirt.

"What the hell did you do, Rook?" muttered Nancy.

Rook shook a piece of flesh off the paper he'd retrieved from the explosive file.

"I just asked him about this."

"And his fucking head exploded!"

"Was he shot?" asked the domme.

"No," said Rook. "He must have had an explosive chip in his head."

Nancy wiped at the gristle on her clothes. "That is some fucked up shit."

"The technology's not new." Rook carefully edged toward the window and scanned the street, checking the other buildings, as well. It was raining hard now. "We use them on a felon's ankle. If he moves out of range or tampers with it, it explodes and takes his leg."

"Jesus."

"Cheaper than jail."

Nancy shook her head. "What could be so important they'd blow President Marion's head off?"

"Same reason they tried to blow our heads off." Rook moved to check on Plesur. "Her." The mod lay on the couch, eyes shut. "She's the key. And one thing's for sure.

Whoever killed the president is sending over the cleanup squad."

Nancy scanned the apartment. "We need some clothes."

The domme pointed down the hall. "There's a wardrobe in the bedroom."

Nancy padded to the room, removing her shirt.

The dominatrix shoved her equipment into a bag and glanced at Rook. "She didn't feel all the pain. Just enough so she'd scream."

"Beating someone who wants it is one thing," growled Rook.

Her eyes met his. "I needed to get to him." She gestured at the headless body. "Look, I was there at Sangacha's when they killed him. I barely escaped."

"Why didn't you report it?"

The blond leather-clad woman laughed. "You're joking, right?"

Rook did not look as if he was joking.

"I thought the killers were after me." She straightened up. "Now I'm *totally* fucked."

"Two clients die on you, might be time for a new job." Nancy returned with an armful of clothes. She tossed a clean blue shirt and a pair of khakis at Rook. "But you did bring us the mod. We owe you for that."

Rook nodded, wadding the clothes into a ball. "Change outside. Don't leave anything here."

"She's waking up." Nancy helped Plesur to her feet. Her head lolled to one side, golden hair spilling across her face.

"Let's move." Rook jammed a fresh ammo clip in his gun.

They started back toward the kitchen, heading for the bootlegger's elevator.

With a terrifying boom, the apartment's front door blew open as dark-suited figures rushed in.

"Nobody move!" bellowed a deep voice.

"You, down on the floor!" A man shoved Rook roughly.

Rook raised his hands slowly, and dropped to his knees as a man in full tac suit pointed an M-25 at him.

"Confirmed. The president is dead," said a voice.

Tac-radios squawked softly among the heavily armored men.

"Get the body bag in here now!" said another voice.

Rook noticed Plesur leaning against Nancy, their backs against the wall. Nancy was adjusting something behind Plesur's right ear. Then one of the tac-team motioned to them with his weapon.

"Down on the floor. Now!" he barked.

"You don't want to do this," Rook called out. "I'm a police officer."

"Shut up!" The man jammed the M-25 against Rook's head. "Bring the mod, kill the others."

How the hell did they know about Plesur?

The world suddenly turned upside down as something knocked the heavy gun away.

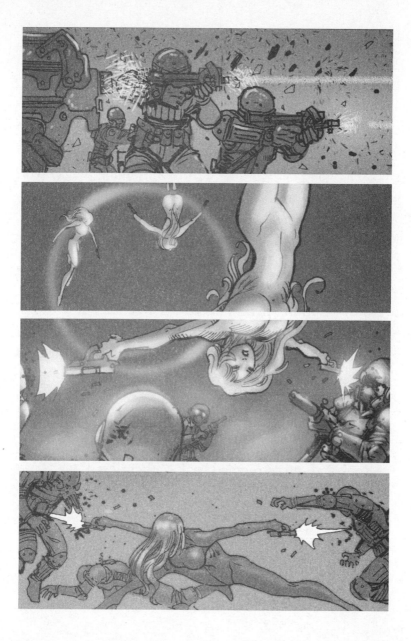

Plesur came off the wall so quickly she was a blur. Rook had never seen a human being move so fast. The guy in front of her went flying through the air with a kick to the stomach, his automatic weapon now in her hands. With blue sparks and a sharp crack, the gun sprayed bullets.

Two members of the tac-squad went down firing wildly.

Rook rolled himself flat on the floor, pulling Julia down. He looked up, saw Nancy stagger as bullets ripped through her in quick succession. She crashed over a table and fell by Rook's side. She grasped his hand, shuddered, and was gone.

Plesur cartwheeled behind a sofa and came up to a vertical position, firing off the whole clip. Three more men went down. Vaulting the sofa, she tossed the commander into the wall, then spun around to shoot the last member of the tac-squad right through the faceplate.

He hit the floor, and there was silence.

The wind suddenly rattled the windows as lightning flashed over the city.

Rook and Julia struggled back to their feet.

"My god!" exclaimed Julia.

"God had nothing to do with it." Rook opened his fist. Nancy had deposited the rest of the earbacks into his hand.

He stood up and faced the killing machine that was Plesur. She studied him through steel-glinted baby blues.

Rook slowly touched her face. "That was really something."

Plesur suddenly focused on Mistress Julia. Her left hand whipped out faster than the eye could follow.

Before Rook could say a word, Plesur backhanded Julia across the face. The domme spun backward, crumpling to the floor.

"I heard they get angry," Julia muttered. There was a vivid red line down one side of her face.

"How do you feel?" Rook asked. Plesur looked at him, her eyes uncertain.

"I know some things, but not others. It is strange."

"You really helped."

The mod faced him, shoulders back, head held high. "I help Plesur now."

"Welcome to the world." He covered Nancy's face with a tablecloth. "The good and the bad."

Julia got to her feet, rubbing her jaw. "If your pleasure mod hadn't gone psycho, we'd all be lying right alongside her."

"Yeah," Rook said dryly, depositing the earbacks in his pocket.

Plesur tossed each of them a raincoat from the closet.

"More like them will come," she announced.

"Where can we go?" Julia asked.

Plesur stopped to think. "74 17 06 97 57 87 56 61."

Rook stopped in his tracks. "What was that?"

"In my head. I am supposed to remember it."

Rook held Plesur's arms, studying her face. "A number?"

"I just remembered."

"What is that?" Julia asked.

Rook pulled out the Nokia. "Ingrid, you catch that?"

"Geographical coordinates," the phone answered. "A location eighty-six miles from here."

Rook felt his heart jump as he slung an M-25 over his shoulder. "I love my phone."

"Thank you," Ingrid buzzed.

Plesur cocked the M-25 and slipped three ammo clips in the waistband of her skirt. "We must go."

"You still want some answers?" Rook asked Julia as they rushed through the kitchen.

"Yes." Julia slipped into the elevator.

"You might just get them."

Outside the rain was hammering down and the wind was gusting fiercely.

"Who are you?" Rook asked the domme.

The woman in leather hesitated, as if debating the answer to the question.

"Just call me Julia." She pulled her coat tight around her. "And who the fuck are you, some supercop?"

"Yes." Plesur smiled. "And a good man."

Turning her face to the rain, gun ready, the ex-pleasure mod led the fugitives into the storm.